God, Spirit, and Human Wholeness

God, Spirit, and Human Wholeness

Appropriating Faith and Culture in West African Style

Elochukwu Eugene Uzukwu C.S.Sp.

PICKWICK *Publications* • Eugene, Oregon

GOD, SPIRIT, AND HUMAN WHOLENESS
Appropriating Faith and Culture in West African Style

Pickwick Publications
An Imprint of Wipf and Stock Publishers
199 W. 8th Av.e, Suite 3
Eugene, OR 97401

www.wipfandstock.com

ISBN 13: 978-1-61097-190-4

Cataloging-in-Publication data:

Uzukwu, E. Elochukwu.

    God, Spirit, and human wholeness : appropriating faith and culture in West African style / Elochukwu Eugene Uzukwu.

    xiv + 268 p. ; 23 cm. Includes bibliographical references and index.

    ISBN 13: 978-1-61097-190-4

    1. Christianity — Africa, West. 2. Theology, Doctrinal — Africa, West. I. Title.

BR1430 .U98 2012

Manufactured in the U.S.A.

To my Parents:

MICHAEL NWOKOLO UZUKWU
and
AGNES ONUKWUBE ASIANYA UZUKWU

who raised me up in my village tradition without being the less Christian; that you may rest in the Lord!

To my eminent predecessors in designing African Christian theology; now resting in the Lord:

MGR MARTIN MADUKA,
from whom I learnt passionate appropriation and integration of Igbo tradition into Christianity;

FATHER GODWIN IKEOBI,
a friend who taught me the value of healing and exorcism in the interface between Christianity and African traditions;

FATHER EMEFIE IKENGA-METUH,
older brother and trailblazer in African religious Studies.

Contents

Foreword and Acknowledgments

THE CONCEPTION OF THIS book project, and its subsequent realization, has taken almost a decade. I am relieved that the thoughts expressed here are finally seeing the light of day.

When I applied to Missio Aachen for partial subsidy to research African theology, at the end of October 2000, I was then interested in a historical overview of African theology. I wanted to highlight stress areas and/or regional perspectives. Missio responded favorably to my request, for which I remain deeply grateful. (My two friends at Missio Institute of Missiology, Josef Estermann and especially Marco Moerschbacher, were particularly supportive during the time I was researching this book). I started research work between 2001 and 2002, using the library resources of the Spiritan Séminaire des Missions, Chevilly Larue, France. I also spent a fruitful two weeks going through the very interesting collections at SEDOS library in Rome, Italy. I am grateful to the then executive director of SEDOS, Fr. Bernard East, op, and his staff. I am also grateful to the librarians at Chevilly (i.e., my Spiritan elder confreres Joseph Gross, Felix Beuzet, and the late Pierre Buis). I will not forget the wonderful hospitality, support, and help of the Spiritan Generalate in Rome during my period of research at SEDOS.

I did not think, initially, that this work would take so long. Researching revealed the wealth of resources available and the complexity of approaches in African theology, at least in English and French speaking Africa. This called for a delimitation of areas to be covered and a sharpening of focus. The preliminary fruit of the project was first tested in two public lectures. The first lecture was delivered at the School of Hebrew, Biblical and Theological Studies, Trinity College, University of Dublin—"Bible and Christian Worship in Africa: Explorations in Inculturation" (February 28, 2002). It was part of Public Lecture Series organized by Trinity College on *The Bible in Christian Life and Thought*. The reworked and expanded version of the paper was presented at the 6th intercontinental conference organized by Missio Aachen on contextual theologies (Mexico City, March 16–20, 2002: *Entre Particularismo y comunicación: Teologías contextuales y reflexion filosófica*). My presentation argued from biblical, historical and liturgical perspectives that Christian life and contextual theology in Africa are not simply culture-specific but Bible-driven. In addition to mainline missionary churches, the immense contribution of African Initiated Churches (AICs), Protestant and Catholic Charismatic movements and new African Pentecostalism in shaping Christian life and theology is clearly noted. The paper was later published in 2003 in the Missio edited *Chakana:* "Bible and Christian Worship in Africa—African Christianity and the Labour of Contextualization."[1]

It became clear to me, as the work progressed, that I have to narrow down the geographical area of my research to the West African region. Second, it was also clear that I have to limit the subject matter to the complex question of God-talk that is Spirit-driven. As soon as I started writing about God that is dynamically experienced, approached and appropriated as and in the Spirit by West African Christians, I looked for opportunities to test the ideas before rushing to publishers. Lectures, conferences and talks in Institut Catholique Paris, Kimmage Mission Institute Dublin, and Milltown Institute Dublin provided the forums.

First, I had the opportunity to test the viability of the project in Paris in 2004 and 2005. In 2004 I gave a lecture at the Institut Catholique on the specificity of the image of God revealed in African religions. I argued that the evidence shows that God distances God's-self from our wars. ("Quand Dieu s'éloigne de nos guerres: l'apport de l'image de Dieu dans la Religion traditionnelle africaine à la théologie des religions")! I noted that this image of God favors a different and perhaps radical perception of religions and human relations. Next, in 2005 I gave another lecture in Paris, under the auspices of the European universities' Erasmus Intensive Programs project—*Translating God(s): Thinking the Divine in interreligious Encounter* (Paris 2005). The focus of my presentation, "Re-evaluating God-Talk from an African Perspective," was a search for ways to develop God-talk that takes God, the Origin of Origins, off the range of violence that plagues our world. As a development of the earlier talk I gave in 2004 I underlined that patient analysis of ATR reveals religion as intending not only

---

1. Uzukwu, "Bible and Christian Worship in Africa."

human flourishing but also ameliorating human relations. I am grateful to the organizers of the Erasmus programs who facilitated my participation in the Project: Norbert Hintersteiner, presently at the Irish School of Ecumenics, Dublin; François Bousquet (Institut Catholique, Paris); and Bede Ukwuije C.S.Sp. (Spiritan International School of Theology, Enugu). The talks are available at the Institut Catholique Paris website; and the Erasmus proceedings will soon be published.

In my former college, Milltown Institute of Theology and Philosophy Dublin, I was in conversation all this while with colleagues who step by step critiqued my assumptions, and challenged me to clarify my methodology and justify the use of sociological and ethnographical material in theology. I found their remarks very helpful. I therefore thank Patrick Claffey SVD, Patrick Roe C.S.Sp., Finbarr Clancy S.J., Patrick Byrne, SM, Thomas Grenham sps, and Thomas Whelan, C.S.Sp. They spared their time and talent to help me sharpen my ideas.

I also developed a lively conversation with my Spiritan confreres over aspects of the themes I treated in this book. James Okoye C.S.Sp., Catholic Theological Union Chicago, was particularly helpful in challenging my biblical interpretations and the way I related ATR to the Bible. Paulinus Odozor C.S.Sp., University of Notre Dame Indiana, made useful and critical remarks that enabled me to clarify my views.

The greatest difficulty I had with organizing my material had to do with methodology. How can one give full airtime to the local, and at the same time address a wider public? I adopted a methodology inspired by the Igbo literary icon, Chinua Achebe. My friends and colleagues in the University of Port Harcourt Nigeria, not only made critical literature available to me for this purpose, but became my sounding board in the development of the necessary second viewpoint on any issue. I thank Professors Charles Nnolim and Christopher Nwodo who made their published and unpublished works available to me. And, in particular I thank my own brother Professor Christopher Ejizu, who not only hosted me but arranged meetings for me with his colleagues and engaged me in interesting discussions. My other friends, close associates, and family in Lagos, Enugu, and Nnewi, Willy and Uche Nzewi, Sr Stella Chibuoke, and Dom, Cyprian and Uche Uzukwu were a great support during the many years of researching and writing this book.

Finally, I must mention Jeffery Gainey of Scranton University Press with whom I held a number of meetings in South Bend Indiana over how to complete this book. The topic is not the most accessible to a North American audience. However, Jeffery, with Paulinus Odozor always prodding, believed from our first conversation that my way of telling the story of the Triune God, encountered in West African Christianity, the attitude of always adopting a second viewpoint, always looking at everything twice, needs to reach the wider North American public. My friends at the Department of Theology, Duquesne University, especially George Worgul and Gerald Boodoo encouraged me to make this story of the Triune God in West African style available to a wider public. I hope readers will experience what they found interesting in my manuscripts.

In completing this book, I decided to dedicate it not only to my late parents, Michael Nwokolo Uzukwu and Agnes Onukwube Asianya Uzukwu, who raised me up in my village tradition while practicing the Christian faith. But I want also to remember colleagues with whom I shared similar feelings and engaged in many conversations about tradition retrieval in African Christian practice and reflection: the late Mgr Martin Maduka, a passionate lover and promoter of Igbo tradition (tradition that must be allowed to fully embrace Christianity), was like a father to me in these matters; the late Father Godwin Ikeobi was a friend with whom I held several conversations about the interface between Christian practice, healing and exorcism; and the late Fr. Emefie Ikenga-Metuh, the first priest from my home town, Nnewi, Anambra State of Nigeria, blazed a trial in African religious studies, and left an example the rest of us follow. Resting in our home of repose with the Lord, they certainly feel the power and sustenance of the same Holy Spirit that led them in Christ from life to life.

Trinity Hall, Duquesne University, Pittsburgh, PA
December 3, 2010

Abbreviations

AIC	African Initiated Church; also called African Independent Church; and even African Initiatives in Christianity (plural AICs)
ATR	African Traditional Religion
C.S.Sp.	Congregation of the Holy Spirit (Spiritans)
P	Priestly Strand of the Pentateuch
S.J.	Society of Jesus (Jesuits)
SM	Society of Mary (Marianists)
SVD	Society of Divine Word
TDNT	Theological Dictionary of the New Testament. 10 vols. Edited by Gerhard Kittel and Gerhard Friedrich. Translated by Geoffrey W. Bromiley. Grand Rapids: Eerdmans, 1964–76
TDOT	Theological Dictionary of the Old Testament. 14 vols. Edited by G. Johannes Botterweck and Helmer Ringgren. Translated by Geoffrey W. Bromiley et al. Grand Rapids: Eerdmans, 1974–2004

PART ONE

General Considerations

WHAT THIS BOOK IS ABOUT

THIS BOOK IS ABOUT a West African approach to the Christian theology of God. It argues that West African Christians, rooted in their history and ancestral context, engage in interesting God-talk that challenges the Jewish-Christian memory. The history of Christianity in postcolonial Africa reveals that "Christian expansion and revival were limited to those societies that preserved the indigenous name of God."[1] West African Christians received the Trinitarian faith from the missionary churches. They embraced the teaching on the economy of the relational God-Christ-Spirit in their Christian communities. However, their faith is marked by the spectacular dominance of *Spirit*. This book argues that the spectacular dominance of Spirit is rooted in the West African map of the universe. In African Initiated Churches or "Spirit Churches" (AICs—also called African Instituted Churches or African Independent Churches) and in Protestant and Catholic Charismatic movements the indwelling Holy Spirit enables the community to experience what one expects from a concerned and providential God; an experience of the liberating, healing or therapeutic hand of God. The ancestral universe is dominated by God, multiple deities, spirits, and ancestors ideally for the enhancement or realization of the destiny of individual humans and the community. The everyday social, economic, and political business of life is displayed before the divine for approval, amelioration, and healing. Human destiny constitutes the core of West African religious practice. Consequently, human dignity, human values and needs control religious

---

1. Sanneh, *Whose Religion Is Christianity?* 31–32.

discourse. Religion is kin-focused. It generates a deep awareness of and respect for one another's (an individual's) destiny under the patronage and inspiration of God, deities, ancestors and spirits. In the absence of a "clash of gods," religion, ideally, is opposed to violence. "Religious fanaticism has little place in African traditions, where a centralised, war-generating force that mobilises people for genocidal projects is hard to conceive."[2] Local war deities that are patrons of violent conflicts and that are instrumentalized for the generation of violence are abundant. But God, the origin of origins, never patronizes nor generates violence. Wars, jihads and crusades are never fought in the name of God as is common in the Jewish-Christian and Islamic traditions.

This book shows that the dominant features of West African Christianity reflect ancestral religious roots. The ancestral religions reflect in turn an ontological structure prevalent in the region's vision of the universe. In this region, duality or multiplicity functions as the constitutive principle of *Life* or *Being*. Relationality, flexibility, fluidity and palaver or dialogue are therefore structural to the socio-political, economic and religious life anywhere and anytime. This structure, this book argues, informs the appropriation of the relational Trinitarian God by West African Christians. The perception of a universe where relationality is the rule holds the key to unlocking the popularity of trance, vision or audition, healing and exorcism under the power of the Holy Spirit in AICs and Charismatic movements. Attention to this relational universe in theological reflection advances, and makes a significant contribution to, the Christian Trinitarian imagination. This book therefore adopts the open-ended flexibility, that the relational structure of the universe suggests, as a working hypothesis or methodological assumption to engage in theological discussion. In doing this, it follows the philosophical assumptions that inspired the works of Chinua Achebe who structured his thinking around duality. Hellenism's preoccupation with *being as one*, with *rest* as opposed to *change* or *motion*, propagated by Western Christian tradition, is being integrated into West African Christian practice on clearly West African relational terms. For: "when something stands, something else will stand beside it." This encourages flexibility, collaboration, dialogue across religions and cultures and could bring together or correlate the gospel ideal and the ideal of secular humanism.

---

2. Eggen, "Mawu Does Not Kill," 359.

Finally, this book argues that the West African Trinitarian imagination displays God-Spirit-Christ, the relational "origin and finisher" of individual and communal destiny (cf. Heb 12:2), as profoundly health-generating. This Trinitarian imagination opens the way to ameliorating relationship among humans; it enables spiritual combat, in the power of God's Holy Spirit, against the evil that endangers relationship symbolized in witchcraft; and it challenges humans to reinvent and re-envision relationship between cultures, civilizations and religions, between all humans who come from God. Instead of the collision course between absolutist claims, of God or gods that are on our side against the others, the ideological "clash of civilizations," it inspires relationship based on flexibility, transparency, and dialogue; and it inspires the enhancement of human dignity and the fulfilment of human needs and longings. West African style of Christianity contains the raw material for renewing Trinitarian theology, for renewing Christian life in the world church, and for renewing human life.

DEVELOPING CONCERNS OF AFRICAN THEOLOGY

This book is a contribution to the developing issues that preoccupy African theology. Over fifty years ago some francophone African and Caribbean priests met in Paris to discuss mission and evangelization. The fruit of their meeting was published in *Des Prêtres noirs s'interrogent* ("Some Black Priests Wonder").[3] Only a few of the contributors to the epoch making book, like Gérard Bissainthe and Robert Dosseh, are still around. Since 1956 theological explorations in Africa have come a long way. Some think that on the whole the numerous publications have made little impact on the life of ordinary African Christians. Perhaps African theologians, preoccupied with classical issues that the academia considers proper to theological discourse, have not engaged seriously the concerns of ordinary Christians or the questions that contexts are raising. It is becoming clearer that the African context should set the full agenda of theological discussion.

In this study I engage some issues that many have discussed these past fifty years. Many summaries of the genesis, concerns and develop-

---

3. *Des Pêtres Noirs S'interrogent.* To commemorate the event, Karthala reedited the book and organised a colloquium in Paris in November 17–18, 2006. Also the Catholic University of West Abidjan, organized a conference February 12–16, 2007 around the book.

ments of theological reflection in the continent exist.[4] My objective is less ambitious. I limit my exploration to one way West Africans are appropriating Christianity, namely, their contextual way of saying, practicing, or better still receiving God-Spirit-Christ as a way of living *human wholeness*. This, I argue, contributes to and challenges the shape and the understanding of world Christianity. It reveals aspects of West African Christian thought and practice that could be shared with the rest of the Christian world. Many of my examples will be drawn from sociocultural groups in Nigeria, Benin Republic, Togo and Ghana. But I indicate the similarity of beliefs and practices beyond West Africa to Eastern and Central African countries to show how certain patterns of naming and relating to God are common in the region and beyond. The similarities could also argue for the mobility of aspects of Christian practice in the region and in other parts of Africa.

The first part of this book will focus on general considerations. I clarify the context and concerns of the whole work and set out my argument for adopting a methodology that is inspired by the dominant features of thought of a West African group—the Igbo (Nigeria) wisdom tradition. The second part will address the prevalent pattern of approaching God-Spirit and its impact on the appropriation of God-Spirit-Christ in West African Christianity. In a world where God-spirits and humans interrelate for the good of humans, the approach to the divine turns around human wholeness.

---

4. *Le Devenir de la Théologie Catholique depuis Vatican II: 1965–1999*, edited by Joseph Doré, contains entries from French and English speaking zones of Africa. See the contributions of Danet & Messi Metogo, "L'afrique Francophone," and Uzukwu, "L'afrique Anglophone." The *Panorama de la Théologie au XXe siècle* edited by Rosino Gibellini includes a bird's eye view of the concerns and orientations of African theology as one among other theological movements in the third world. Gibellini also edited *Paths of African Theology* in an effort to capture the concerns of theology in Africa at the end of the second millennium. Originally, Gibellini, ed., *Percosi Di Teologia Africana*. Earlier publications like Ngindu Mushete, *Les Thèmes Majeurs De La Théologie Africaine*, or Parrat, *A Reader in African Theology*, or even Muzorewa, *Origins and Development of African Theology* are noteworthy attempts to present an overall picture of contributions and trends in African theology.

1

Preliminary Considerations

*History, Culture, Context, and New Methodology for
Interpreting Christianity in West Africa*

THIS STUDY THAT FOCUSES on the interface between West African
Christian practice and the Jewish-Christian memory naturally
leans towards local history and West African ancestral context and traditions. Since I believe that the context generates intriguing questions
about reality and provides adequate language to explore the same, I opt
for methodological assumptions that will enable me to better analyze the
reality. First, theology in our zone has to be attentive to the history of the
various Christian communities in West Africa. Every contextual theology is based on the social history of the groups engaging the Christian
tradition. Second, my methodological assumption is rooted in the structure of the West African approach to reality. This approach is fundamentally plural or multiple and therefore relational. What is not multiple
does not exist. Ideas of twin-ness, duality, relatedness, and ambivalence
dominate West African religion and anthropology. The grounding of
these ideas is ontological—a contextual insight into being and reality.
From Nigeria to Mali, it is the same story. Similar perceptions are found
in Cameroon, Congo, and other central African countries. I will illustrate from the Igbo world and system of thought the relevance of duality,
flexibility and relationality. The wisdom saying *ife kwulu ife akwudebe
ya* (something stands and something else stands beside it) consecrates
relationality and maintains a clear distance from absolutism. Igbo and
West Africans approach reality in a flexible, malleable and relational
way. Such a flexible, malleable and relational world invites a new kind

of methodology or interpretive framework. The world is never simply given, it is interpreted.

My approach is not new. The literary works of West African humanists, especially Chinua Achebe, follows this approach. Chinua Achebe's works that are embedded in Igbo wisdom tradition will be evoked more than any other literary humanistic production of West Africa. My hunch in this study can be stated as follows: the insight that *relational tension mediates being-in-the-world* will enable fruitful exploration of the West African version of world Christianity. The dynamic interaction of Christians in this zone with their social and historical context could teach other Africans and all humans in a globalised world a new approach to the God of Jesus Christ. God approached as Spirit is revealed as the One very close to humans, the One that enables health and wholeness in the human community. Flexibility as methodological starting point will enable African theologians to adopt "a second viewpoint" in the debate over inculturation-liberation, and re-evaluate gender studies and feminist African theology.

ATTENTION TO HISTORY AND CULTURAL CONTEXT:

Historians of Christianity today draw attention to the southward shift of the faith resulting in the emergence of "world Christianity." Walbert Bühlmann years ago called this phenomenon the "coming of the third church." Some are alarmed that this phase of Christian history appears to ignore or to be de-centered from the gains of the Western Enlightenment. Philip Jenkins worries about the inclination of southern Christian practice towards patterns that recall the past of Western Christianity. He forecasts the future of the new Christian phase with the lens of Christendom—"global Christianity." Without minimizing the gains of the Western Enlightenment, I believe that diligent attention to the social history of diverse African peoples and critical exploration of the emerging African Christian story would yield challenging narratives. The emerging story is not a replica of the past of European Christianity.[1] Euro-American Christianity has a lot to learn from it.

African cultural studies have been challenged by Cheikh Anta Diop to be attentive to the historical factor. Diop was one of the best critical

---

1. See Bühlmann, *Coming of the Third Church*. See also Jenkins, *Next Christendom*. See the response of Sanneh to Jenkin's predictions in Sanneh, *Whose Religion Is Christianity?*

minds Africa ever produced. I share his viewpoint that patient historical research unveils not only "the cultural cement that unifies the disparate elements" of peoples of Africa, but it also unveils common or related values, practices and beliefs.[2] Theology in Africa gains mileage from interdisciplinary conversation—a conversation that is *attentive to the historical causes of the expansion of Christianity* in the continent. Historical attention to the spread of Christianity in Africa reveals the local ingenuity and displays the strategy deployed by Africans as a creative response to Western modernity mediated by Christianity. From the period of the encounter with the West (slavery, colonial and postcolonial or independence period) Christianity has always played a major role in African life. But the African ingenuity and strategy are displayed in the way Africans discovered, reinterpreted and repackaged Christianity. They are active rather than passive recipients of Christianity. One overriding pillar of the African strategy, according to Lamin Sanneh, is "mother tongue discernment." The vernacular factor, thanks to missionary ingenuity and local African reception, not only ensured the preservation of the identity of sociocultural groups. It also gave them the initiative in adopting Christianity in accordance with their historical experience and needs. Christianity, for Africans, is a powerful factor in mediating modernity and in reconstructing the identity of persons and communities.[3]

The *history of Christianity in Africa* that unveils the African appropriation and repackaging of Western modernity draws attention to founders of African initiated churches (AICs) without ignoring missionary Christianity. The radical reinterpretation of ATR by AICs in their reception or repackaging of Christianity will be discussed in detail in the second part of this book. For the Catholic Church, the renewal introduced by Vatican Council II (1962–1965) represents the clearest official support of the local appropriation of Christianity as well as modernity. Hans Küng is probably right that unlike Protestantism "Catholicism . . . 'postponed' its response to the Enlightenment until the Second Vatican

---

2. Diop, *Civilization or Barbarism*, 211–12.

3. Sanneh, *Whose Religion Is Christianity?* 55; Sanneh claims that Africa is fast becoming "a Christian continent." See also Walls, *Missionary Movement in Christian History*, 149; and Ross, "Grounding Theology in History," 123. See also the studies of Peel and Meyer that argue for the intellectual struggle to come to terms with Christianity that restructures identity—Peel, *Religious Encounter and the Making of the Yoruba*; Meyer, *Translating the Devil*.

Council."[4] The Council directed attention to the local church and encouraged local creative interpretations of the received Christian faith. Since the irruption of AICs in the 19th century, this local interpretation of Christianity was their principal focus. The emphasis on the "local" in this study should not be construed as self-insulation or ghetto mentality. But reference to local communities helps to exclude or at least limit generalizations such as Africa or African. The social histories of the communities are not reified within an ethnographic present. While I will apply a limited comparative approach to the study of beliefs and practices of West Africans, I depend as far as possible on empirical and descriptive results of research that derive from the communities that discovered Christianity.[5]

African cultures and traditions accessed through *history will neither be ignored nor romanticized.* Vigilant memory or "taking a second look at everything" (Chinua Achebe) will be my watchword. My methodological assumption can be summed up as always "taking a second look at everything." African theologians today insist on the *historical or changing patterns of African cultures and civilizations* and distance themselves from ethnological accounts (emanating from colonial ideology) that viewed African cultures in essentialist or static terms. They also distance themselves from romantic and folkloric narratives of African cultures and traditions. A critical socio-historical approach to African cultures embodies the *memory of our cultural weakness*—a weakness manifest in a rudimentary technological culture. This cultural weakness led to our being vanquished by the West (symbolized by slavery and colonization). Many African authors agree with Hamidou Kane that we must face critically the challenge of Western modernity: "we must learn from them the art of conquering without being in the right."[6] A critical approach enables a creative engagement with the project of cultural globalization facilitated by the incredible progress in information technology. Vigilant memory envisages a *living cultural tradition* which responds to contemporary needs, and a retrieving of dimensions of our heritage that carry the grain for *reinventing the African society.* This is

---

4. Bosch, *Transforming Mission*, 262. Bosch is quoting Hans Küng.

5. In this I follow Metuh's limited comparative method in ATR, Metuh, *Comparative Studies of African Traditional Religions.* But I am attentive to dangers of generalisations; see the interesting study of Owusu, "Ethnography of Africa," 704ff.

6. Kane, *Ambiguous Adventure*, 37.

a project, which, thanks to the critical contributions of Cameroonian and other central African philosophers and theologians, learns from the tribulations, aspirations and expectations or challenges that face African peoples today.[7]

Finally, attention to *cross-cultural and intercultural history* is vital in the postmodern and globalised world. Globalization displays cultural flows not only from the West to the rest of us but also from the South to the North, primarily through migration. This reverse flow displays the dynamics of "world Christianity." In contradistinction from "global Christianity" that embodies the characteristics of Christendom, "world Christianity" embodies southern local characteristics. The reverse cultural flow also highlights how diaspora African culture challenges continental Africa. The "significance of a transatlantic black culture that links the thought and practice of black communities, whether they are in Africa, in North America or Latin America, in the Caribbean or in the wider diaspora of Western Europe" must neither be ignored nor minimized.[8] These "cultural flows" connect African traditional religion (ATR) in West Africa with ATR in the Americas. Explorations into the dynamic and relational perception of God and divinities in West Africa, and its impact on Christian practice, could learn from the creativity and contradictions of the African diaspora—the extensive practice of *vodhun*, *Candomblé*, and *santeria* in Haiti, Brazil, and Cuba.

METHODOLOGICAL ASSUMPTIONS

The flexible, malleable and relational world that one encounters in West Africa invites a new kind of methodology or interpretive framework. Observation of practices or behavior, the comparison of experience from one sociocultural group to another and then weighing or balancing different viewpoints in order to make a decision must never lose touch with the *relational tension that mediates being-in-the-world*.

---

7. See Mana, *Christians and Churches of Africa*; Messi Metogo, *Dieu Peut-Il Mourir En Afrique?* 184–86; Eloi draws from the fundamental philosophical work of Boulaga, *La Crise Du Muntu*, 144–60.

8. Held et al., *Global Transformations*, 371.

Duality and Multiplicity as Foundational
to Accessing Reality in West Africa

To observers or students of the West African sociocultural context, the impact of duality or multiplicity is inescapable. Negatively, what is not related does not exist. Positively, to exist is to be related in a multiplicity of ways; to exist is therefore to be multiple. This runs through myths of origin of the individual, of the human community, and of the universe. The principle of relationship or the idea of relationality is converted into the measure of all things. The fundamental assumption that reality is plural—dual or twinned, multiple or a combination of twinned components—structures the human access to the universe. This is perhaps very well represented in Dogon (Mali) creation myth of the four primordial deities, *Nommo Anagono*. They were created by God in pairs (twinned) male and female. There are also four pairs of the primordial human ancestors, *Anagono Bile*, twinned, male-female.[9] Male-female interrelationship is perceived as the underlying principle of the complementarity of roles. Igbo (Nigeria) convert the male-female interrelationship into the dual-sex and dual-gender social ideology, not only to express gender sensitivity or gender balance. It also enables society to demarcate areas of socio-political and socioeconomic control. This reveals duality in operation; it characterizes traditional African social ideology of matriarchy. The Asante king (Ghana) receives power or authority through the Queen mother; the Ganda king (Uganda) also receives through the queen mother. Marriage among the Jelgobe—a Fulani people in Mali and Burkina Faso—dramatizes the dual-gender complementary relationship of man-woman in the construction of society. The economic role of the man keeps him outside (cattle rearing and arable farming), while the woman controls food processing and constructing the *wuro* (hut—the Jelgobe symbol of culture). The man passes through intricate processes to gain access to the woman. The *wuro* belongs to the woman; the man is an outsider to the *wuro* structure. Marriage rituals and symbolism display "the outsider status of the husband." Indeed, "[t]he new bride builds the hut. The young husband is forced into the hut, and he takes flight when he is forced into his wife's bed. For the first two years, he goes in there only as a thief; he is said to 'steal' the woman."[10] This re-

9. See Laléyé, "Les Religion De L'Afrique Noire," 651–58.

10. Amadiume, *Re-Inventing Africa*, 37–39. Amadiume is using the work of Riesman, *Freedom in Fulani Social Life*. See also her classic, Amadiume, *Male Daughters, Female Husbands*.

veals how *relational tension mediates being-in-the-world*—it is structural to the social health or wholeness of the community.

The principle of duality or multiplicity marks literary productions of the best known Nigerian masters of the art, Chinua Achebe and Wole Soyinka. Achebe, the doyen of African literature, savors duality in the Igbo aphorism, "When Something stands, Another comes to stand beside it." As an artist in search of identity both for himself and his people in a world profoundly destabilized since the experience of slavery and colonialism, Achebe updates the Igbo wisdom tradition and deploys it to respond to the modern/postmodern challenge of creating "a space of imagining a different universe." It serves as a methodological tool for "organising ourselves in a world which holds many perils for black people."[11] In a world that scorns, ignores or holds Black people in disdain, the recuperation of the structural perception of reality as multiple provides a resilient or liberating starting point. It enables one always to search for a "second point of view" or to practice "looking at everything twice." Instead of absolutizing one's conclusions, every resolution to any problem or conclusion to any discussion is left open-ended. This, I think, is a liberating assumption that can help one respond to the methodological crisis in African theology; a crisis that cannot be decoupled from the crisis in metaphysics in post-Enlightenment Western philosophy and theology. I find Victor Anderson's proposal of "creative exchange" in African American philosophical thought, which is attentive to relationality, community sense and ambiguity, very close to my West African assumptions.[12] I will now proceed to describe the challenges of this methodology and illustrate how it operates on the ground especially in the practice of ATR.

Challenge of Duality or Multiplicity

My principal assumption in this research is that duality or twin-ness and plurality—the basis of relationality—structure access to reality! This basic assumption enables me to interpret patterns of world Christianity in West Africa—especially the flexible assimilation of ATR divine qualities into qualities of God and the Holy Spirit.

11. See the study of this aspect of Achebe in Gikandi, *Reading Chinua Achebe*, 3–4.

12. Anderson, *Creative Exchange*. See chapter 1: "Beyond Dichotomies—Toward a Relational Concept of Race in African American Religious Experience."

Duality, the basis of relationality, is the lens through which reality is received—the measure of everything that exists in the West African world. The Igbo say *ife kwulu ife akwudebe ya* ("Whenever Something stands, Something Else will stand beside it"). Nothing stands alone. Life in the universe is relational. Myths, foundation narratives, proverbs and tales, i.e., "language in its original state," embody structures of duality or multiplicity. These are "a philosophical deposit in which are buried expressions and accounts of [peoples'] initial perception of reality, of their primordial exposure to Being."[13]

The challenge of relationality that duality displays lies in the fundamental declaration that reality, e.g., the human as well as the transcendent, is eminently flexible, fluid, relational, and in motion. Isolated uniqueness is abhorrent; so also are non-relational absolutes or absolutist claims. On the ground, from Nigeria to Mali, the Igbo and Yoruba of Nigeria, the Adja-Fon and Ewe of Benin, Togo and Ghana, and the Bambara and Dogon of Mali, and so on, have a horror for unicity, fixity or stasis. They rather delight in multiplicity, fluidity, relationality, and motion. Comparable experiences, widespread throughout the West African coast, show the multiple relational dimensions in the conception of the human person or in narratives about the origin of the universe.[14] The challenge to the non-Igbo or the non-West African, especially the Western pattern of thought is coping with the hypothesis that duality enjoys ontological priority and controls access to the divine. Consequently, duality or multiplicity that constitutes the core principle of Life or Being makes flexibility, fluidity and palaver/dialogue structural to definitions, to relationship among humans, and relationship with God and divinities. Or conversely, the social experience of relationship opens thought to flexibility and relationality. Hellenism's preoccupation with *being* as *one*, as noted above, is very influential in the West and its spheres of influence, including Africa. However, for West Africans, the Hellenistic qualities of being are meaningful only in relationship: when something stands, something else must stand beside it. For Anderson the relational opens an alternative window for African Americans to access reality rather than the "abstract universality, hierarchy, domination, and di-

---

13. See Nwodo, *Philosophical Perspective on Chinua Achebe*, 241. Nwodo is borrowing from Martin Heidegger's description of myth.

14. See *La Notion De La Personne En Afrique Noire*.

chotomies that characterize classical Western metaphysics."[15] In West Africa, ambivalence, collaboration and the hermeneutic of suspicion, especially the suspicion of absolutes, are the rule for accessing reality. This allows room or liberty to always adopt or search for a "second point of view," to practice "looking at everything twice." What is not relational would be degeneration and could harden to intolerance.

Duality and Flexibility—Brief Illustration from Practice of Religion in West Africa

The focus of the practice of religion in West Africa provides a good account of the challenge and relevance of my methodology to the study of the practice of Christianity in the region. Because the inhabitants of this region love flexibility, captured by duality/twin-ness and multiplicity, their perception of and approach to the divine are characterized by flexibility and tolerance.

West African ethnic religions in particular and African religions in general are non-imperial, non-proselytizing, and fundamentally non-absolutizing. In positive terms West Africans extend hospitality to all religions, foreign and local, provided they contribute to a wholesome realization of individual and community destiny. Methodist missionary, Geoffrey Parrinder, complained that among West African peoples there is little hesitation in accepting new types of worship or new divinities. There is no jealous God that forbids adding new beliefs to old ones. Aylward Shorter, from East African field experience, suggested that African Christians did not really have to make a radical break with their past; they simply added one more insurance policy on existing ones. These comments on ritual practice extend to Islam in West Africa. Robert Kaplan, journalist and political analyst, claimed that Islam in West Africa has been structurally weakened by the dominant attitude to religion in this region: "it is being hobbled by syncretization with animism."[16]

While the above comments on practice of religion represent part of the reality, one needs to highlight the structures of thought undergirding the practice. Religions found in this region (as Echeruo observed about the Igbo) are based on local covenants, regulated by domestic institu-

15. Anderson, *Creative Exchange*, 51.

16. Kaplan, *Coming Anarchy*, 35. See also Parrinder, *West African Religion*. And also Shorter, *African Christian Theology*, 10.

tions, for the realization of the destined good of the individual and community. The localization of covenants informs flexibility and results in
a multiplicity of patterns of worship. There is no obligation to worship
only in one way. Echeruo puts it poignantly in his comments on sacrifice
in Igbo religion,

> The Igbo will sacrifice to the Christian God and simultaneously
> to the local gods without embarrassment. The god in front and
> the devil behind must both be appeased. Sacrifice is not only to
> the good gods, but also to the evil ones. Nobody worships ONE
> God, and sacrifices to one god only. Each god is granted its true
> courtesy.[17]

What should not be lost in the above quotation is that it will be naïve
to ritually reduce the relational Igbo universe to one dimensional cult
model. So it is not helpful to interpret ritual practice by resorting to
oversimplification or "isms": "animism" "polytheism" or "henotheism."
Based on the principle of duality or multiplicity, one must confront or
bow to a different type of logic in the perception of hierarchy, power or
force in the universe: hierarchy is fluid or dynamic rather than fixed or
rigid. The Igbo pattern of logic enlarges the domain of reasonableness.
Flexibility structures all areas of life. However, one should not imagine
that models of religious practice are fixed. Yoruba, Adja-Fon, and Ewe
religions that are closely interrelated show, in contradistinction from
Igbo, that one can worship "one" deity—i.e., be a devotee of one *orisa*
or *vodhun*! But the same universe is peopled by multiple deities; one
therefore focuses on those that touch profoundly one's destined course
in life. The Igbo carefully relate to all deities to avert any unpredictable
threat to the realization of the human individual's destiny.

Multiplicity and diversity are the rule and are closely related to individual and community destiny. This principle also draws attention to
the most disconcerting aspect of ATR and African anthropology, the
ambivalence in the behavior of beings, spirits and forces: there is no absolute evil spirit in the West African world—duality is not identical with
Manichean dualism. The evil is in absolutist claims: e.g., positioning a
radically evil matter in opposition to a radically good spirit. For example, the ubiquitous Yoruba deity, *Eshu,* facilitator of all communication,
messenger of the deities, and helper of humans (known among the Fon

---

17. Echeruo, "Religion, Imperialism, and the Question of World Order," 19.

and the African diaspora as *Elêgbara* or *Lêgba*) is also the deity of confusion. *Eshu* illustrates the ambiguity, the ambivalence and the struggle to come to terms with the dynamic West African world. Missionary Christianity called *Eshu* the devil! (Compare with the evolution of Satan in the Book of Job to Satan-Devil in the Book of Revelation.) This is the dominant perception of Christians today with regard to this deity. The contemporary Christian perception of *Eshu* totally misrepresents and oversimplifies the identity and function of *Eshu* from the perspective of West Africa. The evocation of *Eshu* in the African diaspora provides insight into ambivalence and ambiguity in West African religion. *Eshu* was the devil for the slave owners in Brazil; but for the slaves *Eshu* was the guardian angel, angel Gabriel, or St Peter depending on which Candomblé (meeting) one attended. Patrick Claffey and J. D. Y Peel are so fascinated with the position of *Lêgba* (*Eshu*) in the nineteenth century and contemporary Dahomey (Benin) and Yoruba worlds that they baptized *Lêgba* (*Eshu*) the *vodhun/orisa* of the age of confusion.[18] This is only part of the reality. *Eshu* still serves as the deity of the age of communication. This keeps alive *ambivalence* and the *relational tension that mediates being-in-the-world.*

Ontological Underpinnings of West African Religions

The reference to the multiple tendencies in Igbo ritual behavior draws attention to the underlying ontological principle of duality and plurality that is the basis for understanding being and religion in this region. Christopher Nwodo's *Philosophical Perspective on Chinua Achebe* develops Igbo philosophy and insight into Being by focusing on duality.[19] I draw from some of his conclusions. The aphorism "When Something stands, Another comes to stand beside it" is repeated every so often as the ontological principle undergirding the understanding of the emergence of the Igbo human type. Igbo republicanism, their practice of direct democracy and their love for debate or palaver are derived from this principle. Duality or relationality is at the core of religion; it is at the core of the perception of *Chukwu*, the Supreme God. This is captured

18. See Bastide, *Le Candomblé De Bahia (Rite Nagô)*, 109ff.; 282, etc. Claffey, "Looking for a Breakthrough," 91–93. See also Peel, *Religious Encounter and the Making of the Yoruba*, 48–53.

19. Nwodo, *Philosophical Perspective on Chinua Achebe*.

in the founding myth of Nri (the most influential Igbo village-group). Northcote Thomas reported in 1913,

> The traditional account of the origin of kingship is that Ezenri and Ezeadama came from heaven and rested on an ant heap; all was water. Cuku asked who was sitting there and they answered, "We are the kings of Nri and Adama," therefore Cuku and the kings talked. After some conversation Cuku gave them each a piece of yam; yams were that time unknown to man, for human beings walked in the bush like animals.[20]

This cosmogonic myth of the civilizing heroes of Nri and Adama and the founding narrative of agriculture reveal interesting structures. The figure of the hero puts experience of being "on the track of existential structures"; the figure of the hero sums up and recapitulates the human type (Paul Ricœur).[21] What is unmistakable in this narrative is that the figure of the hero or the human type emerges in the context of palaver or conversation. To be is to be related! However, another version of the myth, while retaining the structure of dialogue, shatters the idealism of relationship by introducing the ritual sacrifice of the founding hero's son and daughter at the orders of *Chukwu*. Two marks (stigmata) of civilization followed the sacrifice: the one, human industry and agricultural production; the other, respect for life as foundation of morality. First, "Yam and palm tree grew out of the spot where he buried his son and vegetables and cocoyam grew out of the spot where he buried his daughter." Second, "there was a covenant between earth and man. The earth produces the food that man eats. The earth becomes the greatest supernatural force [*alusi*] . . . No person should defile the earth by spilling human blood in violence on it. This is the covenant."[22] There is no explanation for the command of *Chukwu* to offer human sacrifice. It could indicate the ambivalence in relationship within the human and supra-human worlds. One can also draw the conclusion that because or in spite of the human sacrifice, the Earth (*Ala*) that is spiritualized becomes nourisher and guarantor of the sacredness of human life.

Achebe points to the above myth as a good entry point of discussing the Igbo worldview that stresses palaver as the hub of life captured in the image of the archetypal beings. Among the Igbo, *chi* (the bearer

20. Thomas, *Anthropological Report on the Ibo-Speaking Peoples of Nigeria*, vol. 1, 50.

21. Ricoeur, *Symbolism of Evil*, 162–63.

22. See Isichei, *Igbo Worlds*, 21–24.

of destiny received from *Chukwu* at creation), does not deny one active voice in the determination or choice of destiny: "a man may talk and even bargain with his *chi* at the moment of his creation or when he needs to redress an oppressive destiny." Achebe continues in amazement,

> And what is more, Chukwu Himself in all His power and maj-esty, did not make the Igbo world by fiat. He held conversations with mankind. He talked with those archetypal men of Nri and Adama, and even enlisted their cooperation and good offices.

Nwodo draws the following conclusion from Achebe's statement: "A people who think this way about themselves and even about God are bound to constitute an irritant to others especially those in authority."[23] The finding of Nwodo is not unique to Igbo. The myth of pre-existence and having a predestined course in life involving conversation with God and/or the deity bearing destiny are common. In the complex West African universe humans are not a pawn in the hands of fate or dei-ties. The individual's destiny *Se* (Adja-Fon), *Chi* (Igbo), *Okra* (Asante), *Aklama* (Ewe) is packaged, received or democratically chosen at the ancestral location of pre-existence (e.g., *Bome* of the Ewe).[24]

Without overlaboring the argument, the divine-human dialogue in the Igbo narrative reveals that God, experienced relationally, is for the good of humans: religion is anthropocentric. God for humans values the dignity of humans to the point of engaging them in conversation or dialogue right from creation: they participated in the invention of agriculture; they enjoyed freedom in plotting out their needs and they actively cooperated in searching for ways of realizing their needs in this world.

If the above relational structure of approaching reality and en-countering the divine is a fair interpretation of the Igbo tradition, with similarities and dissimilarities along the West African coast, one can appreciate not only how such a pattern of palaver could be irritat-ing in intercultural social living but also how it could pose enormous problems in the encounter with Islamic and Christian traditions that carry universalist, absolutist and exclusivist claims. Wole Soyinka, in his acknowledgement lecture of the Nobel Prize in literature, took issue

---

23. Nwodo, *Philosophical Perspective on Chinua Achebe*, 274–75. Nwodo quotes from a tape-recording of the address.

24. See Lovell, *Cord of Blood*. Also Eggen, "Mawu Does Not Kill."

with the exclusivist monotheism of Western Christianity that denigrated African religious values. He refuted Hegel's claim (made in *Lectures on the Philosophy of World History)* that monotheism is the symbol of civilization. Soyinka rather declared that the multiple spirits and mediators, like in the Yoruba *orisa* religion, were a more viable option. Soyinka's claim for his Yoruba *Orisa* religion is based on the existential experience of *orisa* cult as flexible, tolerant and respectful of the human person, as opposed to what he considers the Christian totalizing and intolerant monotheistic order that denigrated other ways.[25] Soyinka condemned the intolerance of the two foreign religions found in Africa—Islam and Christianity—because in their exclusivism they do not promote the freedom and dignity of all humans. He aligned himself with the "social vision" transmitted in African religion that he claims to be characterized by tolerance:

> The spirituality of the black continent, as attested, for instance, in the religion of the *orisa*, abhors such principles of coercion or exclusion, and recognizes all manifestations of spiritual urgings as attributes of the complex disposition of godhead. *Tolerance* is synonymous with the spirituality of the black continent, *intolerance* anathema![26]

Soyinka is not simply idealizing African religion. He sees *orisa* religion that embodies flexibility and malleability as profoundly humanist. In his contribution to *Òrìsà Devotion as World Religion: The Globalization of Yorùbá Religious Culture,* he enthused: "It is the profound humanism of the *orisa* that recommends it to a world in need of the elimination of conflict, since the main source of conflict between nations and among peoples is to be found as much in the struggle for economic resources as in the tendency toward the domination of ideas, be these secular or theological."[27] The viewpoint of pioneer African theologian, Bolaji Idowu, goes in the same direction. He believed that a renewed ATR is the only hope for the spiritual renovation of Africans. This could explain why many African intellectuals, of nativistic inclination, actively promote worship and study of African religion that they perceive as more

---

25. Soyinka, *Que Ce Passé Parle À Son Présent.* I am grateful to Bede Ukwuije for drawing my attention to this lecture of Soyinka.

26. Soyinka, *Burden of Memory,* 48.

27. Soyinka, "Tolerant Gods," 48.

viable for providing integral human-world wholeness.[28] While I adopt relationality as foundational to accessing reality and follow the humanist intentionality of ATR, I will contest Soyinka's claim that the two religions that originated from the Near East—Christianity and Islam—are refractory to relationship. West African Christian practice, as I will show in the second part of this study, lives and elaborates this relationship based on the flexibility of both ATR and Christianity.

Risks of Change and Viability of a new Methodology

The above discussion tries to clarify my methodological preference. I find in the saying "Whenever something stands, something else will stand beside it" an underlying ontological principle that provides a sound instrument for accessing the West African universe. It provides a tool for exploring the appropriation of Christianity in West Africa.

Every methodological assumption carries risks. The evocation of myths and the analytical principles I draw from them, especially in the postmodern world that assumes the end of all grand narratives, may sound like cultural romanticism. No science ever claims that its fundamental principles or assumptions, the tacit dimensions of our knowing, are proven. It is necessary to state that part of the problems of African theology is rooted in the crisis of metaphysics in classical West European tradition which abandoned the essentialist pattern of thinking since Heidegger. Existentialism, the philosophy of language and hermeneutics provided new philosophical orientations. African theologians are on tenterhooks over which philosophical system or social science theories to adopt in order to ground their theology.

I have no intention of ignoring the modern or postmodern gains in this study. However, my methodological assumption based on home-spun wisdom tradition allows me the freedom of home rule: it enables me to give weight and attentiveness to contextual history and experience, critically analyze the same, dialogue and compare with other experiences, and reach informed conclusion that still must be left open-ended. Dancing with borrowed dress has its inconveniences. (The owner of the dress may ask for its return in the midst of the dance. Embarrassment!) Dependence on foreign mentors limits one's freedom when one is challenged by the structures of the reality on the ground. The views of

---

28. See Idowu, *African Traditional Religion*, 208; and also Ejizu, "Down but Not Out," 193.

Nigerian historian, the late Adiele Afigbo, that methodological assumptions of African literary works should be based on homespun wisdom traditions do apply to the theological enterprise. One should stop playing the game of others, but design one's own game and set the rules.

> When you agree to play a game already designed by a god or by a man, you offer yourself to be bound hands and feet, for it means you have accepted the rules and regulations invented by the designer to ensure that that game is played according to his rules and may be his desires . . .

However, if you want to "free yourself," you "design your own game and draw up its rules and regulations."[29] Reinventing the wheel on the social, economic, political, philosophical or religious levels is tough job; but it has to be done. The importance of *home rule* will become clear in my analysis of the anthropology and psychology that undergird trance and possession in West African Christianity (see the second part of this study).

The advantage of converting the principle of duality or plurality or the combination of twinned components into a method lies in the fact that on the ground it structures the perception of reality in the West African universe. It obliges one always to take a second look at everything, to question all assumptions without exception, including the African tradition itself. This assumption helps one to appreciate another Igbo aphorism that stresses cross-cultural conversation and the limitations of the local: "one does not watch a masquerade from one spot." "The world is like a Mask dancing. If you want to see it well you do not stand in one place."[30] Life is dynamic, relational, and open to change. Dynamism and openness to change allow one to learn from the other without idolizing the other. Pertinent African theology should neither be hooked unto foreign models nor insulated within essentialist bonding with the ancestral past: "a man must dance the dance prevailing in his time."

The methodology based on duality and motion underlines *change* as implacable: it respects neither individuals, nor community nor divinities. As Nnolim insists from his study of Achebe, "The forces of change

---

29. Afigbo, "Dialogue of Civilizations," 5–6. This article has been republished in the collected works of Afigbo, *Igbo History and Society*, 459–76.

30. Achebe, *Arrow of God*, 51.

are the modern Fates, the Nemesis that must forcefully tame the stubborn individual."[31] Results of works that follow this method could appear eclectic and may annoy purists. Nevertheless, the literary productions of Wole Soyinka and Chinua Achebe, despite their eclecticism, display the liberty and creativity their style generates. It mediates intercultural understanding in our globalizing world; and helps one to narrate in familiar language "to our community what it is that has attracted us elsewhere." It is a subtle instrument of appreciating world Christianity or the discovery of Christianity in West African style. One appreciates that truth is not prisoner of any culture or of any historical period; for, "no culture can stand alone in defining or exemplifying the riches of human aspiration" (David Burrell).[32] As Paulin Hountondji proposed,

> Instead of blindly condemning our traditions on behalf of reason, or rejecting the latter on behalf of the former, or making an absolute of the internal rationality of these traditions, it seems more reasonable to me to try and know our traditions as they were, beyond any mythology and distortion, not merely for the purpose of self-identification or justification, but in order to help us meet the challenges and problems of today.[33]

My methodology, I believe, will help to arrest the dissipation of energy in debates in African theology over adaptation, indigenization, inculturation, liberation, reconstruction, feminist hermeneutics, etc. These theological orientations complement one another. The principle of duality or multiplicity will help our review of the experience of God-Spirit-Christ to reveal the unique and difficult way the West African discovery of Christianity is trying to come to terms with the multiplicity of deities, spirits, ancestors, and mediators interrelating with humans for their good. I believe this provides a creative instrument for approaching human wholeness, for re-envisioning and reinventing a healthy society and a healthy world, guided by God's Holy Spirit.

Needless to say, the wisdom tradition that allows us to take a second look at everything impacts on society and society impacts on it for better

31. Nnolim, *Approaches to the African Novel*. See especially the chapter with title "Technique and Meaning in Achebe's *Arrow of God*" 209–33; 210.

32. Burrell, *Friendship and Ways to the Truth*, 37, 40; and the whole of chapter 3 that has the title, "The Role of Dialogue and Friendship in Cross-Cultural Understanding."

33. Hountondji "Reason and Tradition," 142–43; cited by Mudimbe, *Invention of Africa*, 174–75.

or for worse. There is no guarantee it will survive cultural globalization. Cheikh Anta Diop who postulated goodness, gaiety, optimism, social sense, etc., as dimensions of the African psychic identity that encourage a communitarian ethos (in contradistinction from individualistic social structures that communicate insecurity and pessimism) warned that there is nothing absolute about these psychic reactions since they are in permanent flux.[34] The violence and erosion of human dignity in most West African countries (Sierra Leone, Liberia, Cote d'Ivoire, Nigeria, not to mention the tragedies of Rwanda, the Congo and Sudan) show that the radical transformation of economic and political realities could erode the fundamental relational perception of the world dominant in our region. Persistent misrule, creation of a dominant and oppressive class, and the emergence of dependent-client class, could install feudalism, entrench pessimism and individualism, and jeopardise the freedom of always searching for a second point of view. Achebe taking note of the overall *degeneration* that followed the ambiguous encounter between Africans and Europeans, despite the gains in the encounter, stated: "What happens is that some of the worst elements of the old are retained and some of the worst of the new are added on to them." Things could have been different and can still be different in the meeting of the two cultures: "we could pick out the best in the other and retain the best in our own, and this would be wonderful."[35] In taking the principle of duality as methodological assumption one hopes to retain the best in the encounter of cultures.

I now turn to how my methodology restructures the African theology debate.

34. Diop, *Civilization or Barbarism*, 218–19.

35. Chinua Achebe's keynote address on Igbo worldview given the University of Nigeria Nsukka, quoted by Nwodo, *Philosophical Perspective on Chinua Achebe*, 277.

2

Impact of Openness to Duality or Plurality on the African Theology Debate

"**L**OOKING AT EVERYTHING TWICE" enables one to cope with identity and difference. Pioneer African theologians have been accused of *culturalism,* of being unable to handle the identity crisis as creatively as the creators of the African novel. Their pattern of retrieval of ethnological material reduces their production to ethnophilosophy. Opponents of inculturation argue that the incipient culturalism of the pioneers led them to lock up Africa within an immobile essentialist ethnological past. They are accused of neglecting the historical moment of Africa, the dynamic permutations in culture, the reality of modernity, and the impact of intercultural conversations that were going on in pre-colonial, colonial and post-colonial periods of African history. Oscar Bimwenyi-Kweshi and the Kinshasa school are in the dock.

I refer briefly in this chapter to the history of the African theology debate to draw attention to the theological mileage one gains by anchoring one's discourse on the dynamic patterns of African thought that transcend particularity without ignoring the particular. My methodic focus on plurality or duality, the basis of relationality, argues that relational tension that ontologically mediates being-in-the-world also mediates access to the internal logic of the discourse on divine-human relationship.

BRIEF HISTORY OF THE AFRICAN THEOLOGY DEBATE

The African theology debate erupted in Kinshasa (*Faculté de Théologie Catholique de Kinshasa*—Louvanium) in 1960. It started as a reaction to questions posed by Tharcisse Tshibangu (then a theology student—now Bishop of Mbuju-mayi diocese and retired rector of the universities of Zaire). The respondent then was Canon Alfred Vanneste, the founding rector of Louvanium.

Tshibangu in an argument suffused with the identity crisis of the time, proposed a radical change in the philosophical and cultural sources utilized in Christian theology in Africa; the change was to enable the Christianization of the African mentality through adaptation. Tshibangu proposed a methodological approach that would take onboard the broad outlines of African thought—such as intuition and a global, dynamic or vitalistic view of the universe. The proposed approach echoes *Negritude* poets and Placide Tempels' *Bantu Philosophy*. Tshibangu was not suggesting a mere re-examination of Christian thought or putting external African coating on Christian thought. Rather he was interested in creating a scientific theology in Africa similar to the Jewish-Christian theology in its Graeco-Roman expression. His project is similar to Matteo Ricci's accommodation method practiced in the sixteenth century. Ricci's method proposed to bring Christianity and Chinese traditions into fruitful encounter through friendship, adopting local lifestyle, translation of ideas, identifying common ground, and so on. Tshibangu's theological energy would later be dominated by the passion to explore the scientific nature of Western theology, to justify historically the plurality of theological traditions, and to expose to any doubters the merits of African theology.[1]

Alfred Vanneste captioned his response to Tshibangu, "D'abord une vraie théologie" ("first of all a true theology"). For him "a true theology" for Africa must first and foremost be steeped in "universal thought." Theology must be built on patient and detailed examination of the sources of Christian revelation; it must be in permanent contact with the principal currents of universal thought. Africans should either be steeped in universal theology or risk being relegated to second-class theologians. Only when African theologians have been profoundly

---

1. Tshibangu, *Théologie Comme Science Au Xxème Siècle*; and also his *Théologie Positive Et Théologie Spéculative*. See also Tempels, *Bantu Philosophy*. Kwame Bediako presents an interesting comparison between second-century CE Patristic method in theology and modern African theology; both are preoccupied with the question of identity. Bediako, *Theology and Identity*.

soaked in universal theology would the question of integrating the broad outlines of African thought into "pastoral theology" arise.

Tshibangu captured the widespread crisis of identity of his time. His arguments for pluralism in theology even before Vatican II remain relevant. On the other hand, Vanneste epitomized the paternalism, superiority complex and univocal thinking that characterized the encounter between Africa and the West. However Vanneste's preoccupation with "universal thought" should not be dismissed without further remarks. It provides the healthy "second glance" at the local or contextual. Theology preoccupied with its object God-Spirit-Christ, should, despite its sociocultural context, be able to address all humans coming from God. The weakness of Vanneste's position is the assumption that "universal thought" is identical with Western local thought.[2]

Tshibangu's arguments are inspired first by *Negritude*—"the recognition of the fact of being black, the acceptance of this fact, of our destiny as blacks, of our history and our culture" (Aimé Cesaire).[3] Second, it was influenced by the provocative work of Placide Tempels—*Bantu Philosophy*—the first systematic attempt to draw attention to African presentational thought patterns as philosophy, ethno-philosophy. Tempels claimed a vitalistic undercurrent as cement of Bantu life and thought; this should be perfected and assimilated into European thought. His critics, especially from the Bantu linguistic group, accuse him of prolonging the ideological and colonial project of inferiorizing everything that is non-European. Nevertheless, Tempels' impact on African theological discourse in the Central African region, in works of pioneers like Vincent Mulago, argues for the pertinence of his position. The dynamic patterns of his insight should not be lost.[4]

Des Prêtres noirs s'interrogent, published in 1956, resonated with the gains of *Negritude* and *African Personality* and clearly integrated the philosophical assumptions of Tempels. Francophone African and Haitian priests probed issues related to mission, church, and theology in Africa using terms such as *adaptation, negritude, indigenization,* and

2. Tshibangu and Vanneste, "Débat Sur La Théologie Africaine," 43–58, 169–90. See also the review of the works of Tshibangu and Vanneste by Ntakuritimana in Ntakarutimana, *Vers Une Théologie Africaine: La Théologie Et Les Théologiens Au Congo,* esp. 49–75.

3. Senghor, "Problématique De Négritude," 14.

4. Mulago, "L'union Vitale Bantu."

africanization. Meinrad Hebga in his contribution captured the identity feelings of the time:

> World Christianity should assume in our home a Black aspect
> . . . We desire to present to Christ dishes prepared in our country.
> In philosophy and theology, the unexploited theory of vitalistic
> forces, the metaphysical obsession with mutual interference of
> created causalities, the tendency to have a humble opinion of
> oneself, the desire for patriarchal institutions; in liturgy, the me-
> lodious lamentations which support the collective assemblies of
> contrition, sacred dances, sometimes very forceful, communicat-
> ing religious emotion, simple but beautiful rituals, symbols that
> are very natural; in exegesis, the contact between the linguistic
> genius of the Orient and our own. . . .[5]

This insight of Hebga, despite the inclination towards romanticizing Africa, sums up the underlying missiological thrust of key aspects of African theology—inculturation, liberation, reconstruction, and even interculturation. They are all preoccupied with the relevance of the Christian faith for Africans. They constitute complementary viewpoints.

It is my view that pioneer African theologians were methodologi-cally ill-equipped to interpret the African discovery of Christianity. They were preoccupied with providing answers to questions set else-where—the theological concerns of the academia. On the contrary, the theological interpretation of the African discovery of Christianity is prompted by contextual questions. The answers that are relevant, I argue, are drawn from the dynamic systems of thought of the local that lay a firm bridge for transcending the local. This is the creative art of intercultural understanding that enables us to narrate with clarity "to our community what it is that has attracted us elsewhere."[6]

ADVANTAGES OF METHODOLOGY ANCHORED ON DUALITY OR RELATIONALITY—OPENNESS TO INTERDISCIPLINARY CONVERSATION

The debate in Kinshasa happened within a theology classroom where the dominant theological language was controlled by neo-scholasticism. Catholic pioneer theologians like Vincent Mulago and Charles Nyamiti, who completed their theological education before Vatican II, could not

5. Hebga, "Christianisme Et Négritude," 200.
6. Burrell, *Friendship and Ways to the Truth,* 37.

escape the neo-scholastic circle of discourse. They and their successors adopted the dominant Western philosophical and theological systems as well as the prevailing sociological theories to structure their theology. Even Oscar Bimwenyi-Kweshi, the best exponent of systematic foundations of African theological discourse, relied on the philosophy of language and the existentialism of Martin Heidegger and Rudolf Bultmann to cushion his argument for access to revelation through African religious experience. Barthélémy Adoukonou who brought energy and erudition into the study of *vodhun* in Benin republic in view of the inculturation of Christianity is not weaned off classical Western philosophy and theology. The fear of syncretism perhaps made him to force cultural patterns to be supplanted from their matrix guided solely by pre-established Western Christian theological interest. Even those radically opposed to the narrow ethnological approach of the pioneers (Ela, Kä Mana, and Eboussi-Boulaga) do not deny their dependence on Western philosophical and theological methods. Jean-Marc Ela's liberation theology depends on Latin American theology and on Marxist social analysis. Kä Mana in his evangelicalism rejects inculturation and liberation, but this did not make him less dependent on the philosophical assumptions of Hannah Arendt. Eboussi-Boulaga who called for a radical liberation from epistemological dependence or fetishism in order to follow the christic liberative model in Christian life and thought cannot hide his Hegelianism and inclination to liberal theology.[7]

I made a choice for a methodology anchored on the underlying duality or multiplicity of reality in West Africa because I wish to engage in interdisciplinary conversation with the humanism of the masters of African literature. The *identity crisis* of pioneer African theologians is closely linked with the colonial and postcolonial African context. The response in French-speaking Africa was *Negritude*. English-speaking Africans never accepted the romanticization of Africa captured by Senghor in the oft quoted phrase "emotion is African while reason is Greek." They were inclined towards African Personality that tries to re-conceptualize the anguish of the human (African) person, revaluate (like

---

7. See Bimwenyi-Kweshi, *Discours Théologique Négro-Africain*. Adoukonou is best known for the two volumes of his published thesis: Adoukonou, *Jalons Pour Une Théologie Africaine: Essai D'une Herméneutique Chrétienne Du Vodun Dahoméen*. Sidbe Sempore regards him as pioneer of inculturation in West Africa—Semporé, "Barthélémy Adoukonou—Un Pionnier De L'inculturation En Afrique De L'ouest." See also Danet and Metogo, "L'afrique Francophone."

Negritude) the "neglected humanistic properties" of their cultures, and draw inspiration from their "mystic wisdom that defied materialism."[8] Such re-conceptualization explains the overwhelming lamentation or pessimism that characterized pioneer African literary style revealed in the African novel. Charles Nnolim argues that the pessimistic aesthetic in the African novel goes back to the pioneer African novelist Chinua Achebe.

> Achebe's philosophic pessimism has imbued African literature with a general sense of loss, enough to be part of its aesthetic, so that our fiction, our poetry and our drama are imbued with this circumambient sense of loss—the loss of our heroes, the loss of our culture and values, the loss of our religion, the loss of our land, the loss of our dignity as human beings, the loss of confidence in ourselves, the moral loss among our youth who have unresistingly succumbed to the allure of Europe, the loss of our language, and finally, the loss of that unity which was our bulwark against foreign invasion.[9]

Colonial and postcolonial African novelists like Ngugi wa Thiongo, Cheikh Hamidou Kane, Ferdinand Oyono, Ousmane Sembène, Mongo Beti, Peter Abrahams, Alex Guma drew from this aesthetic.

This general climate of pessimism as aesthetic or literary style impacted on pioneer African theologians. The sense of loss of our heritage is captured poetically by Engelbert Mveng in the rhetoric of anthropological poverty, whose frontiers of deprivation include and therefore are wider than, material poverty.

> When persons are deprived not only of goods and possessions of a material, spiritual, moral, intellectual, cultural, or sociological order, but of everything that makes up the foundation of their being-in-the-world and the specificity of their "ipseity" as individual, society, and history—when persons are bereft of their identity, their dignity, their freedom, their thought, their history, their language, their faith universe, and their basic creativity, deprived of all their rights, their hopes, their ambitions (that is, when they are robbed of their own ways of living and existing)—they sink into a kind of poverty which no longer concerns only exterior or interior goods or possessions but strikes at the very being, essence, and dignity of the human person. It is this

8. Soyinka, *Burden of Memory*, 170.

9. Nnolim, "Achebe's Tragic Heroes," 90.

poverty that we call anthropological poverty. This is an *indigence of being,* the legacy of centuries of slavery and colonization.[10]

This basic lamentation partly informs the defensive or apologetic reaction of pioneer African theologians to the demonization of African religious and cultural traditions. The pioneering works of Bolaji Idowu, Francis Arinze, and Emefie Ikenga-Metuh (Nigeria), John S Mbiti (Kenya), Vincent Mulago (Congo), Alexis Kagamé (Rwanda), and Engelbert Mveng (Cameroon), become thus not only works of religious studies, philosophy and theology, but invaluable documents of cultural retrieval of Africa's past tradition.[11] One should include in this retrieval the works of first generation reactive and apologetic African biblical scholarship that used the comparative method. But of special significance are the numerous conferences and consultations that focused on ATR and the evaluation of the reception of the Christian faith by converted Africans.[12]

Following my methodology of always looking at everything twice or always searching for "a second point of view" I believe that, on the one hand, one must take seriously the hermeneutic of suspicion adopted by theologians and philosophers like Eboussi-Boulaga, Kä Mana, and Jean-Marc Ela toward the apologetic approach and the ethnological claims of the pioneers. The quest for a creative imagination capable of releasing the African potential (Kä Mana) can only be mediated by a methodology that is capable of liberating the theologian from being prisoner of a frozen immobile past. On the other hand, it would be perilous to the project of local theology to deny the creative potential embedded

10. Mveng, "Impoverishment and Liberation," 156.

11. Arinze, *Sacrifice in Ibo Religion*; Idowu, *African Traditional Religion*; Idowu, *Olódùmarè*; Mbiti, *African Religions & Philosophy*; Mbiti, *Concepts of God in Africa*; Mbiti, *Prayers of African Religio*; Ikenga Metuh, *God and Man in African Religion*; Mulago, "L'union Vitale Bantu,"; Mulago, *Un Visage Africain Du Christianisme*; Mveng, *L'afrique Dans L'eglise*; Mveng, *L'art D'afrique Noire*; Kagamé, *La Philosophie Bantu Comparée.*

12. See Baëta, *Christianity in Tropical Africa.* See also the result of a similar seminar held in the university of Jos, Nigeria Fashole-Luke, *Christianity in Independent Africa.* The result of the 1965 Ghana conference convoked by the All Africa Conference of Churches was published in 1969—Dickson and Ellingworth, *Biblical Revelation and African Beliefs.* The Bouake symposium is published—see Monastère bénédictin (Bouaké Ivory Coast), *Les Religions Africaines Traditionnelles.* See also Glasswell and Fashole-Luke, *New Testament Christianity for Africa and the World*; P. Pernot, *Tradition Et Modernisme En Afrique Noire.* See also Ukpong, "Developments in Biblical Interpretation in Africa."

in the African memory and in the dynamic aspects of African thought. For example, the recognition of the creativity of the "galaxy of prophets and founders" of AICs (Kä Mana) as inspiration to reconstruct and re-evangelize, is a commentary on and an acknowledgment of the creative potentials of their local culture that led them to discover or reinterpret Christianity.[13]

Following my methodology, I believe that theological research, open to interdisciplinary conversation, learns from the humanistic properties embedded in African tradition that inspired the creative scholars in African studies and African literature. This involves a revaluation of the religion and cultures of Africa. I feel justified in following Achebe's bold adoption of duality and relationality rooted in Igbo and West African cultural traditions to enhance my theological reflection. This provides a standpoint to look for the best in both the African and non-African traditions without romanticizing any tradition.

INTERDISCIPLINARY CONVERSATION AND CHANGE IN THEOLOGICAL FOCUS

Bimwenyi and the highly criticized Kinshasa school while drawing the flak of colleagues need to be appreciated also for their contribution. Bimwenyi's great merit is that his systematic foundations to theology in Africa go beyond discourse of adaptation and even incarnation; what is incarnated should not be an adaptation of a previous incarnation. His Achilles heel is revealed in his approach to modernity: has modernity swallowed up the African originality? After examining rapid change on the morphological level (dress, housing, roads and transportation, economy, leisure, etc.), slower change on the institutional level (politics and all societal organization), and very slow change on the level of fundamental symbols (religion and worldview), Bimwenyi concluded enthusiastically—"le bosquet initiatique n'a pas flambé"—i.e., the initiation camp is still intact and not torched. He optimistically claimed that on the level of fundamental significations where foundational questions of life, death, God and the invisible hierarchies are raised, African theology pitches its tent.

---

13. See Eboussi Boulaga, *Christianity without Fetishes*. Ela, *African Cry*; Mana, *Christ D'afrique*; Mana, *Christians and Churches of Africa*.

Bimwenyi's work stands out as the most coherent and erudite presentation of the foundations of African theological discourse. However, his optimistic pronouncement about ATR and its worldview could be justified in places like Bé (Togo), Abomey (Benin Republic), Benin City and Ehugbo (Nigeria) where one may encounter aspects of the traditional religious values conceding ground with difficulty to modernity. But these islands of survival are loud proclamations that the camp has been torched. The torching of the camp went along with the sacking or profound transformation of the political, economic and social institutions. The new roads, railways and schools are part and parcel of colonial and Christian implantation; they are part and parcel of modernity. Achebe is on target, "The white man, the new religion, the soldiers, the new road—they are all part of the same thing."[14] Each stands beside the other to support or increase the inroads of modernity. No level is immune to profound change.

Bimwenyi appears to be aware of the necessary reinterpretation of his position. In sharing ideas with his compatriot, Kä Mana, an acerbic critic of the Kinshasa school, he warned "against confusing the core values of a culture with events of the recent or distant past which punctuate its historical evolution." The "initiation grove" should be interpreted metaphorically with emphasis on "initiation" instead of on "grove." The initiation grove "is not a place to inhabit once more, but power to initiate again, to relaunch and to re-envision: a creative breath which makes the initiated a different man, a new being, born again in the spirit of his own culture, his vital force."[15]

The homespun methodological framework that I adopt in this study ensures that interdisciplinarity aligns African theology with the rest of colonial and post-colonial African literary production for the transformation of the continent. Modernity aroused profound questions that call for reinterpretation of all values and doctrines. A balanced methodology enables African theology to be free from being stuck with archaic social science theories. African theology can display the sharp "cutting edge" (Desmond Tutu) as aesthetic discourse that embodies the "spirit" of African cultures, leads to ethical action, and challenges systemic corruption and the systematic brutalization of Africans by post-colonial rulers. Learning about "change" from Achebe's narrative philosophy

14. Achebe, *Arrow of God*, 97.

15. Mana, *Christians and Churches of Africa*, 83.

and Soyinka's social vision, and drawing from the humanistic properties embedded in African religious universe, one can demonstrate that
inculturation and liberation are bedfellows rather than antagonists.
Flexibility, negotiation, and learning from the other are preferred to univocal, absolutist and exclusivist language.

INCULTURATION OR LIBERATION—
ADOPTING "A SECOND POINT OF VIEW"

The quarrel over *material poverty* and *anthropological poverty* highlights
the misunderstanding in the theological debate in Africa over inculturation and liberation. It takes new color when approached through duality, flexibility and openness to the other. Congolese theologian, Ngindu
Mushete, believed that Marxist social analysis could be imperfectly applied to African theological discourse on poverty. While Latin American
theologians stress *material poverty*, African theologians go beyond
material poverty to include cultural, religious, and racial dimensions
of liberation. Thus Ngindu and Mveng assert that liberation theology
started in Africa when AICs declared their selfhood over against racism and adopted Christian worship in African language and symbols.
The positions of these Central African theologians became explosive at
the Ecumenical Association of Third World Theologians (EATWOT)
conference of 1981 in New Delhi. Paragraph 19 of the final declaration
states,

> If the majority [of participants] underlined material poverty,
> others, especially representatives from central Africa, stressed
> anthropological or cultural poverty where they locate the depri-
> vation and suppression of their people. Colonialism provoked
> the loss of their identity, a weakening of their creativity, it dislo-
> cated recklessly their life and tribal organization and destroyed
> indigenous values, religious beliefs, and traditional culture. The
> results of these ravages are today maintained by economic and
> cultural neo-colonialism.[16]

This position inspired Mveng's thesis of anthropological impoverishment—"an *indigence of being*, the legacy of centuries of slavery and
colonization."[17] Espousing such inflexible position explains the conflict

---

16. See Fabella and Torres, *Irruption of the Third World*.

17. Mveng, "Impoverishment and Liberation," 156.

in Francophone African theology. However, my methodology inspired by the West African humanistic perspective that highlights duality, multiplicity, flexibility and openness to change embodies invention and reinvention, only in relationality, and rejects rigid doctrinaire Marxism.

Jean-Marc Ela in 1980 did not address the cultural dimensions of poverty. His numerous works focused on material poverty that trailed the corruption-riddled postcolonial African nation-states. He is the leading figure in critical liberation theology in post-colonial Africa. His compatriot, Eloi Messi Metogo, claimed that the anthropological poverty rhetoric is a *ploy to take the edge off liberation theology in Africa in defense of inculturation.* Nothing has created so much bad blood between Cameroonian and Congolese theologians. Kä Mana is perhaps right that Mveng and Ela could have offered a key to the freedom of Africans were their anthropological and political conceptions of "Christ the liberator" established on a firmer bridge. Ela's recent work tries to do precisely that. His recent discussion of God and Christ addressed the history of oppression, called for liberation, but at the same time affirmed the social and cultural resources of Africa that must be retrieved to rebuild a world and a church where diversity is the rule.[18]

African theology must go beyond the misunderstanding between liberation and inculturation. Duality, plurality or relationality insists that no one view of poverty covers all its dimensions. Ela is therefore correct in drawing attention to the naivety of inculturation theology that ignores the violence and political roguery of the post-colonial ruling Mafiosi. Theology should not be content with liturgical sedation, talking drums that deaden the senses, and ignore the oppressive heavy hands laid on the people, as the Negro Spirituals did with the African American slaves. He is right to call on the Churches to go beyond folkloric inculturation, to challenge the root causes of suffering, and to face the reality of change in the continent. Negatively, one must reject inculturation locked up in mystification and sacralization of structures of power with seductive rhetoric of authenticity and cultural identity. Positively, one adopts inculturation with a social liberating agenda.

18. See Mana, *Christ D'afrique*, 61; see also the study of the thought of Kä Mana by Dedji, *Reconstruction and Renewal in African Christian Theology.* The views of the Kinshasa and Cameroonian schools are contained in the following works, Messi Metogo, *Dieu Peut-Il Mourir En Afrique?* 180–83; see also Mushete, *Les Thèmes Majeurs De La Théologie Africaine*, 97–104; and the recent volume of Ela, *Repenser La Théologie Africaine.*

On the other hand, the cultural, religious, and racial discourse on poverty must be retained. It does not exclude material poverty: "a thing stands and another stands beside it." Liturgical display of the Negro Spirituals and the Zairian rite or even the display in celebrations of AICs and Charismatic Gospel bands instead of being a precept for sedating the worshipping community (Ela) is rather a dimension of liberation. Worship by the oppressed, though threatened by escapism, also proclaims with the Psalmist, "power belongs to God" (Ps 62:2–5). Ela came to be more attentive to this liberating dimension of worship. Liberation theology that omits the historical continuity between the Spirituals, the Black Church, and civil rights movement in the U.S.A. or that ignores the continuity between AICs, their seductive liturgy and Black consciousness movement in South Africa, risks betraying the struggle of African Americans, Black South Africans and other oppressed Africans to claim their human dignity over racism, apartheid and inhuman dictatorship.

The humanistic properties undergirding West African traditions ensures that Marxist analytical tools be at the service of integral good of the community and not absolutized. Marxism is not a fetish that excludes other alternatives. The integration of religion within African humanism for the overall good of the human community, following the flexible spirituality of West Africans, sets aside the atheistic underpinnings of Marxist social analysis.

DUAL-GENDER, DUAL-SEX—
RE-ENVISIONING WOMAN IN AFRICAN THEOLOGY

The methodological assumption that always searches for "a second point of view" gives relational tension an ontological status and could lead to creative re-envisioning of feminism and gender studies in feminist African theology. In her published dissertation, *Overcoming Women's Subordination—an Igbo African Perspective: Envisioning an inclusive Theology with Reference to Women,* Nigerian feminist theologian Rose Uchem observed cynically, "[i]n spite of their goodwill, there is a limit to how much good men can ever do to represent Igbo women's reality accurately enough and with critical consciousness of gender justice." The "head start" that Igbo egalitarian culture has over the West and other African cultures on women's rights (based on its dual-gender, dual-sex ideology) carries, in her view, internal contradictions. Or else, how come "[A] three-year old 'man' is accorded precedence over a mature woman" in the Igbo kola nut ritual? Similarly, the human rights profile of the Catholic Church, as contained in the Church's social teachings, carries internal contradictions. Or else, how come "a young seminarian is set above a fifty-year old woman religious who might have taught him in school"? Indeed, how come "a theologically competent woman is deemed unsuitable to image an unseen 'male God'"? Uchem hinged her theological arguments for radical change on Jesus' parables and his unconventional or subversive wisdom teachings. Jesus' resurrection introduced new sets of values and understanding of his person. Consequently, theological discourse and considerations of vocation to ministry go beyond narrow sexual or ethnic configurations. Uchem calls for radical change and a new evangelization: "only a change in the Catholic Church's stand on women's ordination will send out a message strong enough to initiate the kind of conversion and transformation required by a new evangelization in Africa and in Igbo society".[19]

Other feminist theologians like Teresa Okure (Nigeria) and Amba Oduyoye (Ghana-Nigeria) are emphatic about the radical nature of Jesus' behaviour and teaching with regard to women that contrasts sharply with the uneven ways ethical principles are applied in Africa to men and women.[20] Their arguments are unimpeachable. Nevertheless, one must recognize that in some African societies, e.g., the Igbo, the tense relationship between the "dangerous half" led to balancing or flexibility that demarcates areas of competence. This ensures inclusion of both women and men in socio-political, economic and religious leadership or responsibility. Kamene Okonjo and Ifi Amadiume have demonstrated that Igbo women enjoyed enormous economic and political power. Colonial and Christian policy hastened the erosion of this situation and upset the evenness in gendered responsibility.[21] The Women War of 1929–1930 that engulfed South-eastern Nigeria was a reaction to the rigid one-dimensional colonial gender policy. Colonial and Christian policy found Igbo wisdom based on duality incomprehensible—"When Something stands, Another comes to stand beside it." Indirect rule

19. See Uchem, *Overcoming Women's Subordination*, 12, 72, 121.

20. For example Teresa Okure's book on John's Gospel and her many writings underline the radical nature of Jesus' attitude towards women. See for example Okure, *Johannine Approach to Mission*. See also "Jesus and Women."

21. See Amadiume, *Male Daughters, Female Husbands*. And also, Okonjo, "Dual-Sex Political System in Operation."

through "warrant chiefs" favored excessive use of force that upturned the delicate balance of power normal in egalitarian societies. It introduced distortions in gender relations with disastrous consequences. The women war, fought by Igbo women (involving also Ibibio, Annang, and Efik women), was a major culture shock for the British administration. However, no significant political reforms followed the war. Victorian England was bereft of the experience of female economic and political power.[22] Igbo (Nigerian) men empowered by the colonial state and the Christian church, systematically endangered duality/relationality and flexibility by marginalizing women in politics, economy and religion. Oduyoye after studying some Nigerian and Ghanaian myths drew the shocking conclusion that the only woman-type who is respected in the society is the one that is sacrificed and deified (like Aiyelala—the Okitikpupa deity); this shows where the dangerous erosion of duality and flexibility could lead.[23]

The dual-sex, dual-gender social construct, ontologically based on duality, is a core value to be retrieved to enable West Africans benefit from feminist discourse and to enrich gender studies. Feminist studies should disengage from the narrow one-dimensional Western apron strings for the reinvention of Africa. Gendered *vodhun* religion (among Fon and Ewe of Benin Republic, Togo and Ghana), in which initiates or devotees are mostly women and shrine guardians, men, where ancestral cult is male but ancestral line is female displays the complexity, malleability and sophistication that should be retrieved for the reinvention of Africa and the world. Even masquerades whose performance and cult are oftentimes understood to be exclusive to men could harbor gender balancing. Women of Southeast Nigeria and Western Cameroon (the Ejigham of Cross River) own and operate masquerades just as men do. It is not only the Sandé of Sierra Leone that have women masquerades. The *Gélédé* masquerade in Benin Republic is performed by men but the cult society is entirely in the hands of women.[24] Adopting "a second viewpoint" ensures gendered sharing and redistribution of power in the

---

22. See Allen, "'Aba Riots' or Igbo 'Women's War'?"

23. Oduyoye, *Daughters of Anowa*, 26–29, 33. See also Oduyoye and Kanyoro, *Will to Arise*.

24. See Lovell, *Cord of Blood*, and Claffey, "Looking for a Breakthrough," 76. Also Claffey, *Christian Churches in Dahomey-Benin*; Peek and Yankah, *African Folklore*, 244–46.

social, economic, political and religious domains. It ensures that women not only took charge of women affairs but also of key segments of the economy, politics and religion. For example, the West African "market" was dominated by women. Their power in this area has been systematically eroded or intensively reduced since colonial and postcolonial times. Healing rituals, and even aspects of divination, are dominated by women in some societies. Only AICs and Pentecostals have expanded the social space for women through "prophetic ministries" (e.g., the visionaries of the *Celestial Church of Christ*); the women also enjoy leadership in the Gospel Band. Their dominant role in these ministries enables them to "achieve self-hood and self-actualisation."[25]

While African feminist social scientists like Okonjo and Amadiume are paying attention to the dual-sex and dual-gender ideology, feminist theologians have yet to update their use of the social sciences and appreciate the fundamental values of this ideology to re-envision theology. This is one struggle that all must join to save Africa and humanity from rigid masculinism. African feminist theology suffers the same systemic weakness as every African theology—the dependence on Western methodological assumptions. Feminist "resistance rhetoric" is based on unisex ideology and the masculinization of economy, politics, religion, and social relations. My view is that this one-dimensional focus on reality poses enormous danger for humanity. The injection of fresh ideas into feminist discourse by African theologians in dialogue with African feminist social scientists is vital to history and humanity.

Western feminist rhetoric on patriarchy provides no alternative ideology drawn from Western historical memory apart from the male patriarchal dominance. African feminists can draw from historical memory of matriarchy and matrilineal descent, not of a distant past but as practice still operational in contemporary Africa, despite its radical transformations by modernity. Almost fifty years ago Cheikh Anta Diop drew attention to the social, political, and economic differences between African and Indo-European construction of the world and society based on the image of woman. It is only recently that African scholars are retrieving this saving image; it may even be too late. Amadiume's expansion of her study of Igbo woman to include selected African societies

25. Ojo, "Indigenous Gospel Music and Social Reconstruction in Modern Nigeria," 220. See also de Surgy, *L'église Du Christianisme Céleste*, 205–6.

agrees with Diop on the relevance of the *Cultural Unity of Black Africa* and the possibility of *Re-Inventing Africa* based on *Matriarchy*.[26]

African feminist theology can move theology forward in the continent by learning from the dual structure of perceiving reality in West Africa. For example, Teresa Okure's attempt to retrieve the image of Jesus as prophet and radical messenger, who restored "values that had been lost," dug deep into the Hebrew Scriptures, Judaic and Graeco-Roman social traditions, but unfortunately failed to dig into the African social construct of matriarchy that rejected the indo-European cultural inferiorization of women. The West African social construct is based on the dual structure of accessing reality—nothing stands alone, a thing stands and another stands beside it. Rose Uchem recognizes the existence of this social vision. However, her focus on Igbo in the diaspora (precisely in the U.S.A.) whose sexism (i.e., as practiced by the men) contradicts the Igbo vision prevented her from teasing out the humanistic underpinnings of the dual-gender, dual-sex ideology to embed another kind of interpretation of the Jesus story.

African feminist theology needs to retrieve the regenerating humanistic properties of the African gender diarchy based on primordial duality that ensures relationality and flexibility. This methodological assumption radicalizes relational ethos in behavior as a whole and not only gendered behavior. The ethos is summed up in the southern African term *ubuntu*: "My humanity is caught up, is inextricably bound up, in yours." Mbiti captures it in a popular East African saying: "I am because we are; and since we are therefore I am." It radicalizes the strategic feminine virtue of "mothering" that in the Akan (Ghanaian) tradition is also a male virtue. The strategic kitchen metaphor of *diakonia* that is purposely chosen by Jesus to describe ministry in terms that are politically and religiously counter-cultural is located in that part of the family occupied by the woman. In a theology of ministry informed by duality or relationality, the feminine ensures the fusion of the theological and the ethical; ministry is transformed into nourishing and feeding in all domains of life—political, social, economic and religious.[27]

---

26. See Diop, *Cultural Unity of Black Africa*; Diop, *Civilization or Barbarism*; Diop, *Precolonial Black Africa*; and Amadiume, *Re-Inventing Africa*.

27. See Oduyoye, "Feminist Theology in an African Perspective," 174–76. See also Okure, "Leadership in the New Testament," 85–86.

The above shows the potentials of renewal in African theology informed by a methodology driven by the structure of duality or re-lationality popular among West African peoples. The rest of this study will explore the deployment of my methodology to interpret the West African appropriation of Christianity from the perspective of God-Spirit for human wholeness.

PART TWO

God-Spirit in West Africa
and the God of Jesus Christ

"Western missionaries did not introduce God to Africa—rather,
it was God who brought them to Africa, as carriers of news about
Jesus Christ."[1]

John S Mbiti

OVERVIEW OF PART TWO

THE FOCUS OF THE second part of this book is the question of God-
Spirit and Jesus Christ from a West African perspective. West
African Christians experience God-Spirit as bestower and guarantor of
human wholeness in the Holy Spirit, through the death-resurrection of
Jesus the Christ. They assume continuity between God in ATR world
vision and God as revealed in Jesus Christ. Lamin Sanneh's study of
the spread of Christianity in postcolonial Africa made the stunning
claim: "Christian expansion and revival were limited to those societies
that preserved the indigenous name of God." If this is a hard historical
"fact," then it is a commentary on the flexibility and openness of missionary Christianity. It is also a statement on the openness or porousness
of the ATR world vision and the Jewish Christian world vision to give
and receive development. This blends with my interest in this research:
the malleable, flexible and relational world of West Africans unveils the
intercourse of humans with God-Spirit both in ATR and Christianity
in a unique way. Western Christianity will find the development of my
discussion on God-Spirit in this section comparable, though operating

1. Mbiti, *Bible and Theology in African Christianity*, 11. See also Mbiti, "Encounter
of Christian Faith and African Religion."

41

on a different key, to developments in the Graeco-Roman world on encountering the Jewish-Christian world vision. And this is perhaps not dissimilar from the medieval Christian developments or Western modernity's impact on Western Christianity.

West African ATR presents humans interacting with God and with a plurality of deities, spirits, forces and ancestors. I will explore the impact of this interaction on the contextual Christian experience and expression of God revealed in Jesus Christ, and its relevance for Trinitarian theology. The acknowledgment of One Creator God amidst a plurality of divine beings, in whatever way it is interpreted or named by experts, challenges the theologian to re-examine God in ATR and to tease out the theological implications for reflection on the Triune God of Jesus Christ.

First, I propose a revaluation of ATR as basis or starting point for the West African appropriation of the relational Christian Trinitarian God. This involves discussion and evaluation of scholarly viewpoints on the God that creates and bestows destinies. It also involves discussion on deities and spirits and the various roles they play in the realization of individual and communal destiny. Terms unfamiliar to speakers of English will be explained and included in the glossary.

Second, a critical review of the West African relational approach to the divine enables the second look at God in the Hebrew or Old Testament tradition. It affords the opportunity to retrieve the primitive perception of divinity in the poetic tradition of the Old Testament summed up, especially, in the image of the "divine council" of *El* and Yahweh. The interesting conditions that favored and challenged the development of Jewish monotheism, which matured during the Babylonian exile (Isaiah 40–55), will be explored. This narrative of the historical process and development of the One Yahweh displays flexibility and relationality. The process links up with Jesus' Abba experience (New Testament) that on the Cross reveals God "powerfully weak" in Jesus Christ! Jesus' Abba experience displays the humanity of the relational God, challenging and disarming the intransigent and exclusivist monotheistic doctrines of God that in practice imperil our contemporary world.

Third, in probing the experience, in West African Christian life, of the relational God-Spirit that identified with us on the Cross of Jesus Christ, I draw from the insights of Origen, the Alexandrian Father (c. 185–c. 254 CE). Origen's religious anthropology, his emphasis on the plural dimensions or denominations of Christ and the Holy Spirit will help to reinterpret culturally and theologically the operations and manifestations of the Holy Spirit in AICs and Charismatic movements in West Africa. In the conversation with Origen, I also show that inculturation is the catholic way. From Christian Alexandrian antiquity Origen searched the Scriptures and teased out the dimensions of the relational Trinity through a dynamic reinterpretation and transformation of the categories of the Greek universe.

Finally, one notes that the West African world is not a one-dimensional world: "a thing stands and another stands beside it." There are good and bad spirits. Deities are ambivalent in their relationship with humans. But West Africa (and indeed all of Africa) harbors a perception of evil that appears to be totally opposed to life—witchcraft. Though ambivalence is never totally out of the picture, West Africans, sub-Saharan Africans, consider witchcraft, sorcery, and the negative deployment of occult forces as opposed to human life and destiny. They define evil as that which attacks and distorts relationality; enormous problems of individual and communal responsibility beg for answers. It will therefore be necessary to explore the etiology of evil (witchcraft and the occult) and its relationship to human wholeness. West African Christians struggle against evil, in the power of the Holy Spirit. Life is a spiritual combat! The spiritual energy, created and nourished through the embedding Holy Spirit of God, thanks to the death-resurrection of Jesus, is deployed in the struggle to reinvent relationality in the world and advances the Christian experience and interpretation of the Triune God as author of wholeness.

Naming God in West African Style—Major Challenge for Christianity

The second part of this book therefore critically explores the doctrinal import and relevance of the local appropriation of God-Spirit and Jesus the Christ in West African Christianity. The indigenous ancestral name of God was generally adopted by denominational churches. AICs and Charismatic movements display creative patterns of confessing and celebrating God-Christ-Holy Spirit suffused with local imagery. I will test the theological implications of the fusion of the God of West African experience and the God of Jesus Christ, faithful to my methodology of always searching for a second viewpoint. Is this simply a missionary strategy of accommodation that erects a platform for easy transmission of western Christian cosmological and Christological doctrines? Or is this a fundamental and inevitable correlation of the West African cosmology within the reception of God-Christ-Holy Spirit? In other words, is the adoption of the ancestral name of God, and all the theological risks this involves, part of the display of the "genius of Catholicism"? Integrating the pagan-ness of each cultural group, so as to cater, according to Gesché, not only for the progress of Christianity but also for the preservation of the genius of cultures for the overall good of humanity?[2]

I like to expand, in this overview, the preliminary implications of the Christian adoption of the vernacular name of God that impacts profoundly on discussions all over this second part. By adopting the vernacular name of God missionary Christianity laid a firm foundation for the interpretation of the experience of the relational Trinity in West African terms. Though this is in continuity with the pristine Catholic flexibility, one admires the missionary insight and courage. One, however, needs to proceed with caution so as neither to betray the Christian specificity nor to underestimate the complexity of the West African religious vision of the universe. Perhaps, the adoption of the indigenous name of God is more radical but also more problematical than the experience of Canaanite Baal worshipers in the Old Testament and the Christian implantation in the Graeco-Roman world. We shall discuss the Baals in detail in a later chapter. But to highlight the complexity and the importance of the Christian decision with regard to God in West Africa I quote the comments of Mircea Eliade on the conditions for the persistence of Yahweh over the Baals:

> The "divine form" of Yahweh prevailed over the "divine form" of Baal. . . . This hierophany of Yahweh had the final victory, because it represented a universal modality of the sacred, it was by its very nature open to other cultures; it became by means of Christianity of world-wide religious value. It can be seen, then, that some hierophanies are, or can in this way become, of universal value and significance, whereas others may remain local or of one period—they are not open to other cultures, and fall eventually into oblivion even in the society which produced them.[3]

---

2. Here I adopt as defensible and as applicable to my subject the thesis of Adolphe Gesché expressed in Gesché, "Le Christianisme Comme Athéisme Suspensif—Réflexions Sur Le 'Etsi Deus Non Daretur.'"

3. See Eliade, *Patterns in Comparative Religion*, 1–4.

Eliade highlights "universal modality"; I underline flexibility and openness of different West African world visions, enabling mutual attraction to and from similarly orientated world visions. The adoption of the vernacular name of God underlines an important theological assumption that I retain in my reflection: God, encountered in ATR and Christianity, embodies flexibility, openness to universality, enabling God to have appeal beyond local cultural limitations. This flexibility (God's sign of weakness and strength) saved God of ATR, *Chukwu, Onyame, Olodumare,* and so on, from the fate of the Graeco-Roman Zeus, Jupiter, Venus, Appolos that were radically uprooted and substituted with a vague/generic *deus* or *theos* inscribable either in capital or small letter, masculine or feminine.[4] The Christian adoption of the African name of God, thanks to missionary creativity, is therefore of great moment for Christian theology; despite the need to critically evaluate the advantages and pitfalls that the ATR baggage brings into Christian confession and celebration. But there is need for caution. I elaborate by drawing attention to viewpoints of pioneer theologians.

Proceeding with Caution

Pioneer African theologians, John Mbiti and Bolaji Idowu, affirmed, from the practice of missionary Christianity, the fundamental openness of the African human person to experience the (true) God who is none other than the God revealed in Jesus Christ. Mbiti affirmed identity between the God of African religion and the Christian God.[5] The *same* God brought missionaries to Africa with the message of Jesus Christ. The apologetic approach espoused by Mbiti and many African theologians has advantages but also shortcomings. The theological and missiological advantage of *sameness*, emphasized by pioneer African theologians, is well taken. However, it could lead to ignoring the full weight/implications of the historical and contextual experience of God by particular African sociocultural groups. This historical and contextual experience

4. Bimwenyi discussed this persistence of African God in Bimwenyi-Kweshi, "Religions Africaines, Un 'Lieu' De La Theologie Chrétienne Africaine," 212ff. I made similar arguments in Uzukwu, "Food and Drink in Africa and the Christian Eucharist," 378–80; and in Uzukwu, "Future of Foreign Missionary Congregations in Africa," 338–40.

5. Apart from the text of John Mbiti quoted at the beginning of this section, Mbiti collected diverse names of God in Mbiti, *Concepts of God in Africa*. Also Idowu made his best argument over God in Yoruba religion in Idowu, *Olódùmarè*.

is certainly not identical with the historical self-disclosure of the Jewish Christian God.

Samuel Kibicho, who insists on the autonomy and independence of African religions as ways of salvation, in no way subordinate or inferior to Christianity, is more cautious than Mbiti. He reported a Kikuyu ATR practitioner's viewpoint: "The Kikuyu have always known God and they were always a God-fearing people. What is completely new in the new European religion, and completely incomprehensible to us traditional Kikuyu, is this talk of God having a son who was born into the world."[6] The *same* God! Nevertheless the Kikuyu ATR practitioner sees Christ as introducing a radical difference in the *experience* and therefore the *meaning* of God.

Apologetic theologians are less cautious. This is clear from post-Vatican II liturgical inculturation in East Africa. Catholics co-opted local poetic traditions in creating new Eucharistic Prayers to praise the Trinitarian God revealed in Jesus Christ. The Gaba Pastoral Institute, Eldoret (Kenya), composed a Kenyan Eucharistic Prayer that adopted poetic traditions of Kenyan ethnic groups. For example, the Opening Praise (or Preface) adopts word for word the thanksgiving prayer pronounced by the eponymous ancestor of the Kikuyu as transcribed in Mbiti's *Prayers of African Religion*:

Kikuyu Ancestral Prayer	Kenyan Christian [Catholic] Eucharistic Prayer
O, my Father, great Elder, I have no words to thank you, but with your deep wisdom I am sure that you can see how much I prize your glorious gifts. O my Father, when I look upon your greatness, I am confounded with awe. O great Elder, ruler of all things both on heaven and on earth, I am your warrior, and I am ready to act in accordance with your will.[6]	O Father, Great Elder, we have no words to thank you, But with your deep wisdom We are sure that you can see How we value your glorious gifts. O Father, when we look upon your greatness, We are confounded with awe. O Great Elder, Ruler of all things earthly and heavenly, We are your warriors, Ready to act in accordance with your will.[7]

6. Kibicho, "Interaction of the Traditional Kikuyu Concept of God," 226.

7. Mbiti, *Prayers of African Religion*, 151.

8. See Hearne and Mijere, *Celebration*, vol. 2.

The guiding logic of this retrieval is the optimistic affirmation of identity between the Kikuyu ancestral God and the Jewish Christian God. This overcomes or ignores the embarrassment of the Kikuyu ATR practitioner over the radical Christian God who has a Son. The ATR *prayers* assume new value for Christians. For Christians, this is a legitimate doxological appropriation of ancestral tradition into the Christian faith. Catholics and AICs do this just as Greco-Roman Christians did in the past. But critical African theology has the duty to scrutinize and challenge this type of retrieval. Theologians like Kä Mana and Eboussi Boulaga, opposed to the thesis of uncritical continuity between African ancestral religion and Christianity, insist that Christian practice and reflection must feel the full force of the radical difference introduced to the meaning of God by the experience of Christ. I take note of this radical difference; but I affirm the legitimacy of understanding difference within the logic of continuity. The logic of continuity displays, in the naming of God, a legitimate local theology that brings to Christ the "riches of the nations . . . as an inheritance."[9] The permeability and flexibility, encountered in both the Jewish-Christian and ATR world visions, enable the revelation of the power of God in weakness; this contrasts with the opacity and exclusivism of evangelicalism that breed intolerance.

Nevertheless, West African ancestral map of the universe displays resilience and complexity that one should not underestimate; this at the same time increases difficulty in the God-talk and calls for critical vigilance. Focusing on the peculiarity/difference of the divine in West Africa, Nigerian feminist sociologist, Ifi Amadiume, reproached Igbo Christian theologians for ignoring the full weight of the principle of plurality that undergirds the religious culture. Amadiume also reproached theologians of also ignoring the dominance of female deities in the African (Igbo) universe. Because theologians are preoccupied with propagating the thesis of continuity between ATR and Christianity, she claimed, they reduced "religion to the single truth of a supreme male God." In her estimation, the idea of a supreme male God goes against the grain of "traditional pluralism." It has the negative ethical implication of justifying "patriarchal greed, totalitarian patriarchy, gender oppression, and centrism." Amadiume's criticism is similar to Okot p'Bitek's characterization of African theologians, especially John Mbiti, as "hellenizers"

---

9. Vatican II, *Ad Gentes*, 22.

of ATR.[10] There is little doubt that history and ethnographic particularity must play their full role in discussing God in ATR. Therefore, these critical viewpoints call for additional caution in affirming the worship of the *same* God. From this perspective, the particular and complex West African experience of ATR, practiced in a world that is peopled by female and male deities, challenges not only the West African Christian God-talk but also the meaning of religion.

What we have on the ground point to a minefield of pitfalls and stumbling blocks one must not ignore in developing West African Christian God-talk. AICs from their origins in the 19th century and Charismatic movements, whose impact has been on the increase since the 1980s, presuppose the West African map of the universe in their confession and celebration of God-Christ-Holy Spirit. African theologians of inculturation in their systematic study of Christology and Trinity also presuppose the ancestral universe. Even theologians who are reticent over or opposed to the inculturation discourse (evangelical in orientation) nevertheless think that the ancestral map of the universe provides a preparation for the Gospel (in sharp contrast to the position of the 1910 World Missionary Congress of Edinburgh). Developing God-talk in West African Christian style implies that one must creatively respond to the multiplicity of spirits and deities. How does one relate the deities to the Christian confession of One God? AICs' and Charismatic movements' Spirit-directed faith indicate the solution that must be theologically clarified. For Christians, the deities, that in the West African universe represent God-Spirit's benevolent shadow or presence, are transformed into qualities of the One Holy Spirit of God. Critical theology highlights the theological advantage of this world vision in fostering pneumatology as entry point into Trinitarian theology. But there is more. The dynamic interpretation of divine-human relationship in this region, and the flexibility in the perception and functioning of deities also enable insight into the meaning of religions or ways in our complex world. In West African terms, God-talk and religion *intend the realization of individual and communal destined course in life.* Therefore the multiplicity of religions or ways in our world, reproduced in miniature by the multiplicity of deities and spirits in West African religions, reveals a critical quality of the relational God we want to know: *religions mediate*

10. See p'Bitek, *African Religions in Western Scholarship*; and Amadiume, "Igbo and African Religious Perspectives."

the harmonious interrelationship among religious persons. West Africa provides a good site for evaluating and reengineering interreligious and intercultural relations; Christianity does well to learn from this.

The final preliminary point I make about the naming of God in ATR and its impact on West African Christian talk about the Triune God is to comment on the statement of Lamin Sanneh: "Christian expansion and revival were limited to those societies that preserved the indigenous name of God." Commentators note the enormous cultural and theological ingenuity that went into Bible translation. But Sanneh draws attention to the radical implications of the vernacular name of God: it undergirds the renewal of the social, economic and political structures of African societies, and is presumed to play a similar pivotal role in Christianity.

> The name of God is basic to the structure of traditional societies. It forms and regulates agricultural rituals . . . naming rules, ethics. . . . It's therefore hard to think of viable social systems without the name of God, but easy to envision societies that have become vulnerable because they lost the name or the sense of the transcendent. . . . It follows that the adoption of African names for God in Christianity would carry corresponding implications for social and cultural renewal, with effects on indigenous ethics and historical consciousness. We may summarize the matter as follows: the name of God contained ideas of personhood, economic life, and social/cultural identity; the name of God represented the indigenous theological advantage vis-à-vis missionary initiative . . . theologically God had preceded the missionary in Africa, a fact that Bible translation clinched with decisive authority.[11]

I agree with Sanneh that one should ground the practical arguments for the continuity between African cultures and Christianity in Bible translation. The cultural and theological effort that went into Bible translation constitutes the starting point of inculturation theology. In West Africa, there is the added advantage that the translators, the earliest protestant missionaries, in a place like Nigeria, were African (Nigerian) freed slaves. They were consciously struggling with both the map of the West African universe and of the Jewish-Christian universe. Theirs was as creative an action as the LXX translation that enabled the fertile encounter between Hebrew and Greek cultures, the Old Latin version

---

11. Sanneh, *Whose Religion Is Christianity?* 31–32.

that was translated in Carthage (160–220 CE), and the fourth century translation of the Bible into the Coptic languages. All these cultural and theological efforts curiously took place on African soil. The nineteenth- and twentieth-century translators were not ignorant of the theological advantages and pitfalls of affirming continuity and difference between God in ATR and the God of Jesus Christ. I will bring their experience into the discussion of the name and attributes of God-Christ-Spirit.[12] For example, though Sanneh did not dwell on the complex but radical divergences of naming God in ATR and Christianity, he nevertheless indicated the advantages of continuity for developments in Christology: "In Nigeria Yoruba converts to Christianity, for example, have the rich heritage of Ifa divination to draw upon. . . . The name for savior, *Olugbala*, for instance, is preloaded with older Yoruba theological notions of divine power, solicitude, and redemptive suffering. *Olugbala* accedes to the Jesus of Scripture without dumping the old cargo."[13] I intend to critically cast "a second glance" at this type of appropriation, correlation or "tradition retrieval" that led West African Christians to adopt epithets and qualities of deities as qualities of Jesus or the Holy Spirit.

I sum up once more what I am going to address in this second part: I address issues that bear on the status or revaluation of ATR, the stunning assimilation as well as the radical transformation of its basic assumptions into West African Christianity, and the renewal of theology of the God revealed in Jesus Christ. Naturally, this will start by justifying the revaluation of ATR and highlighting the structures of its universe, with particular focus on West Africa. The aim is to stress that West African love for duality or multiplicity introduces a viewpoint on God that merits further theological scrutiny. Multiplicity of divine beings and their complex relationship to the One God introduce a radical dimension to the meaning of religion. Indeed it calls for a redefinition of the concerns of religion, and invites refocusing the concerns and direction of interreligious relations and Trinitarian theology. It is from my exploration of the structures of ATR universe, that I will review the theological advantages and pitfalls that the mother tongue naming of God in West African Christianity introduces into Trinitarian theology. This will draw attention not only to the flexibility in West African perception of God's transcendence; it will also highlight the crucial role of experts, possessed

---

12. See Adamo, *Reading and Interpreting the Bible*. See also Peel, *Religious Encounter*.

13. Sanneh, *Whose Religion Is Christianity?* 59.

by or entranced into the divine, in the project of realizing the purpose of religion—the realization of human destined course in life as *pax deorum*. Next, my fundamental methodological assumption of relational open-ness, "something stands and another stands beside it," permits the bold though risky foray into Jewish-Christian religious universe, interpreted through the grille or categories of the West African universe. Instead of a *radical displacement* of the indigenous experience of God character-istic of *evangelicalism,* I opt for the more risky and "less pure" *Catholic* perception of *continuity.* West African Christians brought into their new faith, dimensions and potencies of ATR. This enabled local theology to reconsider the bold "rediscovery" of the God of the Old Testament received through Judaism into Christianity as the God that Jesus Christ called "Abba"! The *parrhesia* or boldness of the children of God (cf. 2 Cor 3:12) that enabled West African Christians to assimilate and trans-form God-Spirit raises new problems but also provides fresh insights for Trinitarian theology—especially approached from the perspective of pneumatology. Both the ATR matrix and the received Christian tradi-tion are undergoing development; a process that indicates a dynamic approach to Christian doctrine: understanding better the complexity of the revealing God who maintains distance from humans even in Jesus Christ but whose healing presence is commonly experienced in the Holy Spirit. There is gain rather than loss in the encounter of the African and the Jewish-Christian and Western religious cultures. This encounter is indeed a celebration; a "widening of horizons in the experience of he who cannot be appropriated by any tradition," neither Jewish, nor Graeco-Roman-Western, nor African! And who, Hurbon argues from diaspora African (Haitian) experience, could rightly be called "the es-chatological problem of the encounter of cultures."[14] Finally, I show that understanding the relational Trinity through the West African vision of the universe is the Catholic way. Through dialogue with the religious an-thropology of Origen I argue that this inculturational research is within the catholic tradition. God who is Spirit-Life assures providential care to West Africans and humans all over the world mediated through God's indwelling Holy Spirit that creates human wholeness.

---

14. Again see my discussion in Uzukwu, "Future of Foreign Missionary Congre-gations in Africa." See the views of Hurbon in Hurbon, *Dieu Dans Le Vaudou Haïtien*, 189, 215, 222–23.

3

African Traditional Religion Rediscovered

Reasserting the Value of African Religions

BEYOND THE WESTERN MISUNDERSTANDING
OF AFRICANS AND THEIR RELIGIONS

IN THE COURSE OF centuries Europeans developed an ideological view of others as inferior. This ideology of superiority reached its peak curiously with the Enlightenment celebration of reason and the idea of progress. The evolutionary thesis that societies progressed from primitive to civilized levels of Europe (social Darwinism) was adopted. Africa provided a ready sample. Theorists of religion, like Sir James Frazer, advanced views of "primitive religions" that evolved from magic through polytheism to monotheism. The Jewish-Christian experience is the peak of monotheism; and the last stage of evolution is the triumph of human (European) reason and science. G. W. F. Hegel's *Lectures on the Philosophy of World History* dismissed Africa (Blacks) as having no religion apart from magic. Hegel's transcendental idealism understood history to be nothing more and nothing less than the life of the Spirit, of God the Absolute, the monotheistic incarnate God of Christianity. Africans have no place in this history because they were incapable of conceiving the absolute, of reaching self-consciousness, and of experiencing freedom, law or morality.[1] Slavery, though inhuman, was a privilege for Africans!

This misunderstanding of Africans, their world, cultures and religions became entrenched in the European tradition, especially from the fifteenth century. Missionaries, travelers, colonists, ethnologists,

1. Hegel, *Lectures on the Philosophy of World History: Introduction*.

and anthropologists showed perhaps genuine interest in the religions of Africans. Some of them may not totally accept the thesis of Hegel, but their orientation was suffused with the ideology of European dominance. Very striking about some early writings is the tendentious interpretation of creation myths that focused on the "departure" of the "High God," a *deus otiosus,* no longer interested in the affairs of humans. Having created the world, the "High God" confided its administration to minor deities. Some of these views, though containing elements of truth, are at times inclined towards the exotic and the utterly dissimilar. Some indeed wanted to castigate and dramatize the inferiority of the enslaved/colonized African who is unable to conceptualize God as the enslaving, colonizing and missionizing Christian European. "How can the untutored African conceive God"? queried Emil Ludwig. "Deity is a philosophical concept which savages are incapable of framing."[2] This general denigration of Africans and their religions and cultures justified the three-pronged interrelated movements that followed the abolition of slavery: colonize, civilize, and Christianize. I agree with Chinua Achebe that the portraiture of Africa in some European literature is downright racist. In "An Image of Africa: Racism in Conrad's *Heart of Darkness*" Achebe denounced the representation of Africa in dark and obscure imagery. Joseph Conrad represented an unuttered desire or need embedded in the European psyche "to set Africa up as a foil for Europe, as a place of negations at once remote and vaguely familiar, in comparison with which Europe's own state of spiritual grace will be manifest." The language of civilization evokes the underlying language of "barbarism" and "primitivism."[3] Achebe is on target: "The West seems to suffer deep anxieties about the precariousness of its civilization and to have a need for constant reassurance by comparison with Africa."[4]

2. Cited by Idowu, *African Traditional Religion*, 88.

3. This is critically analysed in Diop, Achebe, and Anderson: Diop, *Civilization or Barbarism*; Anderson, *Creative Exchange*.

4. Achebe, *Hopes and Impediments*. Chapter 1 with title "An Image of Africa: Racism in Conrad's *Heart of Darkness*," 2–3, 17. Joseph Conrad's novel *Heart of Darkness* was published in 1902. Achebe denounces racism in stronger terms in 1998 McMillan-Stewart Lectures, Harvard University: Achebe, *Home and Exile*.

Fury: Africans React to Misunderstandings of their Religious Culture

The fury generated by the prejudiced characterization of Africans, their cultures and religions is understandable (though one should point out that it is discourse on the *Africa that never was*[5]). The fury carried those who romanticize Africa as well as those highly critical of Africa's weaknesses and who would want to reinvent their tradition based on lucid critical analysis. Edward Wilmot Blyden (1832–1912) excluded from the educational curriculum, at the initial stage of the formation of young Africans, the entire literature of modern Europe from the close of the Middle Ages to his own time. The fury carried *Negritude* poets (e.g., Aimé Césaire and Leopold Sédar Senghor) and proponents of *African Personality* (e.g., Kwame Nkrumah). They worked towards what Soyinka called "a revaluation of neglected humanistic properties" entrenched in African traditions, that carry a "mystic wisdom that defied materialism." These movements and literature are part and parcel of the creativity of postmodern Africa.[6]

Soyinka and Achebe, humanists as well as literary critics whose views on duality or multiplicity I endorse, took issue in particular with the Western Christian exclusivist monotheistic order. Against Hegel's monotheistic claims, Soyinka argued, as noted earlier, that the multiple spirits and human mediators, in the *orisa* religion, portray tolerance and human dignity more than the intolerant Christian monotheistic order.[7] The intolerance of the Islamic and Christian missions contrasts sharply with ATR spirituality that is synonymous with tolerance. The "profound humanism of the orisa" religion or ATR makes intolerance anathema![8] But one must note that the Christian missionary adoption of the indigenous names of God contradicts aspects of Soyinka's critique.

Chinua Achebe adopted a methodology that rejected in principle all absolutisms! Absolutist doctrinal claims of Christianity are either a blasphemy or an absurdity from the perspective of Igbo world vision based on always looking at everything twice. He declared, "We are in a period so different from anything else that has happened that everything

---

5. See Hammond and Jablow, *Africa That Never Was.*

6. Soyinka, *Burden of Memory*, 170. See Kenzo, "Thinking Otherwise About Africa."

7. Soyinka, *Que Ce Passé Parle À Son Présent.* See also the more recent Soyinka, "Tolerant Gods."

8. Soyinka, *Burden of Memory*, 48; Soyinka, "Tolerant Gods," 48.

that is presented to us has to be looked at twice."[9] He concludes, evoking Igbo aphorism:

> Whenever Something stands, Something Else will stand beside it. Nothing is absolute. *I am the truth, the way and the life* would be called blasphemous or simply absurd for is it not well known that a man may worship Ogwugwu to perfection and yet be killed by Udo.[10]

Soyinka and Achebe raise issues that one must review when discussing the structures of ATR. One needs to critically scrutinize the impact of ATR structures and the legitimacy of assimilating these structures into Christian practice.

Pioneer African Theologians and the Problem of Identity

African theologians were not outdone by African humanists in the defence of the values transmitted through ATR and the culture it bears. They reacted against the demonization of African religious traditions. The *All Africa Conference of Churches* (AACC—regrouping Anglican and Protestant Churches) endorsed the revaluation of the humanistic properties of African tradition; and accepted these properties as capital for the future progress of Christianity in Africa. AACC organised a conference in Ibadan (Nigeria), in 1965, on the encounter between African religious cultures and Christianity. The purpose of the conference was to carefully evaluate, from the perspective of traditional religious culture, the reaction of the converted Africans to their new faith. Participants in the conference adopted the following resolution that has methodological import for views on God-Spirit and Jesus Christ in the African context:

> We recognise the radical quality of God's self-revelation in Jesus Christ; and yet it is because of this revelation we can discern what is truly of God in our pre-Christian heritage: this knowledge of God is not totally discontinuous with our people's previous traditional knowledge of Him.[11]

9. Achebe in Interview with Bill Moyers, cited by Gikandi, *Reading Chinua Achebe*, 1.

10. Achebe, *Morning yet on Creation Day*, 94; cited by Gikandi, *Reading Chinua Achebe*, 20–21.

11. The result of the conference was published in 1969—Dickson and Ellingworth, *Biblical Revelation and African Beliefs*, 16.

Affirming the *same* God in ATR and Christianity, while recognizing the radical quality of God's self-disclosure in Jesus Christ, buries Hegel and Western prejudice. To deny one's religious cultural past, as a result of conversion, would amount to intellectual suicide. Eboussi-Boulaga remarked, "A living community's past cannot be contradistinguished from its present as 'true' or 'false.' What has given one's ancestors reasons for living and dying cannot simply be repudiated as absurd and senseless by one who finds oneself in human continuity with them."[12] Literary critics and humanists, Soyinka and Achebe, would add a caveat: only life-enhancing narratives or practices of the past (ATR) and the present (Christianity) that reinvent the human person and the African world are worth preserving.

The Ibadan statement affirmed that biblical revelation rather than being destructive of the religious cultures of Africa confirms and strengthens them. True, biblical revelation judges African religious cultures; but in the process of judging and sifting the religious cultures it sharpens the West African perception of the God that is powerfully weak that is revealed in Jesus Christ. This nuanced position of AACC is informed by a hermeneutic of identity and continuity adopted in Bible translation. As a matter of fact, before the Bible was translated into any sub-Saharan African language, the Nigerian liberated slave, Olaudah Equiano, writing in 1789 displayed the hermeneutic of continuity. He enthused about the Bible: "I was wonderfully surprised to see the laws and rules of my own country written almost exactly here; a circumstance which I believe tended to impress our manners and customs deeply on my memory."[13] This is an assertion of the porousness, and therefore openness to universality, of the Jewish-Christian and ATR world visions. They share a similarity in narrative structure; this enabled West African Christians to bring to their new faith the conviction that the intense interreligious and cultural conversation concerns the *same* God. I share aspects of the hermeneutic of identity that affirms continuity between ATR and the Jewish-Christian worldview; but I underline a proviso—the radical dimension of God's revelation in Jesus Christ is not compromised.

---

12. Eboussi Boulaga, *Christianity without Fetishes*, 4. See also Bediako, "How Is Jesus Christ Lord?"

13. Equiano, *Interesting Narrative of the Life of Olaudah Equiano*, 83–84.

God in African theology opens a discourse that touches the heart of Christian life in Africa: the complex interface between identity and conversion. It is therefore not surprising that God and African religion dominated the thinking of pioneer African theologians. J. B. Danquah, Bolaji Idowu, Harry Sawyer, Francis Arinze, Gabriel Setiloane, Vincent Mulago, Kwesi Dickson, John Mbiti, Charles Nyamiti, and others, argued in favor of a hierarchy in the perception of divinity in Africa. They rightly affirmed the presence and action of one "Supreme" God in African religion. Sacrifices to the "Supreme Being" are rare. However, they claimed, with little attention to ethnographic detail, that all sacrifices find their way ultimately to the "Supreme Being." For this kind of generalization, they could be rightly accused of taking the eye off the complexity of African religious contexts. Even the adoption of the language of "Supreme Being" that originated from deist philosophers and later was co-opted by evolutionist anthropologists is severely criticized. The identification of "Supreme Being" with ATR God and God of Jesus Christ is inspired by the nineteenth-century Catholic natural theology and liberal protestant theology. Though the terms were applied to historically identifiable and living deities, the apologetic interest of pioneer theologians is clear: a stout affirmation of continuity between the God of ancestral religion and the monotheistic Western Christian God revealed in Jesus Christ. The intentionality is a Christianization of the pre-Christian religious heritage.[14]

Bible translation into African languages (by African and European missionaries) charted the path toward the option for continuity that has strengths and weaknesses. Positively, through Bible translation, the African ancestral world that started encountering Western modernity through slavery and colonization has expanded. Jewish-Christian cosmology enmeshes with the African religious world; it expands, on the one hand, the African world, and, on the other hand, sets the stage for the expansion of notions of the God of Jesus Christ in African Christian practice: a fusion of horizons. Lamin Sanneh sums up the dynamics of

---

14. Peter Kwesi Sarpong asserted the position of pioneer African theologians on sacrifice as a truism in his summary of the ancestral beliefs of the Asante: Sarpong, "Rôle Des Ancêtres Dans Une Religion Africaine." See Bediako, *Christianity in Africa*, 82–83. A very good recent critique of pioneer African theologians can be found in Ukwuije, "L'humanité De Dieu."

this encounter for the African world in terms that reflect Robin Horton's intellectualist approach to conversion from ATR to Christianity:

> . . . while it might be possible in the pre-Christian period for Africans to think of God in highly refracted social and ethnic terms, now a new scale of identity was introduced that included critical self-reflection in the transcribed medium of language, a language, in the bargain, that retained the marks of the people's tongue . . . What is illuminating in the indigenous cultural process then, is how the Christian Scriptures, cast as a vernacular oracle, gave the native idiom and the aspirations it enshrined a historic cause, allowing Africans to fashion fresh terms for their own advancement and possibility.[15]

Being Attentive to the Complexity of ATR

While making good use of the abundant research results of pioneer African theologians and endorsing aspects of the hermeneutic of identity, I distance myself from the apologetics that diminish the complexity of ATR, that obscure the sociocultural and complex perception of the human person, and the diversity of expressions of beliefs and practices in West Africa. The complexity is better perceived where one recognizes dynamic interrelationship and delight in multiplicity as foundational to the West African notion of life, the human person and the world. Dynamic interrelationship and multiplicity impact on social arrangements, economy, politics and religion despite historical mutations, distortions and contradictions.

Dynamism and creativity guide the integrality of human life! Though Nigerian pioneers like Idowu rejected the exaggerations in Placide Tempels' vitalistic philosophy, they appreciated, from ethnographic data, a fundamental dynamism in the notion of the human person (anthropology) and in human relationship to deity. There is wide relational exploitation or instrumentalization of mystical powers for good and for ill. Plurality and relationality dictate patterns of human recreation and reinvention of the world. Multiplicity of spirits or divine

15. Sanneh, *Encountering the West*, 86. Robin Horton in a series of articles outlined his influential intellectualist approach to ATR: Horton, "African Conversion"; Horton, "African Traditional Thought and Western Science—Part 2. The 'Closed' and 'Open' Predicaments"; Horton, "African Traditional Thought and Western Science—Part 1. From Tradition to Science"; Horton, "Judaeo-Christian Spectacles: Boon or Bane to the Study of African Religions"; Horton, "Ritual Man in Africa."

beings displays a West African divine economy. For example, numerous deities or spirits in the Yoruba, Fon or Ewe pantheon (*orisa,* Yoruba, and *vodhun* Fon and Ewe) function within a divine economy that is dominantly therapeutic. Multiple divine beings are legitimately interpreted as displaying the dispersal of responsibility or competence in the spiritual world as a health-focused design of God for the integral wellbeing of humans. Bolaji Idowu and some pioneer African theologians who claim strict pyramidal hierarchy in divinity (i.e., radical monarchical monotheism) actually diminish rather than increase the contribution of West African ATR to the God-talk.

Multiple deities, complementary roles, relationality, and flexibility maximize the agency of deities, spirits, ancestors, and human mediators, in dynamic relationship to the benevolent purpose of the one Creator God, for integral human wellbeing.[16] The reverse is also painfully true. The exploitation and instrumentalization of the powers or deities for selfish ends jeopardize human wellbeing and raise fundamental questions of morality. Human mediators, diviner-doctors and/or priests, draw their power from the same source as the sorcerer and the witch. They are not destined to be evil, rather they decide to be evil. Mary Douglas correctly describes the witch as "a spoiled priest": "As power is one, and knowledge is one, the sorcerer taps into the same channels as the priest and diviner . . . The more he is trained in religious techniques for more ensuring fertility, curing sickness, and sterility, the more he has at his fingertips the techniques for striking with barrenness and killing. The difference is entirely moral."[17]

Critical reflection on the complex West African religious culture, expanded through contact with Christianity and modernity, enables insight into the broader horizon of West African Christian practice and reflection. It facilitates the appreciation of the contribution of West African Christian experience to Christian theology as such. For example, AICs declare: "*The renewal of the Holy Spirit* is continuous with and greater than the spirits around us." Consequently, the interpenetration of ideas on "spirits around us" and "Holy Spirit" of Christianity enables theological reflection in West Africa to become a critical pneumatologi-

---

16. Chinweizu in an unpublished paper insists that monotheism has done untold harm to African social organisation. See Chinweizu, "Gender and Monotheism."

17. Douglas, "Problem of Evil among the Lele," 29.

cal (spirit-focused) review of the catholic tradition to reinvent this tradition.[18] Pneumatology becomes a viable entry point to the God-talk.

All I am trying to stress is the importance of a critical revaluation of ATR as practiced in West Africa. From the scholarly evaluation of the matter, one can point to abundant resources that forbid the cavalier and racist dismissal of Africans from history, and from religious, human and cultural creativity. However, critical vigilance forbids romanticizing African history, religions and cultures. By examining the structures of ATR in West Africa one comes to appreciate the vitality of a benevolent God, deities, spirits and ancestors preoccupied with human flourishing and the transformation of the world. In the study, samples will be drawn from particular sociocultural groups (living principally in Nigeria, Ghana, Benin, Togo, and Mali) to portray a complex universe peopled by a multiplicity of divine beings. Multiplicity does not undermine hierarchy; rather it redefines hierarchy, making it flexible or malleable. The dominant structures of this religion constitute the basis for appreciating a reinterpretation of the Holy Spirit in AICs and Charismatic movements. At first glance my approach could be condemned as an uncritical assimilation of the operations of multiple ATR deities into Christianity. But exploring the issue from the perspective of "always searching for a second viewpoint," one struggles with the insight of West African Christianity—pointing towards a creative pneumatological, synthesis. The "spirits" (some of the deities and spirits) are dimensions (denominations according to Origen) of the one Holy Spirit.

STRUCTURES OF THE WEST AFRICAN RELIGIOUS UNIVERSE—PRECEPT FOR THE REDEFINITION OF THE CONCERNS OF RELIGION

West African religious universe is open-ended and fundamentally relational. Achebe and Soyinka re-echo the ground rule of this universe when they reject absolutism and monism in favor of plurality and diversity. This universe is also fundamentally anthropocentric, i.e., focused on full realization of human life and destiny. Ruled by relationality, the perception of human society and deity is characterized by flexibility despite the stout acknowledgement of hierarchy. Mediators and therapists

---

18. This is contained in 1996 AIC's manifesto recorded in Pobee and Ositelu II, *African Initiatives in Christianity*, 71. See also Anderson, *African Reformation*, 238.

are empowered by specific spirits or divine beings, ancestors, and rulers or leaders to perform tasks for the good of the human community.

First of all, I proceed by summarizing briefly five models of the universe encountered in West Africa, namely, the pyramidal, ecological, cosmic, social and oval models. Second, I isolate four structural elements that generally determine attitudes towards divine beings and humans in the complex West African world. These are (a) the world is created good, (b) life in the world is guided by relationality, (c) dynamic or relational hierarchy is the rule of life in this world, and (d) mediators are firmly empowered to act in favor of human wellbeing (this power is open to abuse). The four structural elements that guide access to the West African universe could in my view contribute to the reinvention of Africa and the world and the renewal of God-talk and interreligious relations. They embody potentials that perhaps open a window for us to appreciate that rather than promoting conflict, *religions mediate the harmonious interrelationship among religious persons.* The structural elements are assimilated into West African Christian practice and influence the renewal of the Christian perception of and relationship to the Trinity.

Five Possible Models of West African Image of the Universe

Emefie Ikenga-Metuh in *Comparative Studies of African Traditional Religions* drew attention to four models of "African worldview" that reveal how Africans understand and organize individual and communal life anchored in unseen powers. To discuss models of the universe in the African context, one must take account of five interrelated spiritual beings, namely, God, deities or divine beings, spirits or rather spirit-forces, and ancestors or the living dead.

"*God*" refers to the Spirit that has overall supremacy within the dynamic and relational West African world. Some legitimately question the use of the term "supremacy" in view of the flexible and malleable poles of power. Nevertheless, I keep the term because myths of origin go back to God as beginning (e.g., God is first Ancestor according to the Asante of Ghana). However, West African myths declare without ambiguity that "God" does not diminish the agency of deities or spirits and ancestors. *Ancestors* or the Living-Dead are closer to humans. *Deities* are divine beings living with God as consultors or collaborators; they are also described as related to or as being identical with natural forces—

"nature deities": "They are personal, spiritual and powerful beings, and exercise immense power over human life and destiny."

Spirits or better *spirit-forces* differ from deities because "they have not acquired a distinct personality and cult." They could upset human forecasts, run amok, and act irrationally. But also they could be manipulated or instrumentalized by experts for good or for ill.[19] West African imaginative creativity struggles to come to terms with uncanny phenomena in a way evocative of the thesis of "post-mechanistic animism" that postulates "a world in which an invisible field, which is also causative, pervades every system."[20] Spirit-forces become adopted as divine beings through the process of domestication or "grounding" within a sanctuary; they are then provided with priest and devotees.

These spiritual beings that perhaps distinguish West Africa and the diaspora from the rest of Africa are best encountered in *orisa* and *vodhun* religion that dominates Western Nigeria, Benin Republic, Togo and parts of Ghana. They have seen adaptations in Haitian *vodun*, Brazilian *candomble*, and Cuban *santeria*. Undomesticated, *vodhun* is wild, lacks a name or identity, exists on a general cosmological or metaphysical level, and remains potentially harmful to humans. When domesticated, *vodhun* has a name, is "grounded and contained in earthen pots for humans to worship them," it further provides location or habitation to a group and has devotees, and so on.[21]

Finally, *Medicine* or *Charms* or *Magic* is the field of experts. In West African languages the one term covers medicinal herbs, medication and potent fabrications for self-preservation or attack on enemies, or even for "sporting" contests: *ogwu* of the Igbo, *suman* of the Akan, *gbo* of the Ewe, *òògun* of the Yoruba, etc. The expert occupies a strategic position to mediate medicine, and is variously named: *dibia* of the Igbo, *nganga* of the Bantu, *babalawo* of the Yoruba, *bokọnọ* of the Adja-Fon, and so on. *Medicine* is ubiquitous in this universe dominated by a therapeutic economy. Through the services of *experts or mediators*, the human community maintains relationship with the non-human world, and strives to understand, predict, control and reinvent their world.

---

19. Metuh, *Comparative Studies of African Traditional Religions*, 40, 55.

20. See Nwankwo, "From Power Christianity to Christianity that Empowers," 474.

21. See Lovell, *Cord of Blood*, 42, and chapter 4 "Grounding Vodhun, Unmaking Gender."

Metuh outlined four models to explore this complex universe—the pyramidal, ecological, cosmic, and social models.[22] I will summarize his presentation of the four models and add a fifth one, the oval model of the Dogon that merits to be treated separately. The *pyramidal* or triangular model is proposed by Edwin W. Smith. In this vision of the world God is at the apex, nature deities and ancestors are on both flanks, and magical powers are at the base. The pyramidal model is interested in the hierarchal structure or the pecking order within divinity. Hierarchy is crucial to the organization of the human and spiritual worlds. However, in West Africa hierarchy is perceived in highly dynamic, complex and relational ways as will be shown in the discussion below.

The *ecological* model is based on Asante (Ghanaian) myths. Also the Kalabari of Nigeria, who live in the creeks of the Niger delta, have an ecological model of the universe. The Asante image the dynamic flow of divinity (and all existents) like a river from *Onyame* (God), the source of all beings (*Nana*—Ancestor). The nature deities, sons of *Onyame,* are sent to bless humans. They become manifest as rivers, lakes and sea: *Tano* and *Bea* rivers, *Bosamtwe* lake, and *Opo* (the sea). Their offshoots become also spirits or spirit-forces. Along with ancestral spirits they course into and interrelate harmoniously with the human community. Each human is the indwelling of a divine spark, *kra* or *okra that* returns to God at one's death. Spirit-forces, charms (*suman*), evil spirits and witches threaten human life. Consequently the ministration of mediators or experts is crucial in the human world for the realisation of human destiny.

The *cosmic* model derives from the Igbo (Nigerian) perception of the universe. The cosmic order is generally presided over by *Chukwu* (God) resident in the sky and surrounded by sky deities *Anyanwu* (Sun deity), *Amadioha* (Thunder deity), *Igwe* (Sky deity) and so on. On the land, the Earth Mother, *Ala*—wife of *Chukwu*—presides over innumerable deities. *Ala* and Ancestors (*Ndi-ichie,* i.e., Elders, or *Nna-a-ha,* i.e., the Fathers) preside over morality. The important earth deities include *Agwu* (deity of divination, knowledge and health), *Njoku-ji* (Yam deity overseeing agriculture), *Idemili* (Pillar of Water, daughter of *Chukwu* and *Ala,* divinity of peace), *Ekwensu* (deity of war, associated with violence), *Agbara* (deity of coercion), and so on. *Agbara* is also a generic term for unnamed and undomesticated spirit-force. The human community and

22. See Metuh, *Comparative Studies of African Traditional Religions,* chapter 4.

individual humans, centre of this world, interrelate with these divinities. Each human is created unique by *Chukwu* who assigns divine destiny in the form of a personal spirit, *chi* (the equivalent of Asante *kra* or *okra*). *Ala,* ancestors and *chi* are the most visible and influential spirits in Igbo religious practice.

The *social* model is suggested by the Yoruba (Nigerian) pattern of social organisation. The Yoruba model focused on *orisa* is replicated in *vodhun* religion found in Benin Republic, Togo and Ghana, and in the diaspora (Brazil, Haiti, and Cuba). In this model *Olodumare* or *Olorun* (God) is a distant king. The *orisa* (deities) are God's sub-chiefs, while the *ebora* are subordinates of the *orisa*. The major deities are *Orisanla* also called *Obatala,* the demiurge or arch-deity, entrusted with the creation of the universe; *Oduduwa,* mythical hero, founder of kingship and of Ile-Ife, centre of the world (axis mundi), in terms of Yoruba cosmology; *Onile* (Earth mother); *Orunmila* or *Ifa* (deity of divination, wisdom and health); *Ogun* (deity of iron and war); *Shango* (deity of thunder); and the ubiquitous *Eshu* (also known in the region and the diaspora as *Elêgbara* or *Lêgba*) messenger of the deities, helper of humans and facilitator of all communication. *Eshu* has been maligned by West African missionary Christianity and slaveholders in the Americas as the devil. At the bottom of the hierarchical ladder are human beings, who are subject, and engage in worship. Humans are susceptible to possession by the *orisa* that 'mount the *ori* (head)' of the chosen ones empowering them to render specific services for humans in the world. *Orisa* (and *vodhun*) depend on humans for their popularity as much as humans depend on them for the realization of their destiny. Therefore putting humans at the bottom of the hierarchical ladder must be understood in relational and highly flexible terms.

The *oval* (ovum—egg) model is derived from the Dogon of Mali. Creation myths emphasize the seminal, oval or verbal generation of the universe. Creation emerged from a tiny primordial egg, *Amma* (God), very small indeed, though it is taboo to speak about this. Next, there is *fonio,* the primordial very tiny grain found within the originary egg; and within the grain is the primordial speck or life. *Amma* carefully mixed the dynamic elements of creation within the grain. *Amma's* chemistry is described as 'speaking' his creation or turning the grain into wind or word! In this way *Amma* impressed the vibrations of his word into what he was creating. *Amma's* creative work is an art of sophisticated chemistry. Elements are so carefully mixed to ensure happy interrelationship or twinness within the universe to avoid chaos. Interrelationship is such an overriding condition for existents that the myth narrates error in the first creation: *Amma* was superposing elements that should be carefully intermingled. The error (not a moral error, there was yet no time) led to the escape of the key element, water, which functions as internal relational energy. The first creation was abandoned. No trace of it exists. The second creation based on favorable relational intermingling of elements was successful. *Amma* united with his consort the Earth to bring forth in pairs (male and female) *Nommo Anagono,* the four primordial deities. Much later, there was no hurry in creation, four pairs of primordial human ancestors (*Anagono Bile*) were created one after the other—male and female. The interesting perspective introduced by this fifth model is that creation emerged twinned from the egg, seed or word of *Amma*. One is captivated by the imaginative creativity of this myth—primordial deities, human ancestors, and material things emerged from the tiny primordial egg (*Amma*), and the primordial very tiny grain (*fonio*) within the egg, and finally the primordial speck or life within the grain. Creation is *Amma's* image or extension.[23] After describing these five models, I proceed to explain four elements that structure discourse on the universe.

Four Elements Structural to the Image of this Universe

Whatever the model one uses to describe the universe certain fundamental or structural elements undergird the perception of this complex universe. First, the *world created for human habitation is good.* This positive or optimistic dimension of the created universe is common across Africa. It generates an optimistic view of humans in the world. Some myths introduce a discordant note despite the optimism. In Yoruba social model, *Obatala,* the demiurge charged by *Olodumare* to create the universe, brought his personal characteristics into the performance of his task with imperfections. This explains the presence of the infirm, the lame, the blind, etc. In Dogon oval model, the impatience of the fourth *Nommo,* one of the primordial deities created by God (*Amma*), led him to emerge from the cosmic placenta before the full formation of his twin

---

23. Laléyé, "L'accès À Dieu Dans Les Religions Négro-Africaines Traditionnelles," 50–51. More detailed description in Laléyé, "Les Religion De L'afrique Noire," 643–713, esp. 651–58.

sister. This horrid and solitary emergence generated (created) impure (non-twinned) beings. Amma had to intervene to correct the anomaly to re-establish twinness. But overall, optimism dominates. Zeusse asserts justifiably, "The relative material world is not the imperfect nor the compromised. It is the sole realm of reality and is good. God is concerned above all to cooperate in maintaining a world in which crops will grow and health will abound. But because of this, God is not the usual center of worship."[24]

Second, *relationship or relatedness is the overriding criterion of being in the world. To be is to interact or to interrelate.* Nigerian philosopher, K. C. Anyanwu prefers the present participle "life-ing" to "being" to highlight the active (living) interactional dimension of all "beings" in the world.[25] *Relationship* ameliorates *harmony* in the universe. It is the key to being *human,* and it defines the human person, who rather than being a monad is a composite of dynamic interrelationships. Individual identity is always interlinked with plural relationships. The Dogon myth stresses a foundational relationality or twinness, just as Igbo wisdom tradition insists, *ife kwulu ife akwudebe ya*—"Whenever Something stands, Something Else will stand beside it." A colonial official in Igboland made a diary entry in 1920 captioned: *The Pagan Creed* that states, "I believe that all things in this world have their spiritual counterpart, of which their material appearance is but their expression in corporal being."[26] This illustrates the essential duality or twinness of all being. One of the intriguing dimensions of relationality is the consistency in balancing male-female areas of competence on divine and human spheres. *Vodhun* religion (among the Ewe) is, on the one hand, radically rooted in matrifiliation and dominated by female initiates. But, on the other hand, the guardianship of shrines is in the hands of men. The focus on the mother or on matrifocality in Igbo clan and kinship system counterbalances patriarchal dominance, just as the focus on female earth deities counterbalances the male sky deities. This counterbalancing or partnership ameliorates human life and relationship; it engenders human flourish-

24. Zeusse, "Perseverance and Transmutation in African Traditional Religions," 174.

25. Anyanwu, "Meaning of Ultimate Reality in Igbo Cultural Experience."

26. See Metuh, *Comparative Studies of African Traditional Religions,* 51 citing MINLOC, 17/1/1920. Part 1, chapter 1. *The Pagan Creed,* 2156–157. See also Uzukwu, *Listening Church,* chapter 3, esp. "The Relational Notion of Person and Human Rights," 35–38.

ing. Since female deities, led by the Earth Mother (*Ala* that presides over morality), exclude violence, greed and oppression, the counterbalancing has beneficent impact on politics, social life, economy, and religion; it favors egalitarian ethos rather than the dominance and oppression that instrumentalized religion dispenses.[27]

Third, *hierarchy is perceived in dynamic or relational terms*. This element is connected with the second and is *foundational to the perception of order in the universe*. It constitutes the cornerstone of West African religion. There appears no easy way out of a controversy in a religious view of the universe where there is one God and then numerous divine beings fully competent in their areas of operation. Polytheism, a concept based on Graeco-Roman pantheon of competing gods, is an inadequate term. Diffused monotheism falls into the trap of hellenization. Myth narratives and ritual practice rather suggest dynamic or relational hierarchy in divinity as more adequate description. Since this is an area full of pitfalls as well as possibilities for the reinvention of the God-talk, I devote the next section to discuss it in detail.

The final block in the West African religious universe is the vital role of *mediators or therapists*. The importance of their role is intimately connected with the other three structural elements. These men and women, the elect of tutelary deities, are crucial for appreciating West African universe that revolves around human interest—the full realization of human destiny. They operate under the inspiration or guidance of tutelary deities (e.g., *orisa* of the Yoruba, *agwu* of the Igbo, *vodhun* of the Fon).

I proceed to explore the impact of dynamic or relational hierarchy on the meaning and concerns of religion. This will be followed by an examination of the role of mediators or therapists in the West African religious universe; the discussion will also highlight the dangers of the instrumentalization of religion by religious and political hierarchs.

27. See Amadiume, "Igbo and African Religious Perspectives." See also Agbasiere, *Women in Igbo Life and Thought*. For gender balancing in vodhun see Lovell, *Cord of Blood*.

DYNAMIC RELATIONAL HIERARCHY IN DIVINITY—
A PRIVILEGED WEST AFRICAN EXPERIENCE
OF TRANSCENDENCE

The principle of dynamic relational hierarchy is an overriding molding block in the West African view of the universe. This fundamental element of ATR led to West African religion being described as polytheistic or even henotheistic. I already referred to Parrinder's frustration with West Africans who have little hesitation in accepting new types of worship or deities. Their religion acknowledges no jealous God that forbids adding new beliefs to old ones. Aylward Shorter also suggests that African conversion to Christianity may not really include a radical break with the past. It is merely an addition of one more insurance policy on existing ones.[28] The critical questions for ATR that I address here are: "Is there justification for stressing One God (Supreme) and a multiplicity of deities? What mode of relationship exists between God and the deities, and what theological message does this West African experience carry for religions"? There are critical questions also for West African Christians who confess the *same God* and thereby introduce novel accents into world Christianity: "Where lies the novelty of the faith-experience of God-Christ-Holy Spirit in view of the fundamental assumptions of West African ATR? Is there nothing radically new in West African confession of God-Jesus Christ-Holy Spirit, as Shorter insinuates"?

To orientate my answer, I assume that multiplicity of divine beings, following the structure of West African perception of reality, is geared towards a therapeutic economy: deities exercise functions for the good of humans in the world. Because of the freedom with which deities exercise roles, it will be argued that the "supremacy" of One God is meaningful only within a flexible divine hierarchy. God's overall supremacy is inclusive, dynamic and relational. This rejects, on the one hand, a supreme and exclusive jealous God encountered in Deuteronomistic theology of the Hebrew Scriptures. (This will be addressed in detail in a later chapter). There is no evidence of theomachy similar to what is encountered in Semitic or Mesopotamian mythology. Flexible interrelationship ensures the absence of conflict between God and the deities. "Nyame" of the Asante "is the Great Ancestor, the Founder and Builder

---

28. Parrinder, *West African Religion*. And, see also Shorter, *African Christian Theology*, 10.

of community, of which he is the Head. . . . The other spirits are never in competition with Nyame."[29] But, on the other hand distance or transcendence is of the nature of the One God. Distance does not mean otiose: an otiose African "High God" does not exist except in the mind of missionaries and anthropologists. I do not agree with the "expert viewpoint" of Mircea Eliade that myths and religions originate from the void left by the departure of God—the otiose "High God" that plays no role in the religious experience of the "primitives." Eliade's claim that God's transcendence "is confused and coincides with his eclipse," or that "true religion" begins only when God withdraws from the world does not apply to West Africa, or indeed to Africa. I do not agree, as Thomas and Luneau appear to do, with the "fundamental theology" that informed Eliade's viewpoint on "Sky gods" described in the trite phrase recorded in his journal entry of 8 November 1959: "the impulse of the religious person towards the 'transcendent' makes me think sometimes of a gesture of desperation of an orphan that is left alone in the world."[30] I argue on the contrary that in West Africa God's transcendence or distance creates the condition for the dynamics of relationship to come fully into play, for the amelioration of the human world. Louis-Vincent Thomas and René Luneau had an initial and correct hunch of a possible but foundational West African metaphysical imperative which insists that what exists must be plural or it is non-existent. Copious field evidence indicated to them that myths about God's departure or God's distance open a window to contemplate the dynamic and unique West African experience of God's transcendence. Yet our two authors, weighed down by the "experts'" (Eliade's) viewpoint, failed to give full value to the contribution of the West African experience to our understanding of religion.[31]

Myths that narrate God's departure from the human world turn out to provide firm security for the inter-relational agency of humans, ancestors, deities and God for the good of humans in the world. The positive theological message that this carries for religions is that *the multiplicity of religions or ways is fundamentally good.* West Africa re-

---

29. Fisher, *West African Religious Traditions*, 139.

30. Eliade, *Fragments D'un Journal,* entry of November 8, 305. The same journal entry quoted by Thomas and Luneau, *Les Sages Dépossédés*, 163.

31. Field evidence in the following publications, "Les Noms Théophores"; "Les Noms Théophores Ii"; "Les Noms Théophores Iii"; Luneau, *Noms Théophores D'afrique, Série Ii, Mémoires Et Monographies.*

produces the world of religions in miniature through its innumerable deities and through its dogged confession of One (Supreme) God. This experience teaches the world of religions that *religions are multiple because they fulfill their intentionality or tacit end by facilitating harmonious interrelationship among religious persons.* Nevertheless there is a negative message even a threat that accompanies multiplicity. Relationality, so radicalized, enables witches and wizards, capricious spirit-forces and offended ancestors and deities to make their envy and displeasure felt; they thereby threaten individual and communal destined course of life. This explains the fear of spirits, the frequency of rituals and sacrifices in West African religion and cries out for the need of renewal in ATR. It explains the advantage of conversion to Christianity as a liberating option. The struggle to cope with the possible ambiguities within the complex structures of West African religion could lead to syncretism. Echeruo captured this in the facility with which the Igbo would simultaneously sacrifice to the Christian God and the deities: "The god in front and the devil behind must both be appeased."[32] On the other hand, the recourse to therapy (healing and exorcism for liberation and wholeness) in AICs and Charismatic movements and the dominant role of the Holy Spirit argue for a successful Christian assumption of West African characteristics. Indeed AICs assume a leadership role in assimilating or transforming the qualities of deities into the charismatic gifts of the Holy Spirit.

I go on to further clarify the relational operation of One God and multiple deities as well as the theological contribution West African ATR makes to our understanding of religion. The overall contribution of the structures of West African ATR to further insight into aspects of the Hebrew Yahweh and the God of Jesus Christ will be explored in relevant chapters below.

One "Supreme" God and Multiplicity of Deities— Transcendence Facilitating Diffused Agency

In the Yoruba social model of the universe *Olorun* or *Olodumare* (God) created through a demiurge *Obatala* (*Orisanla*). The deputed *orisa* performed the assigned task in all liberty—including the errors in creation that arose from his weaknesses (being drunk with palm-wine.) The model of deputizing for one's superior is the practice in the administra-

---

32. Echeruo, "Religion, Imperialism, and the Question of World Order," 19.

tion of West African kingdoms. For example, *Asantehene* (the Asante king) and *Oba* (the Yoruba king) are shielded by intermediaries and district heads who are closer to the people: every king has "a talking mouth."[33] The distancing of the king in the socio-political arrangement is reproduced in the narrative and perception of relationship between God, divine beings and humans. Yoruba myths portray divine administrators *(orisa)* as representatives of God; they enhance the authority of the creator but at the same time shield *Olodumare* from immediate commerce with humans. This imagery of distance displays, in the view of Ryan, the "absolute uniqueness of God." This feature of West African religion is applicable to the kingdom building Yoruba, Asante, and ancient Dahomey as well as to the Igbo, Ijaw, and Ewe groups that favor decentralized or "anti-state" social structures. Ryan is right that West Africans, the Yoruba and Akan, "are better equipped linguistically than are Semites, Greeks, Romans and their inheritors to express the absolute uniqueness of God. There is no need for *Olodumare (Olorun)* or *Onyame (Onyankopon)* to arise above the 'other gods,' as Psalm 82 bids Him."[34]

The rule in typical West African kingdoms is that kings are withdrawn. Persons involved in the administration of the kingdom, representing all major groupings (regional village councils and chiefs, queen-mother, rain-makers, priests, aristocratic lineages, etc.), become prominent in a *diffused exercise of power*. This socio-political option or oligarchic monarchy neutralizes dictatorship and autocracy. "The Yoruba," says Metuh, "lived in city-state kingdoms with centralised administration under a supreme chief *(oba)*, whose authority in practice was compromised by district heads who were closer to the people."[35] "Closer to the people" engenders popular participation in state affairs, and is designed to "compromise" autocracy. African oligarchic monarchies, geared towards "compromise," enjoy the advantage of being "closer to the people" over autocratic monarchies introduced under Islamic influence. Autocratic monarchies reproduce something similar to what Congar criticized as the pre-Trinitarian or a-Trinitarian conception of God that characterized Christendom. It entrenched a political and social monotheism introduced into Christian theology based on Greek cul-

---

33. See Fisher, *West African Religious Traditions*, chapter 2.

34. See Zeusse, "Perseverance and Transmutation in African Traditional Religions," 174; and Ryan, "'Arise, O God!' the Problem of Gods in West Africa," 169.

35. Metuh, *Comparative Studies of African Traditional Religions*, 60.

tural assumptions.[36] This monotheism operates with the exclusiveness that Soyinka criticized, as mentioned above.

The Dogon, Asante, and Yoruba insist that contact with sacredness (human or divine) must be mediated. Nearness to a monarch, who has right over life and death, could be dangerous. *Asantehene* veiled his face since his direct glance and presence could destroy subjects. This enhances the sacredness or awesomeness of authority but paradoxically guards against autocracy. Instead of *authority* being threatened by the many levels of participatory administration, it is enhanced and even mystified; at the same time it is checked and balanced. This socio-political model that informs the analysis of narratives and perceptions of the divine could explain Idowu's choice of "diffused monotheism" instead of "polytheism" to describe the complex reality of God amidst the multiplicity of deities in Yoruba religion. Zeusse applies the social model unequivocally to interpret the perception of the divine: "Power unmediated is terrific and breaks boundaries. Power as it is disseminated in articulated divine order is good." Consequently, "God does not involve himself too directly in the world that he sustains, for too particular and intense an involvement might destroy the fabric of the divine order he sustains."[37] The Igbo whose social structure is radically decentralized also image relationship with God as mediated; or at least they insist that certain areas of government are assigned to deities. Achebe captures this in the myth of *Idemili* (deity of peace):

> Power rampaged through our world, naked. So the Almighty, looking at his creation through the round undying eye of the Sun, saw and pondered and finally decided to send his daughter, Idemili, to bear witness to the moral nature of authority by wrapping around Power's rude waist a loincloth of peace and modesty.[38]

However, the complex West African cosmos is only partially captured by the language of mediation. The deity (e.g., *Idemili*), the tutelary *vodhun* or *orisa* (e.g., *Obatala*) executes in all freedom assigned tasks, influences communities and individuals without appearing to render account to God. Deities of course neither compete with nor threaten

36. See Congar, "Le Monthéisme Politique Et Le Dieu Trinité."

37. Zeusse, "Perseverance and Transmutation in African Traditional Religions," 175, 174.

38. Achebe, *Anthills of the Savannah*, 93.

the transcendent God. The transcendent and distant God is beneficent and provident, and does not come across as the dangerous or threatening God that Zeusse suggests. If one could draw one lesson from the myth-narrative of Igbo founding kings, the kings of Nri and Adama, God (*Chukwu*) in his inscrutable wisdom chose to exercise power in a weak and consultative way:

> The traditional account of the origin of kingship is that Ezenri and Ezeadama came from heaven and rested on an ant heap; all was water. Cuku asked who was sitting there and they answered, "We are the kings of Nri and Adama," therefore Cuku and the kings talked. After some conversation Cuku gave them each a piece of yam; yams were that time unknown to man, for human beings walked in the bush like animals.[39]

Achebe expressed in amazement: "Chukwu Himself in all His power and majesty, did not make the Igbo world by fiat. He held conversations with mankind. He talked with those archetypal men of Nri and Adama, and even enlisted their cooperation and good offices."[40] What is the nature of God's transcendence?

The transcendent nature of the One God is captured with startling clarity in mythologies of social groups that opt for the ecological and oval models of the universe. *Onyame* of the Asante and *Amma* of the Dogon assume exclusive prerogative for creation instead of confiding creation to a demiurge. The imagery and language used to depict the *nature of the Creator God* suggest an interesting insight by West Africans into God-talk; the imagery helps to clarify the nature and purpose of God's transcendence and requires further comments.

The *first characteristic* that helps us interpret God's transcendence is embodied in myths. According to Issiaka Laléyé, myths portray *God* ("Supreme Being") *always with a name* but rarely and perhaps almost *never with a face* or an image. The aniconic, i.e., *imageless*, character of God, the Origin of origins, is the foundational rule of God's transcendence. It could be connected with the restricted cult of God in West Africa. The elusive *Mawu,* or better the dual gendered *Mawu-Lisa,* of the Ewe and Fon (Togo, Benin, and Ghana) has no human form like the *vodhun*—*vodhun* are "grounded," molded and worshipped. This characteristic sets *Mawu* apart! She is "likened to the wind, an amorphous

39. Thomas, *Anthropological Report on the Ibo-Speaking Peoples of Nigeria*, 50.
40. See Nwodo, *Philosophical Perspective on Chinua Achebe*, 274–75.

and undefined yet powerful element which imbues terrestrial existence with its essence and vitality." *Mawu* is full of "grandeur, mercy, patience, goodness, tenderness and sweetness."[41] The presence of *Mawu* is felt, but She can neither be captured in human form nor grounded in a shrine like *vodhun*.

The closest one comes to projecting an image of God is the Asante *Nyamedua*—"God's tree"! Positioned at the entrance of compounds, this three-pronged branch planted in the ground contains on top a pot of rainwater—"God's water": "holy water" sprinkled on family members and others to secure divine blessings. Ancestors drink from it as well.[42] Perhaps this symbolic closeness of *Onyame* through "God's tree" explains the frequent prayers and offerings made to God—a practice that is exceptional in the West African religion. *Nyamedua* is however neither a face nor strictly an image: *Nyamedua* is a symbol of God's providential care for humans revealed within an ecologically friendly divine economy.

The transcendent imageless God embodies a paradox that appears to me part of the purpose of the uniqueness of God in West African religion. It is a matter for wonder that God's distance does not reduce God's providential presence or nearness, nor God's tenderness and sweetness, nor God's continued involvement in imbuing terrestrial existence with vitality. If creation came out of the very being of God (*Amma* of the Dogon) to transmit vitality to all existents, if creation flowed out of *Onyame* as divine rivers for human good, the mythical language of God's departure or distance can never be interpreted as absence. Rather it could be called an imaginative device to affirm strongly equal distance and equal nearness of all existents from God. Wherever God is concerned there is no place of privilege, no privileged person or community, no chosen people. *Deities* (e.g., in *vodhun* and *orisa* religion) can be grounded, can choose privileged and initiated devotees, can even be instrumentalized by hierarchs, but never God. This is the foundation for the power and weakness of God: anyone can address prayers to God anywhere and at anytime to renew vitality. But the imageless God—*Amma, Onyame, Olodumare*, or *Chukwu*—has no institutionalized priesthood; nevertheless God can be invoked by each person and be approached by the community through its leaders.

---

41. See Lovell, *Cord of Blood*, 25; and Claffey, "Looking for a Breakthrough," 124.

42. Fisher, *West African Religious Traditions*, 141.

God's transcendence engenders the enhancement of relationship for a better world. This *second characteristic of God's transcendence* is displayed sharply on *the rare occasions when direct sacrifices are offered to God*. In times of extreme drought, the Sar of Chad (Central African region) have recourse to communal worship of God that takes the form of a celebration of wider familial inter-relationship. Two procedures are possible. First, the initiated elders could sacrifice an animal or fish (caught during hunting or fishing); part of the victim is offered to the tutelary spirit and the rest eaten by the initiated. A second type of sacrifice involves *direct worship of God*. After hunting or fishing, the catch is cooked and brought to the public square. *No specific portion of the victim is offered to God*. Rather the whole community without exception as to gender, age, or sex, celebrate and eat a communal meal. It appears, according to Hillaire, that what pleases God and attracts God's blessing is less presenting a gift than assembling a people to celebrate and overcome their differences and to be united in brotherhood.[43] This orientation in direct worship of God is a major challenge to the perception of religions in the world; it is a challenge that emerges sharply in the encounter of diverse peoples and cultures. From the study of Haitian *vodhun*, Hurbon underlines the point powerfully and persuasively: the "widening of horizons" that follows in the diverse narratives about God among diverse peoples, narratives that argue that no one people appropriates God, displays God as "the eschatological problem of the encounter of cultures."[44] The perspective of transcendence should be repeated time and time again. Thomas and Luneau correctly observed that for almost half a century, spirits and intermediaries between humans and God took "the lions share" of anthropological studies in Africa, no doubt with justification. But this was *at the expense of distorting the true perspectives of African religion:* the grasp of the flexible and dynamic relationship in divinity intending overall human good as *pax deorum*. It was at the expense of not developing in theology a cocktail of captivating epithets that describe God: "God beyond human speech," "God that departs from men," "God of daily existence," "God without equal," "God beyond contradiction and absurdity," "God whose speech is the world," etc. Reviewing these epithets Thomas and Luneau drew the interesting conclusion,

---

43. Hillaire, "Quand L'homme Africain Parle De Dieu," 139.
44. See Hurbon, *Dieu Dans Le Vaudou Haïtien*, 222–23.

> Whether one says that God is distant or near, God remains the
> essential *reference* in the commonplace nature of everyday exis-
> tence. Research in the future led by Africans themselves, would
> without doubt enable us to discover the wealth of an approach
> to the mystery of God which remains for us virtually unknown.[45]

The rediscovery of the West African "approach to the mystery of God" in my view provides a new point of departure for our understanding of religions. It introduces a shift in the discourse of religious dialogue; and could inject freshness in the review of questions and answers over the meaning of the many religions and ways in the world.

The *equal distance and equal nearness of the One transcendent God* explain the very important place assigned to destiny (individual and communal) in narratives and religious practice. Destiny is packaged for and/or is chosen by each individual in the presence of God at pre-exis-tence. In Ewe and Fon tradition (Benin Republic, Togo and Ghana), one assumes, despite the independent agency of *vodhun*, that one's destiny *se* (the counterpart of *chi* of the Igbo, *okra* of the Asante) is packaged, received and chosen at the ancestral location of pre-existence (*Bome*) before *Segbo* (the great *Se*) an aspect of *Mawu* that guards destiny. *Se* is the individualised roadmap in life.[46] Consequently, each human, each community is destined, is special, and is chosen: each is unique, equally near to the distant God, and endowed with its particular gifts to flourish and accomplish its mission in the world. The indwelling "divine spark" in each human embodies God's providential care. The life or existence of each individual or community is weighed in terms of realizing destined course in life. There is a high level of effort or struggle to realize one's destiny. It is in the struggle to realize the destined course in life that the vulnerability or fragility of individuals and the human community is exposed. Evil, jealous or dissatisfied deities, spirit-forces that are not grounded, could threaten one's course in life. Asante myth imaginatively pictures the Creator (*Odomankoma*) positioning powerful spirits in riv-ers, forests and rocks to ensure the protection of humans from "elemen-tal evil."[47] The struggle to realize one's destiny, to revitalize or renew one's

---

45. Thomas and Luneau, *Les Sages Dépossédés*, 169. Both scholars are highly es-teemed in French speaking world. Interesting works include, Luneau, *Laisse Aller Mon Peuple!*; Thomas and Luneau, *La Terre Africaine Et Ses Religions*.

46. Eggen, "Mawu Does Not Kill," 349. See also Eggen, "Parenté Du Dieu Qui Ne Tue Pas," 133–35.

47. Fisher, *West African Religious Traditions*, 139.

life, and to ensure security explains the importance of deities, mediators and experts in West African religion. Deities, ancestors and mediators dominate ritual practice to the point of giving the impression that God the Creator is eclipsed.

Scholars who claim that God is ordinarily approached through deputies ignore aspects of the reality on the ground. While admitting that such is the case, one must immediately add that West African experience testifies to operational independence of deities in their relation to humans, and that direct prayers and offerings are made to God. Ecologically friendly symbols like *Nyamedua* and the frequent invocations and prayers addressed to God without recourse to ancestors and deities call for caution in claiming that societal structures are replicated in the perception of divinity. This explains my preference for flexibility in understanding hierarchy in divinity. What is the mode of relationship between God and the deities?

GOD'S TRANSCENDENCE MEDIATING INCLUSIVE RATHER THAN EXCLUSIVE SUPREMACY

The paradox in the relationship between God and deities for the good of humans is the most controversial area of West African religious practice and theory. One admits the distance between humans and God without denying nearness. The ubiquity or nearness of deities and ancestors is incontrovertible because of frequent rituals and sacrifices. But there is also the mediatory role of deities between humans and God, and yet they neither appear to account to God nor are they in competition with God. How does one understand the cluster of relationships?

Some argue that the term "supremacy" is an aberration in understanding religion in this region. Others quarrel over symbols and epithets of the nebulous "supreme" God. I argue that in the West African coast (from Nigeria, Benin Republic, Togo, Ghana, to Mali), whether one is focusing on kingdom building peoples with centralized authority or the more numerous sociocultural groups that practice decentralization or "anti-state" ideology,[48] the perception of hierarchy is relational and dynamic. God's supremacy is inclusive rather than exclusive. The power

---

48. There are many interesting studies on African political systems. See Amadiume, *Re-Inventing Africa*. See also Diop, *Precolonial Black Africa*; Niane, *General History of Africa*, vol. 4. Ogot, *General History of Africa*, vol. 5. Also Daigne, *Pouvoir Politique Traditionnel En Afrique Occidentale*; Fortes and Evans-Pritchard, *African Political Systems*. I reviewed these systems in chapter 2 of Uzukwu, *Listening Church*.

of the deities that are immediate administrators of the inhabited world is comprehensible within a notion of "supremacy" that is inclusive.

The suggestive Durkheimian scheme that society reproduces itself in its perception of the divine could mean, on the one hand, that the kingdom building societies, with structural diffusion of power in the political sphere, replicate this structure in their image of the divine. On the other hand, the more common egalitarian or decentralized structure could project an image of the divine that is highly decentralized. This is the crux of the argument of Nigerian literary critic Donatus Nwoga who claimed in a monograph that the "Supreme Being," *Chukwu*, is "a stranger in Igbo life and thought." The republican structure of Igbo society makes the concept of "supremacy" an aberration. *Chukwu* (Great *Chi*) as Supreme Being, according to Nwoga, was the invention of missionaries and anthropologists. The immediacy and power of *Chi* that embodies destiny, *Ala* (Earth deity) and the multiplicity of powerful deities are proof of the absence of a "supreme being." There is no need for one. Nwoga's thesis is attractive, especially from the perspective of *Ala* in Igbo religious practice. *Ala* is a popular and non-controverted deity that dispenses justice with speed. Loved as mother and feared as unbending dispenser of justice, She is a deity that is "beyond the capriciousness of Igbo man."[49] Amadiume argues that studies in Igbo religion should be reviewed in favor of the primacy of the *Ala* and other female deities that ameliorate relationship and exclude violence, greed and patriarchal dominance. Nwoga went further to claim that *Chukwu* provides a clear case of the instrumentalization of Igbo religion by the powerful slave trading Aro clan. They produced an oracle—the *Ibiniukpabe*—converted it into *Chukwu* oracle that made their town, Arochukwu, known and feared to this day. On the whole, while accepting the Durkheimian scheme as partially true, I argue that West African theism resists reductionist categorization.

Igbo theologians, philosophers and literary critics are divided over Nwoga's views on supremacy. Christopher Ezekwugo is the only theologian who partially endorses Nwoga's position. His thesis, defended before Nwoga's monograph appeared, is entitled, *Chi, the True God in Igbo Religion*.[50] *Chi* and not *Chukwu* (*Chi-ukwu*—the great *Chi*) is "supreme

---

49. Nwoga, *Supreme God as Stranger*, 28; also Echeruo, *Matter of Identity*, 18; and Amadiume, "Igbo and African Religious Perspectives."

50. Ezekwugo, *Chi, the True God in Igbo Religion*.

being"—the term *Chi* is used for God as well as for the individualised personal spirit embodying destiny. Ezekwugo supports the claim that the Arochukwu clan is responsible for instrumentalizing and popularizing *Chukwu*. It is instructive to note that attempts to instrumentalize God during the slave trading era were made in the slaving kingdom of Abomey (Dahomey); there, foreign deities including *Mawu-Lisa* were placed under the control of priests of the royal cult. This was an attempt to convert *Mawu* that is probably of Ewe provenance into a *vodhun*.[51] But it is impossible to reduce *Mawu* to *vodhun* that must be molded and given human form. The same impossibility would apply to *Chukwu*. Metuh, in defence of the originality of *Chukwu*, drew attention to resources from earliest CMS missionary archives that recorded *Chukwu, Chineke, and Chi* as epithets used for God in different regions of the Igbo country. Evidence on the ground showed that many Igbo communities (e.g., Nsukka and Awka that are outside Arochukwu influence) not only erected shrines but also practiced direct worship of *Chukwu*. Achebe, literary critic, rejected claims that *Chukwu* was the invention of the Arochukwu clan or of the missionaries. Such claims cannot withstand critical historical scrutiny. The missionary interest was to expose the weaknesses of Igbo religious system. The same missionaries cannot use the *Chukwu* epithet in their preaching unless the epithet was popular. Records of ancient myths and legends and proper names contain the *Chukwu* epithet. These testify to the originality of *Chukwu* as "Supreme Being" (*Chi-ukwu*—Great *Chi*). Umeh, a *dibia* (expert of all knowledge,) in *After God is Dibia*, written from the perspective of the initiate, lends support to Achebe's position. He provides abundant proof, from esoteric lore, of the originality and antiquity of *Chukwu*. *Chineke* (*Chi* the creator) however cannot be ruled out as invented by missionaries. The epithet was reported by early CMS missionaries as in use in the Owerri region. It could be a fusion of two entities *Chi* and *eke* (*Chi*, the bearer of destinies; *eke*, the returnee ancestor reincarnate in a newborn). *Chineke* is canonized through Bible translation and is adopted by both Catholics and Protestants.[52]

51. For extensive discussion of Abomey and instrumentalization of Mawu see, Claffey, "Looking for a Breakthrough," esp. 102–8.

52. See Metuh, *God and Man in African Religion*, esp. Intro. to 2nd ed., 7–19. The reference to Achebe is reported by Chris Nwodo in his *Philosophical Perspective on Chinua Achebe*, ch. 10. Nwodo got his information from the tape of Achebe's Keynote Address on *Igbo World-view* available in Institute of African Studies at University of

The Igbo example of controversy among scholars over the supremacy of God highlights the paradox in the relationship between deities
and God; it also provides insight into the potency of the West African
religious language. The distant aniconic *Chukwu* (Supreme God) is not
as actively present to the community as *Ala* who oversees morality,
influences politics, economy and social life, or *chi* that embodies individual destiny coming from *Chukwu*. The two deities, *Ala* and *chi*, and
the ancestors are obvious in the everyday life of the Igbo. The question is,
if *Chukwu* exercises supreme power, how come that *Ala* controls morality and *chi* individualises each human? The answer is that divine beings
other than God operate with liberty and responsibility for the good of
humans in the areas of their competence. God (*Chukwu, Olodumare,
Amma,* or *Onyame*) is not rendered "less" but "more" in this relational
hierarchy: a flexible and dynamic hierarchy in divinity, an inclusive rather than exclusive supremacy. This suggests a different focus on religion.
Religion intends the realisation of the human destined course in life, to
promote peace and exclude conflict. I pursue the argument to show the
contribution of this image of the divine to the God-talk.

Reinventing Pax Deorum—*Exceptional West African Contribution to the Interpretation of Religion*

A perception of transcendence or supremacy that is not threatened by
multiplicity of divine beings has unique contributions to make to the
study of religions and naturally to the common human project in the
world. It highlights not only coherence in the West African vision of
the universe, but also makes a vital contribution to the meaning of religion. It has potential for renewing Trinitarian theology. From the West
African perspective religions should be viewed less as systems, creeds
or even rituals, and more as the way *groups* of people follow "to attain

---

Nigeria, Nsukka. Edwards and Shaw, "Invisible *Chi* in Equiano's *Interesting Narrative.*"
The linguistic meaning of the gender-neutral *chi* remains unclear. In the non-cosmological usage it is "dawn" or "daylight." Victor Manfredi relates it to *uwa*—the preferred
name for the "male personal spirit" (embodying destiny) among the Ehugbo [Afikpo]
Igbo. Linguistically the root–*wa* in Ehugbo means "arrive home." Manfredi relates *chi* to
"returning" as in *chi-azu* or *logha-chi* [return]. Cosmologically *chi* may be a returning
spirit; this connects with the non-cosmological *chi*, "dawn" or the return of "daylight."
Manfredi's linguistic hypothesis that links *chi* to a "returning" ancestor that partially
reincarnates appears unlikely for *chi* individualises all existents (male and female).
Manfredi, "Igbo Initiation: Phallus or Umbilicus?" esp. 174–78.

what they see as the goal of life:"[53] the integral flourishing, wellbeing or destiny of the group and the individual.

West African ancestral religions, based on local covenants, are cosmic religions; and as such focus on the basic everyday needs. Religions satisfy the quest for explanation, prediction, control and reinvention of the universe. Their focus on the structure of the everyday does not reduce their soteriological thrust because as therapeutic religions their stress on wellbeing or salvation and fullness of life link intimately the here and hereafter. This is in contradistinction from Asian cosmic religions where the soteriological has been subsumed by the gnosis-inclined Hinduism, Buddhism, and Taoism.[54]

Transcendence understood in *dynamic* or *relational* terms argues that God's supremacy does not impede the operational autonomy of deities or spirits. As Zeusse says: "God is concerned above all to cooperate in maintaining a world in which crops will grow and health will abound. But because of this, God is not the usual center of worship."[55] In most cases there is no established priesthood, no clan dedicated to God's service, and no sacrifices or sacrifices only on rare occasions. Unsuspecting students of ATR fall prey to generalizations and a univocal instead of a malleable, dynamic interpretation of God's "distance." Instead of declaring the African "high God" otiose (Eliade), one should rather appreciate that deities, ancestors and humans participate in realizing the purpose of creation—*pax deorum,* as God's plan for humans.

West African religious universe is vibrant, dynamic and relational. Interconnections at all levels between humans, ancestors, divine beings, and God, nourish life in this universe. God's distance that sometimes translates into almost total lack of cult, as in the case of the Yoruba *Olodumare*, testifies to "his absolute transcendence" rather than "Olodumare's otiose nature"[56] This way of understanding God's *exercise of supreme power* protects West African world vision from being confused with the polytheism of the Graeco-Roman world; and preserves its unique contribution to understanding religion for the good of humankind. It bears repeating that God's absolute transcendence and

---

53. Amaladoss, *Making Harmony,* 141–42.

54. See Pieris, *Asian Liberation of Theology,* 71–74.

55. Zeusse, "Perseverance and Transmutation in African Traditional Religions," 174.

56. See Ryan, "'Arise, O God!' the Problem of Gods in West Africa," 166.

exercise of supreme power explain why creation is *Onyame's* prerogative excluding every other deity, and why *Amma* created out of his very being. Igbo cosmogony recognizes *Chukwu* as creator or as the one who sent the founding ancestor. The first action of the civilizing hero (founding ancestor) was the covenant with *Ala*—establishing *pax deorum* that excluded bloodshed on earth.[57]

Vodhun religion that still has enormous impact on Ewe and Fon in Benin Republic, Togo, and Ghana presents one of the most striking illustrations of dynamic interrelationship at all levels and the reality of God's absolute transcendence that ensures the reign of *pax deorum*. *Vodhun* as cosmic or metaphysical beings—children of *Mawu-Lisa*—are not in doubt. Related to wild untamed nature, *vodhun* could cause harm to humans. Consequently, *Vodhun* must be grounded, named or domesticated to give identity, location and settlement (territory) to a community and to ensure the community's survival, enjoyment of abundant health and the good things of life. The relationship and resemblance between woman and *vodhun* are not fortuitous in this culture area. Women, associated with nature, are likened to wild animals (bush meat) that are hunted and grounded (possessed through marriage). *Vodhun* possess women who serve and interpret (possess) the wishes of *vodhun* and mediate their blessings to the community. Men who are guardians of *vodhun* shrines, the *vodhun* themselves who possess women, and women initiates all co-act in the grounding of *vodhun*, in establishing a particular *vodhun* cult in its sanctuary. *Vodhun* are divine beings, children or creatures of God, that orient, govern and direct the destiny of humans. They are constituted governors of the world, plenipotentiary ministers, and administrators of the world or such parts allocated to them by God for the human good. They hardly account to God, *Mawu-Lisa*—the undefined, likened to the wind, good and powerful, who "imbues terrestrial existence with its essence and vitality."[58]

The above is the ideal human expectation in the hierarchical and relational economy of *Mawu* and *vodhun*—God and the deities. *Vodhun* or deities in the West African universe destabilize through possession (this will be treated in detail, next). They are open to instrumentaliza-

---

57. See Onwuejeogwu, *Igbo Civilization*. Details of this in Uzukwu, *Worship as Body Language*.

58. See Lovell, *Cord of Blood*, 25; and Agossou, *Christianisme Africain*, 82–83. Agossou cites the unpublished notes of G. Montilus.

tion and are instrumentalized for evil. This is the case not only in the slave trading kingdom of Dahomey, the slave oracle of Arochukwu, but also the numerous deities whose shrines still function as law courts (e.g., *Ogwugwu* of Okija, Eastern Nigeria) and deities of war (from the less potent *Ogun* of the Yoruba or *Ekwensu* of the Igbo to the flourishing *Egbesu* of the Ijaw, all of Nigeria). They provide ancient and contemporary imagery of instrumentalization of deities in West African religion. Since they are instrumentalized for evil, they cause evil. One hears people in distress cry—*Eshu or Legba or Ekwensu* has killed me! (Similar exclamations by Christians are directed to *chi, Jesus* or *Chukwu*.)

Deities, in their independent operation, lend themselves to be interpreted as centers of energy that escape the grasp, understanding and control of the human community. In their relationship to *Mawu, vodhun* cannot be understood as "subservient deities" under the authority of a "Supreme Creator God," their ruler. True, people believe they can "get reprieve" from *Mawu* when "cornered by any of the junior deities"; but *Mawu* does not deny the deities "autonomy of action." Wiel Eggen is right in his critique of missionaries and anthropologists that claim *Mawu* is "unsurpassable."[59] If one must use the term "unsurpassable" for *Mawu, Onyame, Olodumare, Chukwu* etc., it is only in dynamic relational and flexible terms as opposed to absolutist and exclusivist terms.

Pax Deorum *and Human Destiny*

God-talk or *vodhun*-talk is about *human destiny*—its interpretation and its realization. This critical focus on human destiny stresses that humans are not a pawn in the hands of fate or of deities—destinies are not only given, they are chosen. When individuals and communities learn and embrace the rules of relationship—i.e., the will of God and deities for the human good (*pax deorum*)—they realize their destined course in life. Here lies the strength and weakness of ATR in its West African contours. Its strength lies in the preoccupation with human destiny and human good—religion pursues the realization of integral human wellbeing (*pax deorum*). Its weakness lies in the excessive or consummate devotion to tutelary deities in order to achieve destiny. Devotees (initiates), guardians of shrines and healers could be converted into propagandists of dei-

---

59. Eggen, "Mawu Does Not Kill," 349. See also Eggen, "Parenté Du Dieu Qui Ne Tue Pas," 133–35.

ties. The competition and instrumentalization that emerge lend support to the view that in West Africa "man makes gods."

The dangers and abuses that are part of the ambiguity of religion should not let one lose sight of the West African creative divine economy informed by dynamic hierarchy focused on the human good: *God and God's creation are in dynamic concourse to improve the world of human habitation.* This order, *pax deorum,* originates from God, first Ancestor. Religion is therefore at the service of the human good. Eastern and Central Africa, characterized by what Kibicho calls "simple monotheism," have no highly developed nature deities, yet the human person and community remain the centre of religion. The *transcendent and One God*—described by Kagame in Thomistic-Aristotelian language as the Initial or Eternal Existent, beyond human perception, beyond human linguistic classification of essences (neither human, nor a thing, nor place-time, nor mode of being)—is concerned fundamentally with the integral wellbeing of humans.[60]

Despite centuries of prejudice, a careful study of West African religious resources produces the evidence that God's transcendence in Africa is sharper than among Semites and Indo-Europeans. This rules out the chances of instrumentalizing God by hierarchs—for this would reduce God to a deity (the slave trading kingdom of Dahomey made such an attempt). No religious wars as such will be possible. This statement needs to be clarified. West Africa is peopled by war deities—*Ogun, Ekwensu, Egbesu* (of the Yoruba, Igbo, and Ijaw of Nigeria). Even the Sky-Thunder deity (*Shango, Hevioso, or Amadioha*—Yoruba, Fon, and Igbo*)* whose thunderbolts are connected with the rare direct punishment from God (Kikuyu and Igbo) or with God's benevolent choice (Nilotic peoples) can be instrumentalized for war. But the transcendent One God is removed from direct participation in wars. West Africa has no experience similar to the Mesopotamian violent theogony (Marduk vs. Tiamat) or the hostility in the West Semitic universe (Yahweh vs. Baal.) Such opposition would reduce God to deities (children of God) that are generally ambivalent in behavior. The advantage of West African "kin-focused religion," according to Eggen, is that it provides a perfect antidote against violence. Ancestral or cosmic religions produce deep awareness and respect of one another's destiny—*pax deorum.* Eggen

---

60. See Kibicho, "Interaction of the Traditional Kikuyu Concept of God," 215, and Kagamé, "La Place De Dieu Et De L'homme Dans La Religion Des Bantu."

insists, "Even without idealising the kinship-order, one must admit that religious fanaticism has little place in African traditions, where a centralised, war-generating force that mobilises people for genocidal projects is hard to conceive. The Ruandan or Angolan experiences rather prove than disprove this."[61]

Africa is so difficult to classify in the *clash of civilizations* of Samuel Huntingdon because of the absence of a militant religion, with universalistic and exclusivist claims, supplying the flame that nourishes violence in each civilization. Robert Kaplan, social and political analyst, on this score despairs over Africa's future: there is structural absence of a religion that generates violence. Islam, that in places like Iran or North Africa carries the image of "religion that is prepared to *fight*," a religion that is attractive to the downtrodden, has become domesticated in West Africa. "Though Islam is spreading in West Africa, it is being hobbled by syncretization with animism: this makes new converts less apt to become anti-Western extremists, but it also makes for a weakened version of the faith, which is less effective as an antidote to crime."[62] The successful West African syncretization of Islam and Christianity takes the edge off their exclusivist, extremist and absolutist claims. This is a major act of the retrieval of ATR by Christians and Moslems. It provides a window of opportunity for refocusing the theory and practice of religion in West Africa and the world towards peaceful amelioration of human life. This humanist focus and tolerant, non-coercive dimension of religion makes Soyinka to recommend *orisa* religion: "Orisa, being profoundly humanist, separates the regulation of community from communion with the spirit, even while maintaining a mythological structure that weaves together the living community and the unseen world. But that world of the spirit does not assume any competitive posture whatever over the pragmatic claims of this world."[63]

There are wars and violence in West Africa, past and present, directed by war deities. But there are no religious wars, crusades or jihads prior to the introduction of the two Semitic religions (Judeo-Christianity and Islam.) The jihad still fresh in the memory of Nigerians is the eighteenth/nineteenth century Uthman dan Fodio jihad. The sanguinary literature of the Hebrew Scriptures, the epic narratives of wars and deci-

---

61. Eggen, "Mawu Does Not Kill," 359.

62. Kaplan, *Coming Anarchy*, 35.

63. Soyinka, "Tolerant Gods," 48.

mation of peoples to prove that one god is greater than another, even that Yahweh is the true God, is a scandal from the perspective of West African religious universe. Unfortunately, the reception of these narratives into West African Christianity, especially in Pentecostalism, has radically modified the image of God.[64] Ideally, God, deities, spirits, and ancestors co-act in fashioning and refashioning the world for harmonious and peaceful human habitation. The radical focus on the realization of human needs and destined course in life projects the power of deities and gives the impression that God's power is powerlessness. Christian theology, which is never absent nor excluded from the best anthropological researches, must address more creatively the question of deities. Dispatching them to the category of demons creates a Manichean dualism that is strange to the West African universe. What theological message has the understanding of God and deities, and flexible hierarchy in divinity for the world of religions?

Redefining the Focus of Religion— Promoting Wellbeing and Excluding Conflict

I have tried to show that the principle of multiplicity is not a deficit for the study of ATR in West Africa. Ideally it enhances divine and human agency and ameliorates relationship: God, the Origin, deities, spirits and ancestors relate to humans for their good. Relational flexible hierarchy, structural to encountering the divine, redefines the focus of religion. *Religion that is focused on integral wellbeing has the purpose of realizing destined course in life, and ameliorating human life and human relationships in the world.* This viewpoint on religion *could be an antidote against violence.* The reflection of Bolaji Idowu in the 1970s about a prospective *future for ATR* should not be dismissed offhand. Citing the New Testament, First Letter of John (1 Jn 3:2), "It does not yet appear what we shall be," Idowu affirms optimistically: "This sums up what can be said with certainty about the future of African Traditional Religion."[65] He maintained that ATR is *the* religion of the majority of Africans, and the senior partner in the emerging syncretization of Islam and Christianity in Africa and the diaspora. I think that refocusing on relational hierarchy and the structural elimination of competition between God and

---

64. See among others Meyer, *Translating the Devil*.

65. Idowu, *African Traditional Religion*, 208; see the critical remarks of Bediako, *Christianity in Africa*, 116.

deities would make enduring contribution to the future of Africans and ATR and also make an enduring contribution to the meaning of the multiplicity of religions. The structural elimination of violent competition within divinity, based on the perception of transcendence, does not reduce the transcendent One to an aloof God, "a deist God." Rather, as Fisher correctly states: "Nyame is the Great Ancestor, the Founder and Builder of community, of which he is the Head. Nyame is not selfish and aggressive but tolerant and all-embracing. He makes life within family in the large sense. The other spirits are never in competition with Nyame. He rules over all for the sake of his human children."[66]

There is really no competition among the deities. What is displayed on the ground is the self-involvement of devotees in the cult of their particular deity; this and the propaganda of priests and guardians of shrines and oracles fuel competition. This situation prevails in Igbo myths and legends of the sky deity (*Igwe*) that is proclaimed greater than the Earth deity (*Ala*) by priests of the sky deity. Amadiume interprets this as conflict between matriarchy and patriarchy. But I think it is rather an example of the instrumentalization of religion for economic and political purposes. Barber draws the same conclusion with regard to Yoruba religion: "The *orisa* themselves are not particularly competitive; it is their devotees who try to raise them higher than other *orisa*."[67] This makes a lot of sense: despite the innumerable deities in the Yoruba, Fon and Ewe universes, "possession," the sacred experience of a specific *orisa/vodhun* mounting the "head" of the elect during public worship, is strictly "mono-theistic" (i.e., mono-*orisa/vodhun*). One can be possessed only by a particular *orisa* or *vodhun*. *Ogun* never possesses devotees of *Sango* and vice versa. (Only in the new world, and perhaps among the Gã of Ghana, have there been evidence of serial possession of a single devotee by multiple deities). God, *Olodumare* or *Mawu-Lisa*, the origin of origins, never ever "mounts" anybody because God is never ever compressed into a given mode of manifestation. In this sense, Eliade's "universal modality" of the sacred applies. Possession, dispersed in the multiple deities related to lineage or kin-groups, intends the accomplishment of tasks that fall within the expertise of the possessing spirit. Devotees and guardians publish activities of such deities.

66. Fisher, *West African Religious Traditions*, 139.
67. See Barber, "How Man Makes God in West Africa," 407.

The *structural exclusion of mythological narratives of conflict in divinity* lays the foundation for a West African contribution to the meaning of religion/s and dialogue of religions. It lays the foundation for the struggle against the instrumentalization of religion for political and economic ends—a phenomenon that is very common in Africa and the world. The multiplicity of religions or ways in our world, reproduced in miniature by the multiplicity of deities and spirits in the West African universe, can be theologically defended and interpreted as a potent speech by God, the origin of origins. God through West African religious practice declares: *religions mediate the harmonious interrelationship among religious persons.* This palpable divine speech, based on West African religious perception of transcendence, must be repeated again and again in our world scarred by religious violence. All should join hands to ensure the realization of this mission.

Mediators, therapists or experts, because of their major role in the perception of the divine in West Africa, are crucial for realizing or endangering the purpose of religion. They form the final molding block in the study of religion in this region.

MEDIATORS, THERAPISTS, OR EXPERTS (*DIBIA, NGANGA, BABALAWO, BOKǪNǪ*): ELECT OF DEITIES FOR INTEGRAL HUMAN WHOLENESS

In the West African universe, specialists or experts inspired (or possessed) by tutelary deities (like *agwu* of the Igbo or *orunmila-ifa* of the Yoruba) render services for the overall health and progress of the human community. Their role in the interpretation and practical realization of community and individual destined course in life make them indispensable. They are a key molding block for understanding the West African world. My objective here is to argue that the creative agency of humans, gifted and inspired by tutelary deities, is structural for understanding the West African world. In a world of multiple and ambivalent deities, the experts become men and women of power; and communities and individuals could enjoy relative freedom to choose from alternative centers of power. This characteristic of West African religion, i.e. the role of gifted and inspired women and men, opens an interpretive framework for appreciating the "gifts of the Holy Spirit" and the importance of "powerful men and women of God" in West African Christianity. I begin first with a definition of the expert, then a description of the turbulence that accompanies their call, and finally the ethical imperatives surrounding their practice.

Who is Dibia, Nganga, Babalawo, Bokọnọ?

I consider it important to begin by pointing out that no area of the study of ATR is blocked with prejudice and misunderstanding as the ministry of mediators of health and wholeness within community. Mutual suspicion and conflict existed between missionaries and the experts. They and the deities were denounced by missionaries. The experts resisted missionary presence; but both grudgingly learned from one another. It is a matter of interest, as Peel shows from CMS archival records of mission among the Yoruba, that the *babalawo,* "whose specialism was interpretation", were the principal interlocutors of missionaries. Their hermeneutical assumptions have a major impact on how "Yoruba traditional religion" is viewed.[68] I present two descriptions of the expert by two initiates, Eric de Rosny (French Jesuit) and John Ananechukwu Umeh (Nigerian academic), to disabuse our minds of the prejudicial literature on these indispensable functionaries in the West African world.

De Rosny prefers to call the experts *nganga* because it is the dominant term in Bantu languages of Central and Southern Africa. *Nganga,* defined as "traditional medical practitioners" by the World Health Organization, is preferred to "healers." Experts or healers operating in parts of rural Europe do not have the breadth of social power and esteem enjoyed by *nganga.*[69] De Rosny was initiated as "seer," *ngambi*; and is highly respected in Cameroon. Though he is not *nganga,* yet his clients know "in one way or another that a *nganga,* that is, an heir to the traditional practice of medicine, 'opened my eyes.'"[70] The critical role of *nganga* led him to call ATR a therapeutic religion. In ATR *nganga* stand out and continue to command influence even after the collapse of all patterns of African socio-political and economic structures. *Nganga* display the capacity to recapitulate and reintegrate all aspects of life and world—cosmic, social, psychological, religious, and pharmaceutical—into one great struggle against violence, against the enemies of life, espe-

68. Peel, *Religious Encounter and the Making of the Yoruba,* 13.

69. De Rosny, *Les Yeux De Ma Chèvre,* 48–49. See English translation, De Rosny, *Healers in the Night.* De Rosny also gives a detailed report on his own initiation.

70. De Rosny, "For a Mission of Vision," 95.

cially against witchcraft and sorcery, in order to re-establish order in life. "Fetish-" or "witch-doctor" is derogatory. It fails to capture the depth of the operations of *nganga*. Similarly, the Yoruba term *babalawo* captures the dimension of divination, interpretation, esoteric knowledge, knowledge of herbs and healing. Those initiated, following possession, into *orisa* or *vodhun* cult—*vodhunsi* or *iya-orisa*—may turn out not to be healers or herbalists, but they always render service to the community according to the area of specialization of their *vodhun* or *orisa*.

Ananechukwu Umeh, a university professor, was initiated in 1947. In his two volume work, *After God is Dibia*[71] (a literal translation of the popular Igbo saying, *Chukwu welu olu dibia*), Umeh gives a detailed account of the *dibia*.

> The terminology *Dibia*, in demotic Igbo language, is made up of two words namely *Di* and *Abia*, *Di* means, husband, Adept or Master. Abia means knowledge and wisdom. So while Igbos call *Chukwu* (God) *Abia Ama*, that is, the Knowledge and the Wisdom that reveals Himself, they call *Dibia* the *Adept* or Master of Knowledge and Wisdom.[72]

Consequently, to call the *dibia* healer, psychologist, destroyer of witches, mender of broken bones, etc., is a partial description. Intimately linked with the tutelary deity, *Agwu*, the *dibia* is a complex personality: a man or woman whose vocation is tied to destiny. The vocation could be inherited from matrilineal or patrilineal ancestry, or from pacts made during pre-existence, etc. The link with *Agwu* is transformative,

> Being blessed with *Agwu*, the Holy Spirit's possession, the *Dibia*, sometimes is so taken with complete possession that he or she virtually becomes *Agwu*. He or she speaks the voice of the Holy Spirit, thinks the thoughts of the Holy Spirit, performs the skills, miracles and the feats of *Agwu* the Holy Spirit, sees with the vision of the Holy Spirit and hears with the divine Ears of the Holy Spirit.[73]

---

71. Umeh, *After God Is Dibia*, vol. 1 and 2.

72. Ibid., vol. 1, 76.

73. Ibid., vol. 1, 76, 78. Umeh sees the Christian Holy Spirit as only comparable term for Agwu in English language.

In *vodhun* religion, possession creates, according to Lovell, a "merging of identities of the possessed and the spirit that possesses." "Container and contained become fused." The fusion abolishes gender boundaries![74]

These experts are very well known in West Africa, all over Africa and in the Americas. The overwhelming impact of the tutelary spirit in the life of a prospective *dibia, babalawo, nganga,* or *bokọnọ*, as well as the numerous initiates of *vodhun* or *orisa* (*vodhunsi* or *iya-orisa*—wife of *vodhun* or *orisa*) affects profoundly relationship in the family and social group. The chosen must pass through a rigorous initiation. Their delicate function, which takes them to and from spirit-land, makes them share the ambiguities surrounding spirits in the West African universe.

Signals of Vocation

There is no *dibia* or relatives of *dibia* that have no stories to tell about turbulent events affecting them on the bio-physiological, social, economic or psychological levels. This explains the awe and fear of deities like *Agwu* among Igbo non-initiates, and the general thinking that *Agwu* is a mischievous spirit, a spirit of madness.[75] Similarly, the *contexts in which vodhun appear* are those "where illness, possession, suffering and affliction take pride of place." Immediate signs of appearance of *vodhun* include sudden trance, bulging eyes, contorted mouth, flailing limbs, and foaming; and the general symptoms are in the form of "a sudden and violent, or progressive and prolonged, episode of illness, incurable elsewhere." Diagnosis is followed by treatment; and recovery followed by initiation into a *vodhun* secret society or erection of a shrine. In one case recorded by Lovell among Watchi Ewe (south-east Togo) a *vodhun* whose name is unknown struck a girl with paralysis, making her very ill and unable or unwilling to speak. In another case a *vodhun* struck a young man with madness, making him display "extremely aggressive behaviour, lashing out at people, insulting them, shouting at them, threatening to strike." Healers intervened! *Hevioso* (deity of thunder) was identified as the *vodhun* that struck the girl. She retired into the enclosure of the *vodhun* for initiation into the secret society of *Hevioso*. On the other hand, when treatment of the young man was stopped, he was advised to install a shrine on behalf of a *vodhun*. "As long as he

74. Lovell, *Cord of Blood*, 97.

75. See the detailed study of Aguwa that had not the benefit of the work of Umeh, Aguwa, *Agwu Deity in Igbo Religion*, esp. ch. 2.

continued to care for this deity properly, he would be afforded future protection."[76]

Gendered identity and matrifiliation are also fundamental to the manifestation of *vodhun*, according to Lovell; and not limited only to issues of health. A *vodhun* striking a girl or a woman leads or drives her (the elect) to its shrine, oftentimes linked to a departed grandmother. The woman is allowed to go through the process of possession without interference. Older women follow and remove dangerous objects from her path. "The *vodhun* causing the episode of possession is believed to lead its future initiate to a shrine bearing its name. . . . Once she has arrived at the designated shrine, she collapses in exhaustion."[77] This serves the sociological function of keeping alive the memory of kin-groups—matrifiliation. In *vodhun* religion, the call highlights the dual gender ideology in some West African societies. Whether one is called to become a member of a secret society (mostly women), or guardian of *vodhun* shrine (mostly men), or healer (both men and women) the attack of a *vodhun* whose identity must be diagnosed is a prerequisite. Complex initiation rites then follow.

One appreciates the concern of families and clans disturbed by the invasion of deities. However, initiates are indignant over uninformed negative perception of the deities! Reacting to the negative characterization of *Agwu* by the uninitiated, Umeh explodes, "*Agwu* is what is called the Holy Spirit in the English language. *Agwu* does not do evil. And that is the reason why all great *Dibias* in Igboland desist from doing evil in the face of extreme provocation."[78] Initiates like Umeh, defend, magnify and propagate the holiness and power of *Agwu*, *vodhun*, or *orisa*, and draw attention to the ethical imperatives required of the expert. But one can neither ignore nor deny the preliminary psychological destabilization of those called into the service of deities and the suffering this entails for their families. The suffering and conflict often persist until initiation. After initiation, possession assumes organized ritual mode. Persistent violent possession after initiation could signal infidelity to one's deity.

The psychological destabilization that accompanies the vocation of the expert calls for the "unmasking of the deities"—are they evil, tricksters? Why do the violent seizures, extraordinary misfortunes, etc., form

76. Lovell, *Cord of Blood*, 17, 49–53.

77. Ibid., 69, 81.

78. Umeh, *After God Is Dibia*, vol. 1, 107.

part and parcel of the deity's manifestation? Umeh is eloquent in his defense: "it is definitely not true that *Agwu* is responsible for mental illness. Every *Dibia* worth his/her name knows the causes and types of mental illnesses . . . Commentators on *Agwu* have tended to forget the countless spirits in the service and entourage of *Agwu*."[79] Possession by a deity among the Peki Ewe (Togo) is described in epithets that include madness: "it comes to catch a person," "it is or comes upon a person," "he or she is 'beaten' by *tro* [deity]," "he or she is out of his/her mind, in a rage."[80] Those called to this thankless task oftentimes do not want to serve because of the taboos and restrictions involved. They may require a "shake up" from spirits in the service of powerful deities like *agwu* or *orunmila*. The call is a blessing tied to one's destiny; and compliance is part and parcel of realizing one's destined course in life. The deities are generally irresistible. When *Agwu* bestows her favors, there is little room for freedom. Umeh clarifies,

> . . . if the *Ayagha Agwu* [i.e., spirit of destabilisation in the service of *Agwu*] decides to shake up an unwilling candidate for *Dibiaship* into rising up to his/her responsibility and God-given calling, someone who does not know what has happened or what is happening would conclude that *Agwu* is spirit of *Ayagha* or spirit of chaos and confusion. The person being shaken up is merely being reminded by the appropriate servant of *Agwu* that he or she is called upon to the high and divine service as a *Dibia*; and as soon as compliance is achieved all the troubles would disappear.[81]

Mmaduwugwu Ufondu (now over eighty years) from my village discussed with me, over ten years ago, his endless struggle with *Agwu*. His deceased uncle, Nwokeke Ufondu, came often in the company of *Agwu* to disturb his peace. He did not want to assume the "exalted" office of *Dibia* that his late uncle performed. To shake off the favors of *Agwu* he left the Catholic Church and joined the highly syncretistic Sabbath church that was reputed to provide cures against all attacks of evil spirits. He did not consider *agwu* a good or friendly spirit. But the intrepid *Agwu* and his deceased uncle followed him to the Sabbath church, often making him to trip. They normally sat beside him in the church. After

79. Ibid.
80. Meyer, *Translating the Devil*, 67–68.
81. Umeh, *After God Is Dibia*, 107.

many years of resistance he finally complied. Without any special initiation he prepared herbs for numerous clients with formulas revealed to him in visions. By the time he discussed with me, his travail was not over because *Agwu* did not allow him to make savings to maintain his family. The existence of the deity is not in question. The interest of the deity in the survival of the human community (even in this modern time of confusion) appears also not to be in question. (In a recent conversation, Ufondu asserts he has left *Agwu* and gone back to the Catholic Church— one does not serve God and the Devil. The flourishing of healing and charismatic gifts in the Christian Churches provides alternative sites for gifted people who desire not to serve *Agwu* to realise their vocation.)

The elect of deities come not only from rural or village communities but also city dwellers—Christian or ATR practitioners. The opinion is widespread and is perhaps correct that prospective *Dibia, Bokono, Nganga, Babalawo, Vodhunsi* have melted into AICs where they perform tasks similar to the ones performed in ATR. The cases of psychological destabilization that are discerned by experts as signal of the call of an elect to undertake the sociological function of the integral healing-wholeness of members of the community, raise questions about the nature of the deities. The fascination and fear are transferred to the experts who serve and propagate the image of the deity. They could abuse their power and use it to kill instead of to save life. This calls for a word on the moral imperatives surrounding the expert.

Moral Imperatives Surrounding the Initiates

Awe, respect, unease and fear are popular reactions to the *nganga, dibia, babalawo* or *bokono*. A high ethical standard is generally set or claimed. Umeh's study narrates the feats performed by *dibia*, their extraordinary knowledge of herbs, etc., but also stresses the ethics of *dibia*. First, the last stage of initiation displays the candidate as human-spirit:

> As for the *Dibia*, as soon as he or she is fully formally admitted ritually, he or she would have his/her left-half of the body ritually painted with the white chalk (*ima nzu; iba nzu*) and thereafter sent out on a lone stay in the dangerous wilderness for *Izu Asaa* (Seven Igbo weeks or one Igbo month or 28 days) and on triumphant return home thereafter is so overwhelmingly spiritual and so little human that he or she is approximated to the spirit.[82]

82. Umeh, *After God Is Dibia*, vol. 2, 208. See the arresting photo of a *dibia* just initiated in Basden, *Among the Ibos of Southern Nigeria*. See also Basden, *Niger Ibos*.

This extraordinary power—arising from knowledge of herbs (*ama* of Ewe, *mgbologwu* of Igbo), esoteric knowledge (related to *ifa*, Yoruba; *afa*, Igbo), manipulation of the deity and manipulation of charms—is controlled by ethics. The most fundamental norms are expressed thus:

I malu nso Chukwu	If you know and keep God's don'ts
Malu Nso Ala/Ana/Ani	And know and keep the don'ts of Ana Land or Earth Goddess
Onwero ife I chelu aka	There is nothing you stretch your hand to do or accomplish
Ghalu ime ya	That you will not succeed in carrying out or achieving[83]

Ali Nweke, a *dibia* interviewed by Jude Aguwa during his fieldwork, was initiated by revelation made through dreams and visions directly "granted to him by the sheer benevolence of the gods." He was "instructed to observe certain ethical norms": "never to commit murder or to hurt other people." He is fully committed to saving life. The ambiguity surrounding the deity is shared by the expert. But the good or evil use of herbs, charms and esoteric powers is resolved on the basis of morality. Judgment resides on the level of intention.[84] The *dibia*, *bokọnọ*, *nganga*, or *babalawo* holds the key for understanding creative agency, the flexible intermingling of spirits and humans, and the dynamic hierarchy in the West African universe; they are a key molding block not only in health delivery but in realizing the community's destined course in life. But they walk the tight rope of right and wrong.

Many African societies underline the imperative of drawing the line between the right and wrong use of gifts, the right or wrong deployment of esoteric powers, and resort to the language of witchcraft and occult to sharpen the ethical imagination. Even here a lot of room for flexibility and ambivalence exists. André Mary's study of *Bwiti* cult in Gabon described the prophets that carry out anti-witchcraft crusades as experts who are admired but feared. In the *Bwiti* worldview humans in their relationship to *evu* (i.e., the evil force of witchcraft) are classified into three categories: the *nnem* have a strong, uncontrollable and evil *evu*; the *ngolongolo* are masters of the art of dual personality and can overcome

---

83. Umeh, *After God Is Dibia*, 243.

84. Aguwa, *Agwu Deity in Igbo Religion*, 142. See Lovell, *Cord of Blood*, 106.

the *beyem* (witches); finally the *miêmiê* are naïve, either they have no *evu* or have very weak ones. The expert or prophet that combats evil forces is not the naïve; rather he is holy but wise, even sly as a serpent. Prophets are comparable to the expert (*beyem mam*) who have knowledge of all things, and are able to master the two faces of reality that the possession of *evu* guarantees.[85] A more complex image of the two faces of the expert is recorded among the Lele of Congo—witchcraft goes back to *Nzambi* (God): "It was God who made sorcery. He gave it to a Lele chief (the chiefs are all sorcerers to this day); the chief revealed the secret to his friend, and so knowledge of sorcery spread."[86] While *vodhun* religion does not trace witchcraft back to *Mawu-Lisa*, Lovell is of the view that *ebo* (or *gbo*—charms) and witchcraft need the complicity of *vodhun* to be effective. "Witchcraft as a technical means of inflicting harm requires the spiritual involvement of deities to achieve its aims. Equally, treating witchcraft will involve the divine in restoring order."[87] The ability to inflict harm or do outrageous things with impunity is characteristic of Yoruba *orisa* religion. Devotees propagate the perception of their *orisa*, their protector, as capable of inflicting evil on their enemies.[88] All these increase the ambivalence and ambiguity surrounding the expert chosen by the deity.

Despite the complex image of the expert, the ethical imperatives are not taken lightly. He or she is well aware of the dreadful consequences of turning the healing power into a killing power—fabricating destructive medicine instead of protective ones. The ethical imperative would generally prevent the expert from daring to upset the peaceful intermingling and cohabitation in creation to protect difference, and to realize one's destined course in life. True, the leopard can dismember the goat for its dinner, yet both walk peacefully along their tracks. As the Yoruba hunting oral recital chants:

> Let not the civet-cat trespass on the cane-rat's track.
> Let the cane-rat avoid trespassing on the civet-cat's path.
> Let each animal follow the smooth stretch of its own road.[89]

85. Mary, *Le Défi Du Syncrétisme*, 65–66.

86. Douglas, "Problem of Evil among the Lele," 29.

87. Lovell, *Cord of Blood*, 104.

88. See Barber, "How Man Makes God in West Africa," 405.

89. Babalola, *Content and Form of Yoruba Ijala*, 62 cited by Okpewho, *African Oral Literature*, 39.

Consequently, the humane service of the expert is highlighted, though the shadow side remains. Igbo *dibia* declare, "*Ayi bu onwa,* / *Ayi aha-etiwa ji,* / *Nke ayi na-etiwa ede* (We are the shining light of the world like the moon, / being the moon, our light neither scorches the yam plants, / Nor scorches the coco-yam plants"). The expert who indulges in unethical practices, who "scorches" instead of being "shining light," faces peril that could run in the family for generations. "*Obuho ita akwu bu mkpa* / *noo otune aga-eji nyu abubo so akwu* (It is not eating the ripe palm fruit that is difficult, / The herculean task is the anus with which to excrete the rough fibrous chaff that is contained in the palm fruit)."[90] The lineal pursuit against unethical behaviour is frightening: *Ona-abu iyi egbughu ogeli* / *o naa ya nnwa* (If the oath deity taken in perjury does not kill a woman / It will surely kill her child or children.)[91] We shall have cause to revisit in a later chapter the evil that imperils relationality and the struggle against it in the power of the Holy Spirit.

Maximizing Creative Agency of Humans and Spirits and Eliminating the Instrumentalization of Religion

The closeness of experts and initiates to their deity and the competition among priests and healers to advertise their deity or their prowess lead to exaggerations. Propaganda and aberrant behavior display the dangers of instrumentalizing religion for personal or group ends. Reform is necessary and ongoing in this area of West African ATR to disarm priests, experts, and political officeholders from abuse of power.

West African kin-focused religion and its egalitarian social structures provide an advantage to curb abuse even though they could also fuel competition. *Individuals and communities could challenge pretentious experts, withdraw their support for a deity and creatively shift allegiance to benevolent spirits for the realisation of their destiny.* However, human agency does not mean independence from the hierarchical structure of the universe, no matter how malleable the West African universe is.

First, anger or jealousy of deities can be provoked either by ignoring them, being ignorant of taboos of a particular *vodhun,* or not respecting the relational order of hierarchy that informs approach to deities. For example, *Eshu* or *Elêgbara* of the Yoruba, also known as *Lêgba* (Fon and

90. Umeh, *After God Is Dibia,* vol. 2, 213.
91. Ibid., 249.

Ewe of Benin and Togo), is the messenger of the deities, their servant and slave (*Orunmila* or *Ifa* in particular) as well as the guard dog of humans. In West Africa and *Candomblé* (African religion in Brazil, also called *vodun* in Haiti and *santeria* in Cuba) *Eshu* is first to receive sacrifice because he opens the way to communication with other deities. If *Eshu* does not receive the required preliminary sacrifice, negligent humans risk having their life upset due to *Eshu's* jealousy or anger. The realization of individual and group destiny requires therefore harmonious interrelationship on both horizontal and vertical levels.

The more common evidence of the instrumentalization of religion, which one encounters in West African ATR (transferred to African Christianity), is revealed in the ambitious experts, priests, healers, etc. The genre of the novel has been successfully used to denounce exploitative experts. African authors are not only critical of missionary Christianity (like Mongo Beti's *Poor Christ of Bomba*), African Christianity (like Wole Soyinka's *Trials of Brother Jero*), but also of ATR (like Achebe's *Arrow of God*). In *Arrow of God*, Chinua Achebe presents a good illustration of how pride, ambition, and jealousy endangered the destined course of life of a community that reposed its confidence on a benevolent deity. Achebe's *Arrow of God* also illustrates a fundamental value in West African religious belief and practice: individuals and community are not a pawn in the hands of deities and experts. The community exercises liberty by withdrawing support from one deity (and its shrine guardian) and transferring it to another deity and shrine guardian. An Ikwerre proverb says it well: "The villagers may belong to a god, but the god also belongs to the villagers."[92] The Yoruba have also the saying: "If humanity were not, the deities would not be."[93] I rely on Achebe to describe the traditional and effective pattern of challenging the instrumentalization of religion.[94]

Primacy of Human Destiny—Integral Human Wellbeing— in Mediating the Intention of Deities

Arrow of God describes with flourish the need for flexibility, openness, and change in mediating the will of deities for the realization of the

92. Quoted by Amadi, *Ethics in Nigerian Culture*, 1.

93. Soyinka, "Tolerant Gods," 48–49.

94. Achebe, *Arrow of God*.

community's destiny. *Arrow of God* is based on a historical event that occurred in Umuchu (renamed Umuaro by Achebe), a village-group in Anambra State of Nigeria.[95] The local deity, *Ulu* (that "saved our fathers from the warriors of Abam"),[96] was the symbol of benevolence for a united Umuaro. Ezeulu was the priest of *Ulu*. The phenomenal entry of *White Man* onto the scene (modernity) precipitated crisis in Umuaro. Achebe crafted the story to demonstrate the implacability of change and the overriding need for individuals, the community and deities to adjust to change so that the community's destined course in life be realized.

Modernity channeled by colonialism and Christianity challenged humans and divine beings. "The white man, the new religion, the soldiers, the new road—they are all part of the same thing."[97] The dramatis personae struggled to coherently interpret and adapt to change—an enterprise full of drama, irony and ambiguity. Igbo wisdom tradition that nourished Achebe's humanism provided the ready to hand aphorism for adjustment to change: "a man must dance the dance prevailing in his time." This is in harmony with the foundational *ife kwulu ife akwudebe ya* ("Whenever Something stands, Something Else will stand beside it"). Achebe cleverly put the aphorism into the mouth of the tragic priest-hero, Ezeulu, to justify Ezeulu's adjustment to modernity and change. The priest-hero sent his son Oduche to a Christian school (and Church) because "The world is like a Mask dancing. If you want to see it well do not stand in one place. My spirit tells me that those who do not befriend the white man today will be saying had we known tomorrow."[98]

The principle of duality, flexibility, and openness to change must be applied across the board. When the *White Man* imprisoned the proud priest-hero for one month ("the proudest man on earth is only his messenger"), he refused to apply the same wisdom tradition to save the village-group from death. His imprisonment prevented him from the ritual eating of one sacred yam on citing the 12th moon. Out of prison he refused to eat two sacred yams on citing the new (13th) moon. In other words he refused to eat the regular 13th yam that should be eaten on citing the 13th moon along with the 12th yam that he was unable to

95. The historical background to the novel is testified by a booklet written in 1953 by S. A. Nnolim, Esq. See Nnolim, *History of Umuchu*.

96. Achebe, *Arrow of God*, 180.

97. Ibid., 97.

98. Ibid., 51.

roast and eat when he was in the White Man's prison. Flexibility and adjustment to change, on his part, would have enabled the village-group to see the year of 13 lunar months to a close, celebrate the new yam festival and begin to eat the new yams. The priest's *refusal to adjust to change along with his stubborn pride is heresy and idolatry.* The individual is being absolutized at the expense of the survival of the community. Ezeulu refused to listen to the elders who reminded him of the aphorism, "a man must dance the dance prevailing in his time." The elders had opposed his dependence on the same aphorism to send one of his sons to the Christian school. They confessed, "we have come—too late—to accept its wisdom." Nevertheless, pride, stubbornness, and an exaggerated perception of his power as priest had the better of Ezeulu. That is why "he would rather see the six villages ruined than eat two yams."[99] Ezeulu symbolised the instrumentalization of religion for personal pride and ambition.

The inability of the hero to perceive that religion is for the good of the human community (i.e., inability to understand the delicate, flexible commingling of humans, divinities, and mediators, yielding *pax deorum*), led him to the destruction of both himself and his deity. He became a sacrificial victim. Ogbuefi Ofoka, a character in *Arrow of God*, mused while conversing with his friend Akuebue, "Let me tell you one thing. A Priest like Ezeulu leads a god to ruin himself. It has happened before." Akuebue modified his friend's statement, "Or perhaps a god like Ulu leads a priest to ruin himself."[100] Nnolim believes Achebe made Ezeulu a sacrificial victim.

The image of the stubborn priest and the idolatrous unilateral perception of his position clearly contradict *Igbo tradition*. (This human tragedy and moral error is similar to the cosmic tragedy narrated in the Dogon mythology—the horrid and immature emergence of the fourth Nommo from the cosmic placenta before the full formation of his twin sister.) Igbo tradition *rejects erecting* (idolizing*) personal ambition, and manipulating deities to that end, at the expense of the destiny of the human community.* Individual worth, progress and achievement, are celebrated and hallowed in titles (*ozo* for men and *ekwe* for women). What is at stake in *Arrow of God* is self-centered pride, a bloated ego that is disdainful of the community's realization of its purpose in life. This pride and

99. Ibid., 232.
100. Ibid., 243.

disdain inserted crisis within the flexible dynamic hierarchy in divinity that characterizes West African cosmologies where humans are not pawns in the hands of deities. To prove that they are not pawns and to safeguard the good of the community the elders told Ezeulu that they were ready to assume responsibility for any consequences that would follow his eating two sacred yams instead of one. *Ulu* and his priest must protect and not destroy the community.

The degeneration of the conflict displays the dialectics of the complex relationship between deities like *Ulu* and the human community in the overall Igbo (West African) perception of reality. Priests, cult leaders, devotees, initiates, healers, etc., through their devotion, knowledge and reputation, increase the deity's popularity and their own reputation. The perpetuation of the deity may depend on the "ability to attract, convince and maintain followers."[101] Consequently, the golden rule guiding this complex relationship is that *deities, spirits and their priests must do what they are expected to do for the good of the community or risk irrelevance.* Selfish orientations of priests and the inordinate or irrational demands of deities are idols to be exorcised. The case between Ezeulu and Umuaro makes this clear:

> And we have all heard how the people of Aninta dealt with their deity when he failed them. Did they not carry him to the boundary between them and their neighbours and set him on fire?
>
> Let us drive him away as our neighbours of Aninta who drove out and burnt Ogba when he left what he was called to do and did other things, when he turned round to kill the people of Aninta instead of their enemies.[102]

Lovell confirms from *vodhun* religion Achebe's findings, "If a vodhun is perceived no longer to satisfy the needs of its human guardians, regardless of its original power or its notional position in the cosmological hierarchy, it will be neglected and eventually forgotten."[103] Eliade's discussion of "local" or "particular" hierophanies in contradistinction from "universal" modes is helpful.

Like God who is aniconic, deities, whose existence are not in doubt, are most powerful when they become icons of the overall good and progress of the community. Guardians of deities struggle to show

---

101. Lovell, *Cord of Blood*, 65.

102. Achebe, *Arrow of God*, 31, 180.

103. Lovell, *Cord of Blood*, 65; also 64–65, 104–5.

that their deity performs. *Arrow of God* concluded with what appears to be an intervention of the deity (*Ulu*) to save the people of Umuaro by making his priest insane. It was too late: the people had abandoned *Ulu* and carried their new yams to the Christian church, whose God, they hoped, would satisfy the needs of the community. The moral to be drawn is clear, revealing a major canon of West African religion: the image and honor of God or divine beings are protected in the realization of the community's destined course in life. *The major concern of religion is the realization of the destiny of the human community* commingled in an unbreakable way with God and divine beings. Achebe's conclusion draws attention to the humanism embedded in Igbo world vision guiding interrelationship between God, deities, ancestors and humans who are not pawns:

> So in the end only Umuaro and its leaders saw the final outcome. To them the issue was simple. Their god had taken sides with them against his headstrong and ambitious priest and thus upheld the wisdom of their ancestors that no man however great was greater than his people; that no man ever won judgment against his clan. If this was so then Ulu had chosen a dangerous time to uphold this wisdom. In destroying his priest he had also brought disaster on himself, like the lizard in the fable who ruined his mother's funeral by his own hand.[104]

My recourse to the genre of the novel to address a key aspect of the theology of ATR rejoins what students of ATR in this region call "limited scepticism" in the African approach to religion. It is not exactly the agnosticism or atheism that Messi-Metogo postulates.[105] The recognition of the existence of God, ancestors and divine beings is not in doubt. But these have to incarnate in the everyday world as beneficence and protection. The power of deities is magnified by devotees for the realization of the God-given destiny of individual and community. This explains the programmatic inculturation of Christianity and Islam in Africa. Robert Kaplan mistakenly interprets this as "syncretization with animism."

Aderemi Bamikunle's study of "Priest-Heroes in the Nigerian Novel" correctly drew the conclusion that *the human has priority over the religious*. But he missed the flexible interrelationship that informs West African religion by claiming, "power is reposed in the hands of

104. Achebe, *Arrow of God*, 261.

105. See Messi Metogo, *Dieu Peut-Il Mourir En Afrique?*

man." Religion, understood as leaving the destiny of the human community in the hands of higher powers is, Bamikunle claims, something on the surface for Nigerian authors.

> God and the gods can only exercise the power that they are given by men. God and the gods mostly provide camouflages or sanctions for what men have determined. What rules is the philosophy of men, the will of the community given greater power and credibility by being forged as the image and will of gods.[106]

Bamikunle's Durkheimian conclusion reflects Karin Barber's thesis about *orisa* religion, as "man making gods" or "limited scepticism" in West African religion. Barber is right in interpreting the enthusiasm of devotees to propagate their *orisa* (who possess or mount them, mono-*orisa*) as "man making gods important." The beneficent and personal deity, receives offerings, gives protection and is magnified enthusiastically over other deities with whom the devotee does not enjoy such intimacy. In a world of multiple deities, the complicity between devotees and deities—through beneficence, protection, and constant praise and propaganda—ensures the survival or disappearance of a particular deity. The paradox of enthusiastic involvement of religious persons with a deity that performs as one expects of a deity and the radical abandonment of a non-performing deity is a phenomenon of kin-focused and destiny obsessed West African religion.[107] The belief in the transcendent One God amidst multiple deities and ancestors, not only fails to produce a jealous God (Parrinder) that can centralize the generation of violence (Eggen). It also fails to render humans impotent or hold the community to ransom before overbearing deities, experts and shrine guardians. *Arrow of God* illustrates the agency of the community, aware of its destined course in life, and also the presence of a limited skepticism about deities. But the existence of the deities is not in doubt; despite the fact that "If humanity were not, the deities would not be" (Yoruba). Deities are experienced and worshiped to enable individuals and community realize their objective in life.

Against Bamikunle's thesis, one must insist that relationship between deities, the human community and experts is not a one-way traffic—"power in the hand of the community," or "power in the hand of

---

106. Bamikunle, "Priest-Heroes in the Nigerian Novel," esp. 338ff., 340.

107. See Barber, "How Man Makes God in West Africa," 405–11. Barber adopts with modification the viewpoints of Robin Horton and Jack Goody.

deities," or "power in the hands of experts and shrine guardians"! Rather, in the complex experience of divinity in West Africa, interrelationship is perceived as malleable and flexible. I do not think that Achebe, in *Arrow of God*, draws the conclusion that "men make gods." Flexibility discards exclusive clauses. Therefore while human communities contribute to the power and popularity of beneficent *deities* who are deeply involved in the destiny of the communities, this does not warrant the interpretation of human spiritual urgings as only "camouflages" of the will of the community as Bamikunle claims. Religion that is relational searches, through harmony, to realize the destined course of the human community in the world as *pax deorum*: God, deities, ancestors, spirit-forces, and humans work together for the good of the human community.

The West African world is dynamic. Interrelationship between humans and a multiplicity of deities is the rule. In the process, humans help to shape the image of their deities, an image transmitted through sacred narratives, initiation rites, erection of shrines, figurines, and art and architecture. On the other hand, the imaged deities shape the present and future of human communities. Deities are real. God, named, though not captured in images, is the ground of all narratives, the origin of origins, of the world, the deities and of humans.

What impact would this West African experience have on the West African reading of the Old and New Testament texts; especially with regard to the multiplicity of deities or gods? What impact has the West African experience on Christian practice? Does the focus on *spirit*, on the Holy Spirit, among West African Christians integrate West African deities within the experience of God of the Hebrew Scriptures, the God of Jesus Christ? Is the West African picture of *spirit* a creative entry into the discussion of the Christian Trinity? I first discuss the impact of the West African perception of God on the Jewish-Christian narratives. This will be limited to aspects of Old Testament and New Testament notions of God—as revealed in Patriarchal and Mosaic religion as well as the prophetic conflict with Baalism (chapter 4). I then proceed to engage the interpretation of God that appears in Origen's religious anthropology, comparable to and yet different from West African anthropology; this opens up pneumatology as entry point into Trinitarian theology (chapter 5). Finally, I engage with the West African Christian practice of the AICs and Charismatic movements to sound their consonance, dissonance and reconciliation with the Great Christian Tradition (chapters 6 and 7).

4

Rediscovering the Depth of God
in the Old Testament through Interaction
with Dynamic West African Categories

T HE EXPLORATION THAT I make into the Jewish-Christian experience of God from the grille of the West African religious universe
has more advantages than pitfalls for contextual experience of the
Trinitarian God. My basic assumption is that the West African is not
utterly dissimilar from the Jewish-Christian experience of God. Because
plurality of active deities that do not threaten the transcendent One God
dominates the West African universe, I opt for a perception of hierarchy
in divinity that is flexible and dynamic to explore aspects of the history of God in the Jewish-Christian tradition. This has the advantage
of paying attention to the mutations and struggles in the emergence
of the One and only Yahweh of Israel from within the religious world
of West Semites. Pre-exilic monotheism, or rather mono-Yahwism, is
not characterised by the antagonism and exclusion presented by the
Deuteronomistic historians. (We shall show later that Hebrew monotheism reached a level of radical and full flourishing during and after the
Babylonian exile.) The Deuteronomistic rhetoric of exclusion was forged
in the process of the creation of mono-Yahwism.

The exploration into the complex theological history of the emergence of the Hebrew One and Only Yahweh helps one to appreciate, ap-
plaud and critique the wide adaptations or inculturation of Christianity
in West Africa. Bible translation that incorporated and reinterpreted
West African cosmology is generally appreciated. But the positioning of
the Holy Spirit as privileged entry point into experiencing the Trinitarian

God in AICs and Charismatic movements needs to be fully addressed. The differentiation of the One and Only Yahweh that had acquired or assumed the qualities associated with West Semitic deities helped to create Israelite monotheism. This matured during the exilic and postexilic period; it was passed on through Judaism into Christianity. I argue that the West African Christian practice must learn from the history of "emergent" Jewish-Christian monotheism that some believe is still in gestation. (Robert Gnuse is of the view that the social or egalitarian and ethical implications of this monotheism would require centuries of practice to be realized.)[1] West African Christians will learn from Hebrew religion how to thread with caution in trying to fuse qualities of deities and conceptual schemes of West African cosmology into their new Trinitarian faith. The caution would reduce dissonance with life-generating experiences of the great Christian tradition.

In this chapter I first cast a second glance on the exclusive monotheism of Deuteronomistic theologians that represents a militant stage in the mutation of Jewish faith in Yahweh that did not always exclude worship of other deities. Informed by West African experience of the transcendent One God and multiplicity of deities that do not threaten God but that are children of God, I distance myself from the militancy of Deuteronomistic History. I learn from the universalistic dimensions of God, *Elohîm* of the Patriarchs, that were in the process of being assumed by the One and Only Yahweh. Then I draw attention to the landmark experience of the divine by Elijah that distances the emerging Yahweh of the universe from instrumentalization; this novel proposal of Yahweh will reach full maturity in Deutero-Isaiah who, in the context of utter weakness, projected Yahweh as the One and Only God. These ideas moved from postexilic Judaism into the features of the God that Jesus addressed as Abba, Father.

CASTING A SECOND GLANCE
AT THE DEUTERONOMIC MONOTHEISM

A review of dominant and emerging scholarly opinion by Gnuse highly suggests that the exclusivist and militant monotheism (mono-Yahwism—Gottwald) that characterizes Deuteronomy and Deuteronomistic History fails to represent the gradual evolution of monotheism in Israel.

---

1. See the discussions of this in Gnuse, *No Other Gods*, ch. 3.

The militant narrative of the exclusion of non-Yahwistic cults from the monarchies of Hezekiah and Josiah and the campaigns of Deuteronomic reformers (seventh century BCE—cf. 2 Kgs 23:15–20), should not be construed as recovering a pre-monarchic monotheism. The account of the destruction of sanctuaries like Bethel illustrates the tenor of Josiah's reform: "Moreover, the altar at Bethel, the high place erected by Jeroboam son of Nebat, who caused Israel to sin—he pulled down that altar along with the high place. He burned the high place, crushing it to dust; he also burned the sacred pole" (2 Kgs 23:15). These sanctuaries had served as centers of Yahwistic cult earlier in patriarchal history (cf. Gen 28:10–22). Asherah was not simply a tree or "sacred pole" but a female deity in the view of most scholars—though some scholars dissent. According to Gnuse, "Most scholars assume that the average Israelite considered Asherah an actual deity, a consort of Yahweh, and that the veneration of her was acceptable throughout most of Israelite and Judahite history."[2] Jeroboam's opposition to Solomonic innovations that ended in secession was in the context of Israelites who worshipped Yahweh and other deities. He was not establishing a non-Yahwistic cult! To do so would have made him lose out in the campaign to woo his people away from the shrine of the ark in Jerusalem. "The state cult in northern Israel" was distinguished by the "worship of Yahweh that included the use of one or more bull calf images" (1 Kgs 12:28–33; 2 Kgs 10:29; 17:16; Hos 10:5f.). Jeroboam's bull images were adopted in opposition to the cherub throne in Jerusalem or were analogous to the ark that shows Yahweh's presence. Jeroboam's sin, according to F. M. Cross, was in setting up a sanctuary to rival Jerusalem rather than the establishment of a non-Yahwistic cult. He chose the popular sanctuary of *El* at Bethel; and the secession of the northern kingdom was sealed with the inauguration of the Bethel cult during the festival of *Sukkot* (1 Kgs 12:25–33).[3]

The Deuteronomistic reformers were intent on generalizing a minority view of the cult of the One and Only Yahweh that radically excluded other cults. Their ideology was based on romanticization of the past of the favored people of Yahweh that should be devoted to the *one cult* of Yahweh (Deut 13) and *one pattern of relationship* with the unique

2. Ibid., 115; 184–86.

3. See Cross, *Canaanite Myth and Hebrew Epic*, 73–74. see also Keel and Uehlinger, *Gods, Goddesses, and Images of God in Ancient Israel*, 191–92 and footnote 9. See also Gnuse, *No Other Gods*, 186–87.

Yahweh (Deut 14). They solidified this ideology, thanks to political support, through the propagation of *one place of cult* (Deuteronomy 12) in the southern kingdom. Covenant liturgy was celebrated in the one and only place that the name is located: "the place that the LORD your God will choose out of all your tribes as his habitation to put his name there" (Deut 12:5, 21).

The Deuteronomistic project, though evolving from older Yahwistic religion, is revolutionary but also legitimate. Judaism, Christianity and Islam are products of this revolutionary program. It is also consonant with the West African perception of religion whereby devotees help to shape the image of the deity, just as the deity shapes the present and future destiny of the human community. But it is radically different from West African experience. In West Africa there is experience of mono-*orisa* or mono-*vodhun* in the cult of devotees; but there is no exclusion of other deities. However, when the ideology of One Yahweh becomes life-denying for dissenting voices, who perhaps prefer the flexibility of the more humane ancestral practices, and when it is projected in antagonistic terms against other sociocultural groups, it must be rejected like every other case of the instrumentalization of religious symbols. Life-giving images of *El* that were being integrated into the image of Yahweh through the intermingling of West Semitic peoples are not accounted for and are being undermined by the Deuteronomistic propaganda of mono-Yahwism. The One and only Yahweh must be the God of all peoples! Though there is slim historical evidence of a capture of Jericho by Joshua yet the idealized sanguinary narrative of the capture seethes with the intolerance of the reformers.

> Joshua said to the people, "Shout! For the LORD has given you the city. The city and all that is in it shall be devoted to the LORD for destruction. Only Rahab the prostitute and all who are with her in her house shall live because she hid the messengers we sent. As for you, keep away from the things devoted to destruction, so as not to covet and take any of the devoted things and make the camp of Israel an object for destruction, bringing trouble upon it. But all silver and gold, and vessels of bronze and iron, are sacred to the LORD; they shall go into the treasury of the LORD." So the people shouted, and the trumpets were blown. As soon as the people heard the sound of the trumpets, they raised a great shout, and the wall fell down flat; so the people charged straight ahead into the city and captured it. Then they devoted to destruction by

the edge of the sword all in the city, both men and women, young
and old, oxen, sheep, and donkeys . . . They burned down the
city, and everything in it; only the silver and gold, and the vessels
of bronze and iron, they put into the treasury of the house of the
LORD. (Jos 6:17–21, 24)

The life-giving image of God (*El, Elohîm*), characteristic of the Patriarchal
narratives, is not integrated within the Deuteronomistic proposition of
the One and Only Yahweh as God. Yahwistic theologians, more interested in fusing the qualities of *El* into the national Yahweh, presented an
image of Yahweh that is humanistic, flexible and universalistic. Martin
Rose argued that the concern of Yahwistic theologians was not the *particularity of Israel's God.* Rather they projected Yahweh as the perfect realization of his function as *Elohîm:* the "God of gods," "the highest God,"
"the quintessence of all divine powers," "the only God who represents
the divine in a comprehensive and absolute way"! Yahweh is *El* that "*ac-
complishes what one expects of a god (Elohîm).*" His name "Yahweh"—"I
am that I am" . . . (Exod 3:14)—is life-giving and life-enhancing. It defines a true and helpful existence. The particular name, Yahweh, steps
behind the universal "Yahweh function"—i.e., *Elohîm,* a deity that does
as he says for his people.[4]

The Deuteronomic reform project, a legitimate elite proposal
of mono-Yahwism, is different from the concerns of earlier Yahwistic
theology that perhaps knew monolatry but not the type of monotheism
presented as Mosaic. This was at the cost of narrow, intolerant and naïve
(Yahwistic) theology that contrasts with the life-giving universalistic
patriarchal *El.* For Saggs, the contrast is like "a tincture of universalism
as against ethnic exclusiveness; mercy and tolerance against intolerance and vindictiveness; a calm prosecution of a predetermined plan as
against aggressive self-assertion and *ad hoc* reaction."[5] The maturing of
Jewish monotheism during the exile (Deutero-Isaiah) presents a better
integration of the universalism of *El.*

4. See Rose, "Names of God in the O T," "(*Elohîm*)"; also Gnuse, *No Other Gods*,
192–94.

5. See Saggs, *Encounter with the Divine in Mesopotamia and Israel*, 38. Compare
Gen 12:3; 26:4; 18:32 and the treatment of Egyptians and Pharaoh, e.g., in Exod 11:3–5.

CHALLENGING DEUTERONOMISTIC INTOLERANCE
FROM THE RESOURCES OF WEST AFRICAN ATR

West African experience of the transcendent One God amidst non-competing deities reflects the qualities of the Patriarchal *Elohîm*. While respecting the history and particular provenance of each deity, the qualities of *Mawu, Onyame, Amma, Chukwu, Olodumare* etc., that were exposed above include goodness, mercy, compassion, providence (bestower of destinies). Other qualities are captured by epithets like "God beyond human speech," "God that departs from men," "God of daily existence," "God without equal," "God beyond contradiction and absurdity," "God whose speech is the world." These universalistic qualities are similar to the religion of the Jewish patriarchs. Indeed they enhance the qualities of the One and Only Yahweh that will reach maturity in postexilic Judaism, and that will be received as the God of Jesus Christ. But West African experience will find totally unacceptable the militancy, violence and intolerance of the Deuteronomic reformers:

> You must demolish completely all the places where the nations whom you are about to dispossess served their gods, on the mountain heights, on the hills, and under every leafy tree. Break down their altars, smash their pillars, burn their sacred poles with fire, and hew down the idols of their gods, and thus blot out their name from their place. (Deut 12:2–3)

Violent West African war deities, e.g., *Ogun, Ekwensu, Egbesu,* are instrumentalized for the destruction of enemies and the subjugation of peoples under conquering and enslaving kingdoms (like Benin, Dahomey, or Oyo) or communities (like Ijaw or Igbo). However, *Mawu, Chukwu, Olodumare, etc.,* maintains distance and cannot be instrumentalized. Yahweh that assumes the qualities of *Elohîm* of the Patriarchs must be shed of the violence, intolerance and exclusivism of Deuteronomistic theology or risk remaining a local deity. In West African terms, such violent, intolerant and exclusivist posturing reduces Yahweh to a local war deity.

The instrumentalization of God for local projects, however noble, obscures the one aniconic face of God, the giver of destinies, beyond manipulation. In reaction to unimpeachable historical evidence of the connection of monotheism with absolutism, forced conversion and tyranny, Gnuse points out that the Jewish monotheistic breakthrough came "from below"! However, it requires millennia of patient development for its egalitarian ethos to permeate society: perhaps "we are still in the formative stages of monotheistic evolution in terms of developing the implications which flow from the experience of more than two millennia past."[6] Gnuse is perhaps inflexible in adopting the model of biological evolution merged with revolution: this incorporates mutations in religion followed by the quantum leap under the influence of prophetic intellectuals. But waiting for millennia for the monotheistic ideology to come into full bloom begs the question. Who will be there to crosscheck? However, we retain the insight of monotheistic breakthrough "from below"; this matured under Deutero-Isaiah.

The Deuteronomistic version of intolerance is shared by Constantinian Christianity (especially from Theodosius) and Islam. Aloys Pieris is perhaps right in claiming that metacosmic religions like Hinduism, Buddhism, Judaism, Christianity, and Islam, cannot coexist. All these monotheistic religions originating from Asia share a common suspicion with regard to each other. Once installed they neither receive nor welcome other religions. Islam and Catholicism were easily established in Indonesia and the Philippines, respectively. In these places they were first to come into contact with cosmic (ancestral) religions. However, in Sri Lanka, Burma, India etc., Islam and Christianity are powerless before Buddhist gnostic soteriologies that dominate.[7]

African religious history displays unique features. ATR is both kin-focused and yet embodies soteriological intent. ATR is therefore able to domesticate Christianity and Islam. This reduces the areas of religious conflict. Indeed Eggen claims that West African "kin-focused religion" is a perfect antidote against violence, being dominated by a keen awareness and respect of one another's destiny—*pax deorum!* The absence of a centralized "war-generating" God, before the introduction of Christianity and Islam, renders religion impotent to mobilise people for "genocidal projects."[8] For Soyinka this is the perfect flourishing of humanism thanks to West African religion: it separates the "regulation of community from communion with spirit." This insight should be retained for peace, human flourishing and good neighborliness in the world. The peroration of Senator Symmachus on behalf of Roman

---

6. Gnuse, *No Other Gods*, 151.

7. Pieris, *Asian Liberation of Theology*, 72.

8. Eggen, "Mawu Does Not Kill," 359.

Senators, faithful to Roman ancestral religion and customs, contains similar insight that should be retained. While presenting his report (384 CE) to the child Emperor Valentinian II, he pleaded for the restoration of the altar of Victory in the Roman Senate declaring: *Aequum est, quidquid omnes colunt, unum putari* (one is justified to consider what all peoples worship as one and the same being.) Symmachus was unaware of the universalistic and humanistic qualities of Yahweh, Elohîm of the Patriarchs. He was unaware of *Mawu, Onyame, Amma, Chukwu, Olodumare,* the benevolent, and providential giver of destinies. But his insight endorsed their universalism and depth: *Uno itinere non potest perueniri ad tam grande secretum* ("One and only way does not suffice to approach such a great mystery"). To be intolerant of diversity or to deny legitimacy to other ways is symptomatic of ignorance of the Mystery.[9] Ambrose of Milan like the Deuteronomistic theologians disagreed. Pope Gregory the Great who called for the respect of the customs and even the altars of the Anglia appears to incline towards the wisdom that Mystery is revealed in diversity. This is the focus of West African narratives and practice. It is from this perspective that I proceed to re-examine aspects of the Hebrew Scriptures that challenge ideological uniqueness. My considerations are limited to two areas: first, the evocation of Yahweh in the council of El; and, second, the conflict with Baalism that led to the renewal of the tradition through Elijah's mystic encounter with the God of the Patriarchs at Horeb revealed as a sound of "sheer silence" (1 Kgs 19:12).

Yahweh in Divine council of El Elyôn

The actuality of the West African perception of divinity enables a redirection of focus towards the formal and informal acculturation that the Hebrew people were constrained to achieve in their struggle for space among their neighbors of the Ancient Near East. This resulted in the internationalization of the local Hebrew deity Yahweh (as *El* and *Elohîm*), revealing not only the concepts of the divine held by ancient Israelites but also the fertile mixing of religious symbols in the Ancient Near East. The place of Yahweh in the divine council, which reflects the socio-political realities of the Ancient Near East, is of particular interest from a West African world vision that is characterized by multiplicity of divine

---

9. *Symmachi Relatio*, art. 10, Prudence, *Psychomachie Contre Symmaque*, vol. 3:110. Quintus Aurelius Memmius Eusebius Symmachus c. 345–402.

beings. Yahweh's relationship with other deities (including the Satan— the adversary that scrutinizes human intentions and protects the honor of Yahweh, Job 1–2) is of great interest. One is challenged to explore the reasons for the later developments in prophetic and Deuteronomistic theology that have transmitted the dominant exclusivist interpretation of Mosaic monotheism.

Hebraic experience, drawing from a primitive West Semitic pool, may not have experienced theomachy described in Babylonian epics. Nevertheless, there was struggle for the dominance of one divine cult over others. The story of this dominance merges with the story of national formation; this directs attention, in the creation of Israel, to the aggressive positioning of Yahweh in the emergence of "Yahweh-Israel." Through careful reading of earlier historical and poetic texts, one discovers not the radical exclusion that characterizes Deuteronomistic history; rather a serene dialogue or learning process, an acculturation that accounts for the emergence of a melody of epithets or qualities of Yahweh the God of Israel. This "convergence" (Mark Smith) is a process of fusing into Yahweh the qualities of Canaanite or West Semitic deities.[10] Apart from the political theological denunciation of Baal cult, for which the Elijah narratives are noted, the relationship of Israel with her neighbors in the Ancient Near East displays a learning relationship rather than a war among divine beings, and by extension among their followers: Israel was learning from more experienced peoples. If this relationship were interpreted negatively (for example as idolatry—as suggested by the Deuteronomic tradition) there would have been an impoverishment of the experience of the divine in Hebrew tradition that depended on similar experiences in the Orient. OT texts testify that most festivals that celebrated the Israelite mountain-god, Yahweh, were adaptations of existing Canaanite festivals. The positive appropriation of the characteristics of West Semitic deities into the Hebrew tradition accounts for the treasury of qualities or epithets attributed to Yahweh the God of Israel, confessed in the New Testament as the God of Jesus Christ. In other words, Yahweh the God of Israel, the God of the Exodus, is incomprehensible if disconnected from the complex history and context of Israel.

Yahweh-Israel and Israel-Yahweh represent an indisputable bonding of people and deity. Whether the ethnic origin of Yahweh goes back to the family of Joseph or to a Qenite pre-Israelite source or outside

10. See Gnuse, *No Other Gods*, 100–102.

Israel "to the south, in the area of Midian," Yahweh-Israel and Israel-Yahweh are understandable within the context of national formation. Old Testament scholarship is persuaded that Yahwism cannot be understood apart from the socio-political community that articulated, transmitted, and practiced the religion of Yahweh.[11] But just as Israel has a complex history, so also Yahweh.

The point I find particularly interesting is the importance of the divine council in the Semitic universe. The council is peopled with divine allies and opponents. Early poetic literature presents Yahweh as a member of the council of *El-Elyôn*; then later Yahweh became the head.[12] *El* is the common Semitic appellation for divinity requiring a concrete locality. The semantic range of *El* is open to expansion—e.g., the Canaanite *El-Elyôn*, "the divinity, the most high." *Elohîm* (plural of *El*) represents the quintessence of what one expects in a god. In the complex relationship between Israel and the Canaanite world, or in the emergence of the nation Israel from the complex social situation of Canaan, a relationship between the primitive creator-god *El-Elyôn* and the national liberator-god Yahweh was unavoidable. The evocation of Yahweh as member of the council of *El-Elyôn* indicates probably an earlier differentiation between the "supranational" creator-god ("*Elyôn*") and Israel's national god Yahweh, the liberator of Israel from Egypt. Deuteronomy 32:8–9 records this in a primitive poetic presentation of Yahweh in the council of *El-Elyôn*,

> When the most High divided to the nations their inheritance, when he separated the sons of Adam, he set the bounds of the people according to the number of the children of Israel. For *the LORD'S portion is his people; Jacob is the lot of his inheritance* [My italics].

This poetic language stands closer to the Canaanite worldview and projects a *divine council* presided over by *El-Elyôn* with Yahweh as member (cf. Ps 82:1, 6). Melchizedek, priest of *El-Elyôn*, naturally blessed Abraham: "Blessed be Abram by God Most High, maker of heaven and

11. See Rose, "Names of God in the OT"; Day, *Yahweh and the Gods and Goddesses of Canaan*, 14–16; see also Gottwald, *Tribes of Yahweh*, 72–73. See also the interesting developments in stricter monotheism (mono-Yahwism) after the exile in the collective work Albertz and Becking, *Yahwism after the Exile*.

12. The summary depends very much on Rose, "Names of God in the OT." "*El-Elyôn*"; see also Gnuse, *No Other Gods*, 180–82.

earth" (Gen 14:19). The superior blessed the inferior in the name of *El-Elyôn* that is also incontestably superior.

The position of Yahweh in the council of *El-Elyôn* is capital for explorations into the Hebrew experience of divinity. Yahweh will later merge with, transform into or displace *El-Elyôn*. Or perhaps poets, theologians and reformers will discover through "inculturation" that Yahweh is *El-Elyôn* and that *El-Elyôn* is Yahweh. In the same patriarchal tradition Abraham confessed Yahweh as *El-Elyôn*: "But Abram said to the king of Sodom, 'I have sworn to the LORD, God Most High, maker of heaven and earth' . . ." (Gen 14:22) It was easy to reduce the divine name *El-Elyôn* to the function of the attributes: "the divinity, the most high." Yahweh, a deity of nomadic provenance, has "become enriched with the dimensions of world creation and the royalty." The theological labor involved in converting *El-Elyôn* into an epithet of Yahweh represents "the last phase of a long process." [13] "Yahweh-Elyôn is terrible, a great king over all the earth" (Ps 47:2). The "long process" or long evolution is best described with the help of process theism to highlight the active presence of God in every historical period and every event—yielding a wider conception of sacred history.[14]

The divine council was such a powerful image in the Hebraic tradition that the prophets who delighted in evoking the majesty and lordship of Yahweh with the epithet *Adonai* (*Lord*—an epithet that replaced the divine name Yahweh when it could no longer be mentioned) described themselves as present (transported in trance) in the divine council. The visions of Isaiah open with, "I saw *Adonai* sitting upon a throne, high and lifted up; and his train filled the temple" (6:1). Jeremiah (23:9–40) denounced prophets as false because they were not present in the divine council: "For who hath stood in the *counsel* of the LORD, and hath perceived and heard his word? who hath marked his word, and heard it"? (23:18). According to the *New Interpreter's Bible* the critical question in OT prophecy and especially in Jeremiah is "how does one know which prophecy is correct"? (Jer 23:18, 21–22; cf. 1 Kgs 22:19–23). The answer, "We learn that *the true word of the Lord comes only to the prophet who has stood in the council of the Lord* [my emphasis], the

---

13. Rose, "Names of God in the OT"; and also Gnuse, *No Other Gods*.
14. See Gnuse, *No Other Gods*, 303–7.

heavenly assembly gathered around the throne of the Lord, and who has received the decree of the Lord that the prophet is to proclaim."[15]

Extensive Assimilation of Pre-Israelite Notions of Deity into the Confession of Yahweh

The extensive appropriation of pre-Israelite traditions into the confession of the national-god Yahweh were favored by royalty—especially during the Davidic and Solomonic eras. There was more latitude and flexibility than what is presented in exilic and postexilic literature. Freedman and O'Connor argue,

> The nature of Mosaic monotheism is often misconstrued as insisting that Yahweh is the only god in existence. This notion is foreign to earliest OT materials. There are other gods, who fall into two categories: those who work for Yahweh (and appear later as angels) and those who oppose him. All these figures derive from pre-Mosaic Yahwistic mythology. Mention of these groups is most common in old poetry.[16]

Yahweh's subordinates, members of the "council of the holy ones" (Ps 89:9), surrounded him as he moved (Deut 33:2f.; Zech 14:5). The texts show that Yahweh is superior (Exod 15:11; Ps 89:6–8), having taken over the characteristics of and displaced the dominant Canaanite deities. Yahweh has been successfully fused with *El*. Yahweh's *bodyguards*, a chthonian entourage, are *deber* (the plague god, in front of him) and *resep* (the pestilence god, behind—Hab 3:5: "Before him went the pestilence, and burning coals went forth at his feet.") "Thus the God of the Hebrew Bible has 'terrors' (*bi'utim*, Job 6:4) corresponding to those of *Mot*, who is called in Job 18:13 'the king of terrors' (*melek ballahot*)"; but "in the eschatological battle described in Isa 25:8, Yahweh swallows up *Mot* forever (*nesehi*)."[17] In later Israelite literature minor deities were transformed into virtues—e.g., *tôb* and *hesed* (*goodness* and *loyalty*—Ps 23:6). Poetic tradition also converted *'emet*, *sedeq*, and *hesed* (three minor deities) into virtues in display: "Steadfast love (*mercy—hesed*) and faithfulness (*truth—'emet*) will meet; righteousness (*sedeq*) and peace

---

15. Miller, "Book of Jeremiah," 751.

16. Freedman and O'Connor, "Yahweh," 519. Gnuse came to the same conclusion from his literature review, Gnuse, *No Other Gods*, 115–23, 180–82.

17. See Lewis, "Mot (Deity)."

will kiss each other. Faithfulness will spring up from the ground, and righteousness will look down from the sky" (Ps 85:10–11).[18]

The context for appreciating the retinue of deities, described sometimes in military language, is the recital of Israel's creation-liberation. Creation is a conflict in which Yahweh emerges victorious. In Mesopotamia, Ugarit, and Israel creation is imaged as a struggle with chaos on the cosmological and political planes. Victory songs and psalms of enthronement evoke Yahweh, creator-liberator, with historical and suprahistorical motifs. Yahweh saves his people from chaos: i.e., a dangerous environment, the sea swarming with frightening creatures, death, suprahistorical phenomena, and the historical enemies of Israel. The songs of Miriam (at the crossing of the Sea of Reeds Exod 15:1–18) and Deborah, and Psalms of enthronement (Jgs 5; Pss, 29; 78; 135; 89) illustrate this. Some of these hymns appropriate motifs and even texts of Canaanite origin (Ps 29 is possibly a Canaanite hymn to Baal appropriated for Yahweh or perhaps an Israelite hymn to Yahweh modeled on Baal mythology).[19]

In OT literature two epithets have been co-opted to stress the militancy and might of Yahweh the God of Israel—*El Shaddai* and *Yahweh Sebaot*. The common meaning "Almighty" given to the terms is based on the LXX *Pantocrator* and the Vulgate *Omnipotens*. It is a free rendering of obscure Hebrew terms. Perhaps the LXX term *Pantocrator* that sometimes translated *El Shaddai* and sometimes *Yahweh Sabaot*—two obscure terms that the LXX translates with other terms—led to the choice by modern translations to limit the meaning of *El Shaddai* to "Almighty." Babut considers the choice of translators totally arbitrary and unjustified. It increases the militant and perhaps misleading image given to the God of the Hebrews and the God of Jesus Christ. The militancy is canonized in the Nicene Creed: "I believe in God the Father Almighty."[20] *Sebaot* does imply the one who has absolute power to recruit others into service. Israel is the first recruit: in the conflict between David and the Philistine, *Yahweh Sebaot* is placed in apposition to "the God of the armies of Israel" (1 Sam 17:45). However, in the Song of

---

18. Freedman and O'Connor, "Yahweh," 520.

19. See Day, *Yahweh and the Gods and Goddesses of Canaan*, 95–98; Schmid, "Creation, Righteousness, and Salvation," 104; Clifford, *Fair Spoken and Persuading*, 59–67; Clifford, "Hebrew Scriptures and the Theology of Creation," 509.

20. Babut, *Le Dieu Puissamment Faible De La Bible*, 15–19.

Deborah (Jgs 5) "Yahweh's power of control reaches widely beyond the *'armies of Israel'*, to encompass the stars that fight on Yahweh's behest": "from heaven fought the stars, from their courses they fought against Sisera" (Jdg 5:20).[21] The stars symbolize "the host of heaven" (e.g., Isa 40:26; 45:12), the recruited powers of heaven that could be present in divine council, the members of a heavenly court of Yahweh (1 Kgs 22:19). The Deuteronomic reform under Josiah banished such symbolism (2 Kgs 23:5; Deut 17:3; Jer 8:2).

The above illustrate developments of fertile inculturation of the Patriarchal religion in the Ancient Near Eastern context. They indicate likely models of interpreting the multiplicity of deities in the reception of Christianity in West Africa. But the crisis over Baalism also illustrates the challenges of plurality and the difficulty of inculturation. I read into the Elijah narratives not only the "differentiation" of Yahweh from Baal and other deities but also the call to deepen the knowledge of God. The revelation of the One and Only Yahweh, who progressively assimilated the characteristics of other deities, embodies enormous surprises in intercultural situations. Process theism, which argues that God is not only present in every event and history but also lies in the future and impacts on humanity's appreciation of the past and present, presents a helpful language: the present draws the past into itself—"concrescence" (Gnuse) and the "future is a 'lure' for the present." God "lies in the future and 'lures' the present and all humanity into future possibilities, which may be described as gracious gifts or opportunities." Therefore, Elijah's experience embodies the divine "lure"—"the persuasive power of God to draw the present into the future."[22] The evolving context and historical conditions of Elijah's time not only challenges Israel to deepen its knowledge of God, who does not remove the veil as the "unknown God" (cf. Acts 17:16). It draws all of humanity to embrace the God we want to know. This became accessible for Elijah paradoxically in the mystical depth of "silence"—the profound depth of God.

21. Rose, "Names of God in the OT." "*Sebaot.*"

22. Gnuse, *No Other Gods*, 305, 307.

"YAHWEH OUR GOD IS ONE YAHWEH"—
PROPHETISM AND THE BAAL PHENOMENON

The *Shemaʿ* is the heart of Israel's confession and worship of God, Yahweh. Even when it was forbidden to pronounce the name, Yahweh must be mentioned in the *Shemaʿ*. The story of Yahweh who came to be confessed in the above fundamental Creed of Israel is a complex one. In addition to the popular epithets already mentioned, Israel's ancestral religion had other names for God, like *Abir* ("Mighty" one of Jacob—Gen 49:24), *Pahad* ("Fear" or "Terror" of Isaac—Gen 31:42, 53b). But none of these names posed a threat comparable to *Baal* due to its dynamism and attraction. Paradoxically, the confrontation with Baalism helped to sharpen the dimensions and demarcations of Yahwism.[23]

The divine name *Baal* denotes "lordship." The sphere over which influence is exercised is defined by the genitive—e.g., Baal-Peor (Baal of Peor—Num 23:28). Originally *baʿal* did not denote a particular divinity, but was attributed to a variety of Semitic gods. Later, it came to denote a divine type, the *Storm god*. Consequently, a variety of gods like Hadad that were called *baʿal* began to recede into the background. Finally, Baal became a divine name.

The encounter with Baal put to severe test the formal and informal acculturation of Israel's Yahweh to the characteristics and epithets of Canaanite deities. Initially dynamic characteristics of Yahweh (a warrior mountain-god that does as he says, the liberator of Israel) found affinity with Baal (a dynamic Storm-god whose rule or lordship must be periodically exercised or demonstrated). Features of Baal were taken over in the worship of Yahweh: Yahweh "rides on the clouds" (Ps 68:5; 104:3; Deut 33:26) and manifests himself in thunder and storm. The lament of Psalm 18 displays the intervention of Yahweh in earthquake, volcano, and especially in the tempest, thunder and flashes of lightening:

> The cords of death encompassed me; the torrents of perdition assailed me the cords of Sheol entangled me; the snares of death confronted me. In my distress I called upon the LORD; to my God I cried for help. From his temple he heard my voice, and my cry to him reached his ears. Then the earth reeled and rocked; the foundations also of the mountains trembled and quaked, because he was angry. Smoke went up from his nostrils, and devouring

23. In what follows I depend especially on Martin Rose and F. M. Cross. Rose, "Names of God in the OT." "Baal"; Cross, *Canaanite Myth and Hebrew Epic*, 190–94.

> fire from his mouth; glowing coals flamed forth from him. He
> bowed the heavens, and came down; thick darkness was under
> his feet. He rode on a cherub, and flew; he came swiftly upon the
> wings of the wind. He made darkness his covering around him,
> his canopy thick clouds dark with water. Out of the brightness
> before him there broke through his clouds hailstones and coals
> of fire. The LORD also thundered in the heavens, and the Most
> High uttered his voice. And he sent out his arrows, and scattered
> them; he flashed forth lightnings, and routed them. (Ps 18:4–14;
> cf. Ps 77:19)

Images of Baal are creatively integrated into a hymn to Yahweh (cf. Ps 29).

After the split of Israel into northern and southern kingdoms and with the reign of non-Israelite kings over Israel, it was becoming not only impolitic to use Baal motifs to designate Yahweh but the epithet was beginning to represent everything foreign and unfaithful to the national god, Yahweh. This came to a head during the reign of Ahab whose wife, Jezebel, a Sidonian princess, forced Israel to encounter Baal not simply as an epithet that could be used for Yahweh, but as a dynamic Phoenician god. The Elijah cycle of narratives shows that "Yahweh" and "Baal" had become incompatible alternatives. It is either Yahweh or Baal. It displays also the dangers or challenges of appropriating attractive suprahistorical motifs in the recitals of the victorious intervention of a warrior-god to save his people. The destruction of historical enemies of Israel and overcoming chthonic forces (suprahistorical motifs—"Sea" or Rahab/Leviathan) are merged in sacred narratives that affirm the effective lordship of Yahweh over Israel. The Elijah cycle of narratives was a clear statement by the growing prophetic tradition of its rejection of Baalism in favour of orthodox Yahwism. The whole confrontation at Carmel between Elijah and the priests of Baal and the subsequent theophany at Horeb were a projection of the Sinai covenant in which Yahweh's mode of appearing was shed of the characteristics of the storm god. It was a veritable polemic against Baal.[24] I examine this more closely and draw attention to insights from exploration of multiplicity of deities in West Africa.

---

24. Rose, "Names of God in the OT," "Baal"; Cross, *Canaanite Myth and Hebrew Epic*, 190–94; also Day, *Yahweh and the Gods and Goddesses of Canaan*, ch. 3; and Uzukwu, *Worship as Body Language*, 159–64.

Elijah and the Jealousy of Yahweh—
Horeb and the Paradox of Universalism

Elijah believed he embodied Yahweh's uniqueness and jealousy. His name *Eli-jah*—Yahweh is *El* (God)—captures in militant and uncompromising terms the attitude of the champion of Yahwistic exclusivism. "I have been very zealous for the LORD, the God of hosts; for the Israelites have forsaken your covenant, thrown down your altars, and killed your prophets with the sword. I alone am left, and they are seeking my life, to take it away" (1 Kgs 19:14). Acculturation to, or better convergence with, Canaanite modes, especially the powerful Phoenician Baal, was intolerable! Baal and Yahweh were "incompatible alternatives." Jezebel, the Sidonian princess, represented the worst in foreign intervention in Israelite politics and religion. Baal was thus a symbol of foreign religious and political domination.

The drama between Elijah and the prophets of Baal on Mount Carmel displayed Yahweh's victory and incomparability (1 Kgs 18–19). The confrontation took place after three years of drought (1 Kgs 18): Baal that dynamically renewed the seasons was shown to be incapable of bringing the rains.[25] The lack of rain was a sign of Yahweh's displeasure. This popular exegesis runs across religions. In the African religious universe (e.g. among the Sar of Chad) drought could ultimately provoke communal approach to God. Senator Symmachus in presenting the position of the Roman Senate to Emperor Valentinian insisted that plagues and famine had befallen the nation because of the abandonment of piety to ancestral religion. Of course Ambrose of Milan rejected this opinion and gave other reasons for the plagues and famine. Augustine in *City of God* gave his own interpretation of the disaster that followed the collapse of ancient Rome.

The victory of Yahweh at Mount Carmel demonstrates that he is lord of heaven and earth, of the seasons, and most importantly the LORD God of Israel. Elijah had challenged the people: "How long will you go limping with two different opinions? If the LORD is God, follow him; but if Baal, then follow him" (1 Kgs 18:21). When "the fire of the LORD fell and consumed the burnt offering, the wood, the stones, and the dust, and even licked up the water that was in the trench," the people

---

25. Day, *Yahweh and the Gods and Goddesses of Canaan*, 76–77.

fell on their faces and said, "The LORD indeed is God; the LORD indeed is God" (1 Kgs 18:38–39).

But the slaughter of the four hundred and fifty priests of Baal by Elijah is a misunderstanding of the God of the Patriarchs. There was a predictable "clash of fundamentalisms"[26]—Elijah's and Jezebel's: "So may the gods do to me, and more also, if I do not make your life like the life of one of them by this time tomorrow" (1 Kgs 19:1). The revelation at Horeb on the one hand was an effort to shed Yahweh of the characteristics of the Storm god (Baal).[27] On the other hand, and from the West African standpoint, it is a sharp critique and rejection of Elijah's political theology, and all previous and consequent theologies of war and violence. I consider this second point more important than the first in searching for a refreshing image of God in intercultural encounter. In contemplation the prophet was going through a process of purification from violence. The LORD that wants to be known was no longer available "in the wind," nor "in the earthquake," nor "in the fire" (1 Kgs 19:11–12). Though these characteristics were contained in hymnic celebrations of Yahweh the liberator (Ps 18) and the Mosaic theophany on Sinai (Exod 19:16) they are now under pressure in the emergent image of Yahweh. These elements of nature that made the people tremble out of fear are critiqued in their function as symbols of Yahweh's presence. They are ruled out in the access to God, especially in intercultural encounter, when they lend themselves to instrumentalization to violence.

The overriding theological point in the narrative turns out to be a *critique of Elijah who deployed violence to prove that the Lord is God*. Religion that is for the service of the human, that humanizes and divinizes, is life-giving and not life-denying. The God that is concerned with peoples' destined course in life is not represented in human bloodletting, violence and fear but in human dignity and love. A pleasant, surprising and shattering revelation was made to the mystic Elijah: Yahweh is sought, found, and contemplated in "a sound of sheer silence" ("and after the fire a sound of fine silence" [1 Kgs 19:12]). "When Elijah heard it, he wrapped his face in his mantle [reproducing the gesture of Moses—Exod 3:6] and went out and stood at the entrance of the cave" (1 Kgs 19:13).

---

26. See Ali, *Clash of Fundamentalism*.

27. See Cross, *Canaanite Myth and Hebrew Epic*, 190–94.

This experience of Elijah demonstrates how mysticism shatters cultural boundaries and brings peoples together. It reveals the God beyond God—i.e., beyond all our habitual patterns of knowing God! The Mystery into which we are drawn, the emerging face of God, reveals God who *chooses discrete withdrawal, distance, and transcendence or silence. In this way God invests humans with greater authority (autonomy) to handle humanely their affairs.* This process of God's empowerment of humans to handle responsibly or humanely interrelationship on earth explains why Yahweh demands account: "Then the LORD said to Cain, 'Where is your brother Abel?' He said, 'I do not know; am I my brother's keeper?' And the LORD said, 'What have you done? Listen; your brother's blood is crying out to me from the ground!'" (Gen 4:9–10). In the NT it is pushed to a mystic-ethical resemblance (*homoiôsis*) of God: "Be perfect, therefore, as your heavenly Father is perfect" (Matt 5:48). Elijah's mystical experience recaptures the challenging image of God of the Patriarchs—the humanistic and universalistic aspects of the patriarchal *El* that contrasts sharply with the narrower, less tolerant and more naïve original Mosaic Yahweh. The critique of Mosaic Yahweh in contrast to the Patriarchal *El* by Saggs is similar to the critique of instrumentalized Dahomean *vodhun* by Gbegnonvi in contrast to *Mawu*. The Patriarchal *El's* universalism, mercy, tolerance, and prosecution of a predetermined plan contrasts sharply with the Mosaic Yahweh's ethnic exclusiveness, intolerance, vindictiveness, aggressive self-assertion and ad hoc reaction. Dahomean *vodhun's* rapaciousness, politics of the belly, and generation of fear contrasts with *Mawu's* "grandeur, mercy, patience, goodness, tenderness and sweetness."[28] God "lures" the prophet, God "lures" peoples, to a more mystical and shattering image of the divine that is transcultural and with wider ethical demands.

The emergent face of God at Horeb, *silence*, is confirmed by West African narrative tradition and practice in respect to *Mawu, Onyame, Amma, Chukwu,* and *Olodumare*. It challenges the intolerance and exclusiveness of religions in our contemporary world. Yahweh the God of the ancestors of Israel, like God in West Africa, is not prisoner to the "clash of civilizations," cannot be co-opted or instrumentalized in the politico-religious struggle. Christian missionaries brought to Africa by God were not wrong to acknowledge identity between God in Africa

---

28. Saggs, *Encounter with the Divine*, 38; and Claffey, "Looking for a Breakthrough," 121–27.

and the new image of God in Elijah's revelation, the same God revealed in Jesus Christ. They were certainly wrong in their dualistic positioning of this God against ATR deities and practice; wrong in positioning Christianity in conflict with what they called "heathendom" or the "kingdom of Satan." Yahweh, the warrior mountain God, the one who enlists armies, armies of Israel and the hosts of heaven (*Sebaot*), has shed off the violent characteristics forged about him in the heat of struggle and national formation. Note that in the heat of combat the following interrelational logic dominates: God creates the people, and the people make God important—Yahweh-Israel, Israel-Yahweh. The emergent image of God at Horeb is beyond the struggle of the gods for dominance, beyond electing portions as God's own people (Israel as portion of Yahweh) to the exclusion of others, and reveals the unique mystery of divinity (*Elohîm*) in discrete distance, "silence."

In the struggle with Baalism, Israel was in an extreme situation of national crisis—a privileged situation where, in West Africa, God is experienced in communal celebration, in the hospitable welcoming of one another. *The revelation at Horeb where distance and silence are preferred modes of divine transcendence and availability to all* created the environment for wider communal celebration and intercultural communication that propagated the knowledge of the relational God. Even though the idea of a jealous Yahweh that emerged probably in the Elijah prophetic circle could be justified in the struggle to differentiate Yahweh from Baal, it does not justify bloodshed. Hosea, perhaps successfully, also employs the imagery of the singularity of betrothal, love, and marriage, rather than violence, to exclude the cult of other deities from the religious practices of *Yahweh's witness*, Israel.

The novelty of the conversion experience may have been surprising to Elijah. In utter humility, face wrapped (like Moses during the originary revelation at Horeb) and standing at the entrance of the cave, Elijah listened to Yahweh's new instructions, suffused with the implications of the new approach to Yahweh. His mission is to go and anoint Israelite and non-Israelite kings, and thereafter to "retire," handover to a successor. The emergent image of Yahweh, the God of Israel, the God of the ancestors, while being particular to Israel is moving beyond exclusivism. Yahweh, God (*Elohîm*—the quintessence of being God) is the God of Israel as well as the God of the Phoenicians, Syrians, or the gentiles. Elijah's commission makes this universalism clear: to anoint Hazael as king of Aram (the Syrian—a task carried out by his successor Elisha), Jehu as king of Israel, and Elisha as his successor. Political and economic problems of the nation, Israel, bonded to Yahweh by covenant, are not resolved by violence ("clash of civilizations"). Whenever and wherever violence occurs, whenever Israel goes to war with its neighbors, Yahweh can no longer be enrolled in the war. Natural phenomena like fire, storm, hailstones or earthquake can no longer be interpreted as the "hosts" of Yahweh, nor as dimensions of a battle-ready Yahweh. Yahweh takes his distance from Israelite politics and is accessible as God of Israel and the nations in "fine silence." Prophets and servants of Yahweh are learning with difficulty to take the back seat, as witnesses of Yahweh the God who is revealed in apparent weakness.

If the idea of silence, distance and transcendence succeeds in enriching theology in the cross fertilization of Hebraic and West African narratives and practice, one should not undermine or underestimate the dynamism of oneness or uniqueness of Yahweh in a theology that involves the encounter of cultures. The relational tension of "convergence" and "differentiation"[29] between Yahweh and the Semitic deities in forging Israelite monotheism, and the benefits therefrom, must not be whittled down. I re-examine mono-Yahwism, election and choice, without ignoring diversity and plurality that are fundamental to any discussion of deity in West Africa.

Mono-Yahwism—Covenantal or Conjugal Relationship and Multiculturality

Deuteronomic theology captures mono-Yahwism, the basis of Israel's faith proclaimed in the *Shema*; "Hear, O Israel: Yahweh our God is one Yahweh" (Deut 6:4). The terms of this confession are rooted in the historical covenantal relationship bonding together Yahweh-Israel and Israel-Yahweh. Jean-Marie Carrière is perhaps correct in drawing attention to the conjugal or affective language of the *Shema*:

> Hear, O Israel: The LORD is our God, the LORD alone. You shall love the LORD your God with all your heart, and with all your soul, and with all your might. Keep these words that I am commanding you today in your heart. (Deut 6:4–6)

---

29. See the discussion of these concepts taken from the works of Mark Smith in Gnuse, *No Other Gods*, 100–102.

Conjugal language directs the process of forging Israelite monotheism away from mathematical unicity, "one Lord," towards Hosea's stress on relationship and intimacy. Hosea's preference for conjugal relationship between Israel and its God was critical of political alliances. Consequently, in the *Shema*, chanted within the conjugal paradigm, love and fidelity emphasize uniqueness in the eyes of the beloved.[30] Instead of a concern with numbers (mono-), the *Shema* focuses on singularity of Yahweh and Israel; the unicity or singularity of "the LORD alone" whose only *witness* is Israel. Israelites rather than being the inventors of monotheism are *witnesses*—credible witnesses who trust *they will be believed*.[31] This tends towards soteriological and kerygmatic monotheism rather than Greek philosophical monotheism or the dogmatic monotheism of Islam. In the context of national crisis or captivity (Deuteronomy and Deutero-Isaiah) Israel has recourse to the "One Lord" of the covenant and not to a unique deity deduced through philosophical reasoning.

From the perspective of conjugal relationship one appreciates the theme of a "jealous Yahweh" and the commandment interdicting the presence of other deities in front of Yahweh (in Yahweh's sanctuary.) Perhaps the emphasis on jealousy is the consequence of the choice made by both partners. The Book of Joshua, edited by Deuteronomistic historians, makes the choice clear, "Now if you are unwilling to serve the LORD, choose this day whom you will serve, whether the gods your ancestors served in the region beyond the River or the gods of the Amorites in whose land you are living; but as for me and my household, we will serve the LORD" (Jos 24:15). The people chose Yahweh, "we also will serve the LORD, for he is our God" (Jos 24:18). Joshua discouraged them, "You cannot serve the LORD, for he is a holy God. He is a jealous God; he will not forgive your transgressions or your sins. If you forsake the LORD and serve foreign gods, then he will turn and do you harm, and consume you, after having done you good." In West African religion it is rare to hear that the transcendent One God "kills"—the rare occasion will be through the Thunder deity as punishment for hidden crimes. It is more common to hear of jealous (ambivalent) *vodhun* or *orisa* who either kill or profoundly disturb the life of backsliders.

The emphasis of Joshua 24 is not that there are no other gods. Rather, in a world of tension and conflicting national deities, the one

30. Carrière, "De l'un à l'autre testament: le travail de l'unicité," 53.

31. Ibid., 55.

choice and no other is permitted. Israel's choice is of Yahweh, the One who acts towards Israel as one expects Elohîm to act. If Israel is mobilized to be loyal, to "will one thing" and none other apart from Yahweh, then other deities, whose existence is not in doubt, are denied "air time."[32]

> I am the LORD your God, who brought you out of the land of Egypt, out of the house of slavery; you shall have no other gods before me. . . . You shall not bow down to them or worship them; for I the LORD your God am a jealous God, punishing children for the iniquity of parents, to the third and fourth generation of those who reject me. (Deut 5: 6–9)

The narrow pre-exilic history of Israel was insufficient to present Yahweh as Elohîm of the wider world.

In *Deutero-Isaiah and in the Wisdom tradition,* Israel was in touch with gentile reality. Exiled Israel was militarily inferior. Exile and oppression challenged Israel. It presented her an opportunity to expand the notion of divinity through the theology of creation integrated with the Exodus experience. In the Semitic world, cosmic creation was the domain of *El.* Deutero-Isaiah proclaimed Yahweh, *El* creator of the universe. For the prophet creation is an unparalleled action of Yahweh, the God of the Exodus-covenant, the lord of history, in favour of his people Israel. During the period of exile or captivity, when a militant Yahweh was totally powerless, the prophet took the combative and extraordinary step of declaring the Babylonian deities "idols" and no gods at all. This is revolutionary; going beyond what Deuteronomy and early Patriarchal history could have imagined, and yet creatively integrating them. *Monotheism is emerging without political support.* Captive Israel is Yahweh's *witness.* The whole world is convoked to unanimously recognize Yahweh as the One and Only God. The totality of Israel's history, i.e., the Exodus-covenantal history, is narrated or recalled (*zkr*) within this novel monotheistic propaganda. Israel as *witness* before the nations is God's *icon* (image Isa 46:8–10). This bold and creative theology is a subtle development of Elijah's vision at Horeb, of the Deuteronomistic stress on one choice, and of the universalistic Patriarchal theology. In utter weakness or *silence* captive Israel becomes the *witness* of Yahweh, indeed the *image* of Yahweh—the quintessential humankind beloved

---

32. Brueggemann, "Book of Exodus," 840. see also, Anderson, "Introduction to Israelite Religion," in *The New Interpreter's Bible, Vol. I*, especially paragraphs on "Canaanite and Israelite Beliefs about the Gods," 272ff.

and witnessing to the quintessential deity (the transcendent One and Only God):[33]

> You are my witnesses, says the LORD, and my servant whom I have chosen, so that you may know and believe me and understand that I am he. Before me no god was formed, nor shall there be any after me. I, I am the LORD, and besides me there is no savior. I declared and saved and proclaimed, when there was no strange god among you; and you are my witnesses, says the LORD. (Isa 43:10–12)

The Priestly tradition of the Pentateuch, in the book of Genesis, sees created humankind as the quintessential representation of *Elohîm*: "Then God said, 'Let us make humankind *in our image*, according to our likeness'" *(kat' eikona hêmeteran—*Gen 1:26).[34] Deutero-Isaiah unequivocally proclaims *Israel witness and icon of Yahweh*. Jeremiah was at pains to declare the end of any special history, insisting that Yahweh as cosmic creator distributes gifts as He saw fit, even giving all lands to Nebuchadnezzar (Jer 27:4–6). But Deutero-Isaiah had the incredible universalistic insight integrated within the particularity of Israel— Yahweh's icon and witness. Universalism is radically embraced: the prophet declared irrelevant Israel's national script, the Exodus, that for the prophet is synonymous with Israel's creation. Shocking blasphemy! But this was to emphasise the "new thing"—*a novel cosmic creation in which Israel has the role as witness!* Yahweh is "approaching Israel with a new action which made the old saving institutions increasingly invalid since from then on life or death for Israel was determined by this future event."[35] No one could imagine or anticipate it on the basis of any earlier story:

> Do not remember the former things, or consider the things of old. I am about to do a new thing; now it springs forth, do you not perceive it? I will make a way in the wilderness and rivers in the desert." (Isa 43:18–19)

---

33. Scharbert, "Brk, Berakah," 245. It is remarkable according to Scharbert that the term, *bara'* (to create), that occurs 49 times in the Hebrew Bible is used most frequently by Deutero-Isaiah (17 times as against 10 times by P).

34. See Westermann, *Genesis 1–11*, 142–58, esp. 157–58.

35. Cross, *Canaanite Myth and Hebrew Epic*, 345; see also 135–36, 343–46; also Clifford, *Fair Spoken and Persuading*, 51, 55.

> From this time forward I make you hear new things, hidden things that you have not known. They are created now, not long ago; before today you have never heard of them, so that you could not say, "I already knew them." (Isa 48:6b–7)

First, Deutero-Isaiah re-appropriated the ancient image of *El* "creator of heaven and earth" and identified Yahweh with *El*. The prophet went back to "re-emphasize certain aspects of the pre-Yahwistic concept of God"; thus he reintroduced "a universalism latent in patriarchal religion but largely lost in the mainstream of Mosaic Yahwism."[36] Second, Israel strengthened in weakness (cf. 2 Cor 12:19) is not shielded from the nations. The Book of Consolation, Isa 40–55, proclaims a message that radically includes the nations and radically restructures Israel's identity. Israel witnesses to the ends of the earth that Yahweh is universal creator. According to Legrand, "the whole history of the nations is inserted into the perspective of the Creator's universal sway."[37] Third, my conclusion is unavoidable, no nation (not even Israel), no cultural group accounts all alone for the mystery of life or of the universe. *Uno itinere non potest perueniri ad tam grande secretum* "One and only way does not suffice to approach such a great mystery." The transcendent One God, *Mawu, Chukwu, Olodumare, Onyame,* and *Amma,* Yahweh, Elohîm of the Patriarchs, in utter weakness ("silence" or distance) experienced radically as Lord of creation, opens a window for a novel perception of universalism. Captive, weak and screaming Israel is witness; but *witnesses come from all over the earth.*

> All is in the hand of God. Cyrus himself, the conquering pagan from Persia, is the Shepherd, the Anointed/Messiah, charged with accomplishing the designs of God (Isa 44:28; 45:1). From this point forward, all human beings are called upon to acknowledge that the God of Israel is the only God, and that there is no other. (45:14)[38]

Israel's Yahweh is God, at a cost (universalism)! Israel is witness at a cost—a radical renewal of identity and with a mission! Nations recognize Yahweh is God at a cost—"there is no other" (conversion)! Conversion in practical terms learns from historical Israel's merging of

---

36. Saggs, *Encounter with the Divine*, 50–51. Creation was originally the prerogative of El, Day, *Yahweh and the Gods and Goddesses of Canaan*, 20–21.

37. Legrand, *Unity and Plurality*, 19.

38. Ibid.

the Patriarchal *El* with Yahweh, the process of transformation of deities into qualities of the transcendent One God, and the absorption of divine epithets of other cultural groups.

The expansion of the Israelite world through the experience of exile inevitably led to a new understanding of particularity—the chosen one is witness. It led to further adaptations of the personality of Yahweh, expressed more and more with trans-cultural and supranational imagery. It enlarged the spectrum of the *chosen*—Israel is not the only *witness* of God (Yahweh); Cyrus of Persia is boldly presented as *messiah*.

This emergent image of God, transcending and at the same time integrating particularity, was assumed with difficulty in the Jewish tradition. The struggle for its clarification continued into the New Testament. Gnuse argues that exile and oppression ensured Israelite monotheism was not triumphalistic but was deeply committed to peace; it did not originate "from above" but "'from below,' from the common people"; this explains the insistence on an "egalitarian ethos." The position of weakness ensured it has no conquering mission like the cult of the victorious Marduk. Judaism, the embodiment of this monotheism of weakness, could then give rise to Christianity "the ultimate missionary religion."[39]

The *Wisdom* traditions that Israel shared with her Ancient Near Eastern neighbors—Mesopotamia, Egypt and Canaan—helped in expanding the image of God. Wisdom, personified and related to God, became part of Israelite literature especially from the third century BCE. Wisdom, shed of the exclusivist political theology that dominated the enterprise of nation building, emphasized universalistic mediation, dialogue and communication. Wisdom that is the art of finding ways and means, without being identical with such ways or means, is versatile and mobile, mediates circulation, communication, between humans and nature, among humans, between men and women, parents and children, and so on. The emergent One Wisdom, according to Carrière, is of interest and valuable for Christian discussion of the One God.[40] Dame Wisdom (Wis 7:22–30) is intelligent, holy, unique, manifold, subtle, mobile. Pure emanation of the Almighty, she is but one and yet can do all things. Consequently, "God loves nothing so much as the person who lives with wisdom" (7:28).

39. Gnuse, *No Other Gods*, 94; drawing from the works of Gerd Theissen, *Biblical Faith*.

40. Carrière, "De l'un à l'autre testament: le travail de l'unicité," 57.

Deutero-Isaiah, in the situation of utter weakness of the "chosen people," proclaimed Yahweh as creator of Jacob and of the whole universe. But Proverbs paints a touching picture of creation cosmogony where Dame Wisdom declares universal creation as play or delight. Wisdom was the first to be created—possibly embodying the qualities of the powerful Asherah and/or the "Queen of Heaven" and neutralizing and subordinating them to Yahweh:[41]

> The LORD created me at the beginning of his work, the first of his acts of long ago. Ages ago I was set up, at the first, before the beginning of the earth. When there were no depths I was brought forth, when there were no springs abounding with water. Before the mountains had been shaped, before the hills, I was brought forth—when he had not yet made earth and fields, or the world's first bits of soil. When he established the heavens, I was there, when he drew a circle on the face of the deep, when he made firm the skies above, when he established the fountains of the deep, when he assigned to the sea its limit, so that the waters might not transgress his command, when he marked out the foundations of the earth, then I was beside him, like a master worker; and I was daily his delight, rejoicing before him always, rejoicing in his inhabited world and delighting in the human race. (Prov 8:22–31)

This expansive experience of the one Wisdom that cuts across the whole of humanity, that declares, "I came forth from the mouth of the Most High, and covered the earth like a mist" (Sir 24:3) nevertheless found settlement in Jacob. The tension between universalism and particularism in the wisdom tradition is noticeable in Sir 24:3–8. The motifs of Mosaic revelation—desert wanderings, pillar of cloud—and even the later temple cult connect with wisdom. Contrary to the author of *1 Enoch* who did not grant any people "exclusive access to divine knowledge," "Ben Sira attributes true wisdom to the Jews."[42] Nevertheless, the particularist claim of Ben Sira, a matter of identity, is possible only within the wider relational mobility of the one universal Wisdom. The all-encompassing reality declares, "Over waves of the sea, over all the earth, and over every people and nation I have held sway" (Sir 24: 6). The acknowledgment of the subtle and boundless mobile Wisdom is prior to the particular incarnations: "Then the Creator of all things gave me a

---

41. See Gnuse, *No Other Gods*, 209, 184–86, echoing the views of Bernard Lang.

42. See Crenshaw, "Book of Sirach," 57.

command, and my Creator chose the place for my tent. He said, 'Make your dwelling in Jacob, and in Israel receive your inheritance'" (Sir 24:8).

The universal all-encompassing Wisdom standing "beside" the Lord Creator, the "delight" of God and "delighting in the human race," radically stands beside any Origin of origins encountered in our envisioning of reality. West Africans, Hebrews, Mesopotamians, Egyptians, Canaanites, etc., confirm, "Nothing stands alone! Something stands, and Something else stands beside it." Multiplicity, plurality, twin-ness is the key to accessing reality. The particular shapes and forms this takes are dimensions of the local appropriation of the one wisdom. Senator Symmachus is right, *Uno itinere non potest perueniri ad tam grande secretum* (One and only way does not suffice to approach such a great mystery). The one wisdom that is uttered from the mouth of the Most High is found all over the earth before incarnating in a particular location, Israel, and all other particular places like West Africa or the Graeco-Roman world. "Nothing stands alone"! The creator does not create except in relationship! Or rather, every narrative of creation anchors on relationality. God is inconceivable without relationship. This dynamic and relational appropriation of divinity constitutes the core of New Testament theology of the incarnation of the Word.

YAHWEH AS THE GOD OF JESUS CHRIST— POWERFULLY WEAK[43]

The developments in OT theology of Yahweh—from the monolatry of pre-exilic period, the process of forging mono-Yahwism, to the full flourishing of monotheism in exilic and postexilic period—were assumed in the New Testament image of the One and Only God that Jesus Christ called *abba* (Father), whose Kingdom Jesus proclaimed. The *abba* relationship and the proclamation of the Kingdom dominated the life and mission of Jesus the Christ. New Testament literature is not directly preoccupied with developing a "theology." Rather than being dominated by the "theology of God" as such it presupposed the One and Only God received through postexilic Judaism. The proclamation of the Crucified-Risen Jesus as the Christ dominated the life and theology of the Church. The doctrine of God presupposed by the NT is radically continuous with the OT image of God and the common interpretations of the OT within

---

43. See Babut, *Le Dieu Puissamment Faible De La Bible.*

later Judaism.[44] What happened to the deities? Their qualities were appropriated by the One and Only God, Yahweh the creator of Israel and the nations. Negatively, as John Day shows, Baal was transformed to Beelzebul—the abominable "prince of demons" that one encounters in the gospels; the "seven-headed Leviathan of Canaanite mythology lives on even in the New Testament"—"seven-headed dragon" (Rev 12), "seven-headed beast" (Rev 13). The book of Revelation is the hunting ground for neo-Pentecostalism, specialized in diabolizing ATR deities in West Africa. Positively, since Yahweh appropriated the characteristics of *El*, "the seventy sons of God, originally denoting the gods of the pantheon under El . . . became demoted to the status of angels, the seventy guardian angels of the nations attested in *1 Enoch*."[45] Angelology is not only the preserve of the mainline missionary churches but also of the AICs, Charismatic movements and new African Pentecostalism.

The Christological preoccupation of NT writings, while maintaining the pre-exilic OT doctrine of one God, displays oneness in a radically relational way. NT and early church affirmations about the dead-risen Jesus were "in accordance with the scriptures" (1 Cor 15:3–4). But the epithet "Lord" and even "God" (John 1:1; 20:28) are accorded the risen one. Nevertheless whatever epithets of exaltation or pre-existence the NT and the early Church accorded the risen one, the *Cross*—the sign of contradiction, the principle of utter weakness—occupied the centre stage, "so that the cross of Christ might not be emptied of its power" (1 Cor 1:17). Koyama prolongs Paul to highlight the intriguing and suggestive quality of the Cross that should be lost on no one—the symbol of weakness, failure and powerlessness, and the "foolishness of God": "There is no handle to the cross"! It is unwieldy; the opposite of a briefcase; it is borne, stumbling, discomfited![46] Ideally the One and Only God of Christianity proposed from the position of weakness, "from below," will embody "egalitarian ethos" and will have nothing to do with tyranny or imperialism.[47]

The radical relational approach to the oneness of God by the nascent Church, dominated by the Spirit is captured in the Pauline *parenesis*: "There is one body and one Spirit, just as you were called to the one hope

---

44. See Bassler, "God in the NT."

45. Day, *Yahweh and the Gods and Goddesses of Canaan*, 232–33, 77–81.

46. Koyama, *No Handle on the Cross*, 7.

47. See Gnuse, *No Other Gods*, 94.

of your calling, one Lord, one faith, one baptism, one God and Father of all, who is above all and through all and in all" (Eph 4:4–6). Jouette M. Bassler in her review of NT notions of God concludes that from the evidence of the NT texts "an intimate relationship of God, Christ, and the Holy Spirit," is indicated. However, "a formal triadic coordination of the three is found in only a few places." Rather, the pairing God-Christ and, less frequently, Christ-Spirit are more common.[48] It is from these texts that carried over OT motifs of the relational God, creator-liberator, that the tradition drew its doctrine of Christology and Trinity.

No one text or narrative captures God's revelation in the Crucified-Risen Jesus Christ. But the impact of the Cross-Resurrection was so overwhelming that the preaching of the early Church moved from the Kingdom of God that dominated Jesus' earthly ministry to the risen Jesus who is the Christ: the preacher is preached. The resurrection is the act of God who in justifying or glorifying Jesus justified Jesus' proclamation of the Kingdom. My interest is restricted to how the reception of the revelation in Jesus Christ brings insight into our understanding of the relational Trinitarian God. The dominant West African pattern of approach to the transcendent One God, amidst a plurality of deities, spirits and ancestors was repudiated and diabolized by missionary Christianity. However, the dramatic focus on demons diametrically at war with God (especially in Pentecostalism) and the radical focus on the Holy Spirit (AICs, Charismatic movements and Pentecostalism) indicate the continuing relevance of West African cosmological ideas and opens a window for a fertile encounter between Christianity and West African ATR. In the first place, the demonization of ATR is internalized. However, it makes present, disturbingly and dualistically, the agency of the devil or Satan; though dualism is alien to the West African world vision. Secondly, AICs and Charismatic movements have created a wider and more potent economy of the Holy Spirit. AICs are called "spirit churches"! This integrates into Christianity the therapeutic roles of devotees or agents of deities—the healing services and the struggle against witchcraft and the occult—without naming the deities. Missionary Christianity totally misunderstood West African ATR and laid the foundation for the dualism which bedevils Christian life and practice. This reaches paroxysm in the excesses and alienation of neo-

48. Bassler, "God in the NT."

Pentecostalism. AICs and Charismatic movements are on the right track in the search for the new image of God—but they need to be critiqued to align with Trinitarian intuitions of the great Christian tradition.

I tried to show in analyzing the OT how the West African experience of dynamic hierarchy in divinity, dominated by relationality, expands or brings an interesting point of view to the notion of religion itself and to the Jewish-Christian notion of God. I prolong this interrogation into the Jewish-Christian tradition to highlight aspects of the economy or relationship of God-Christ-Spirit that have impacted prominently on Christianity in West Africa—especially the dominance of the economy of the Spirit. Deities, spirits, and ancestors, ambivalent in behavior, are closer to the community and mediate for the community the experience of what one expects of a concerned (providential) God. In West African Christianity, the liberating, healing or therapeutic hand of God is best experienced through the Holy Spirit. The relational order in the Trinitarian economy makes the Holy Spirit's "delighting in the human race" (Prov. 8:31) understandable and theologically defensible in the context. Origen of Alexandria proves this convincingly in his religious and theological anthropology. He exposed the life-giving dimension of God, who is Spirit, through an interesting exegesis of NT texts embedded in Greek cosmological ideas that find profound echoes and even identities with West African cosmology. I move on to present Origen's ideas on the economy of the Spirit as building block for my argument that the Spirit is the most fertile entry point into Trinitarian theology in West African Christianity.

5

The Economy of Spirit in the Dynamic Access to the Trinitarian God

Aspects of the Theology of Origen of Alexandria

THE PRIMARY ROLE OF *Spirit* in Jesus' life and in the mission of the Church is clear in the writings of Luke and Paul. In John's Gospel the Spirit is Paraclete (14:16, 26; 15:26; 16:7), the Promise of the Father that abides with the community. Indeed, God is Spirit.

The relational dimension of access to God as Spirit appears to be stressed by the Fourth Gospel in the "missionary dialogue" between Jesus and the Samaritans. Nigerian exegete, Teresa Okure, in her study of chapter four of John's Gospel, suggests that the dialogue with the Samaritan woman is not only "universally recognized" as "the most overtly concerned with mission in the Gospel," but also as "a minia-ture of the whole gospel."[1] The contemplative in the Beloved Disciple emerges in discussing mission originating from God who is Spirit and Life. Mission in John is Trinitarian and relational. John 17, the great mis-sionary prayer, echoes relationship: "as you have sent me . . . so I have sent them . . ." (17:18). The closing dialogue in John 20:21 envelopes the Lord and disciples within the one mission of God: "As the Father has sent me, so I send you." In the dialogue with the Samaritan woman, God and mission are presented in a new key: worship of God, who is Life and Spirit, is freed from imprisonment within the traditional conflict between Jews and Samaritans. The Fourth Gospel moves the dialogue onto the eschatological plane where worship is "in spirit and truth"

---

1. Okure, *Johannine Approach to Mission*, 285. See also Köstenberger, *Missions of Jesus and the Disciples*.

(vv. 23–24). It presents a new "form of worship that reflects and is shaped by the character of God"[2]—dynamic and relational ("God is Spirit"). The expression, "God is Spirit," according to Okure, "defines not the nature of God as such but the mode of his creative, life-giving action in human beings. . . ."[3]

Earlier in this study (chapter 3) I pointed out that the creative and life-giving dimension that defines God as *Spirit* is structural to ATR: *Mawu* "imbues terrestrial existence with its essence and vitality." In West African Christianity, AICs and Charismatic movements display this in their worship and healing rites—an experiential insight into the life-giving creativity of God who is Spirit. There is an interesting homology between the Johannine definition, *God is Spirit,* and West African Christian practice that I interpret as a *recapture and fusion* into Christianity of ATR experience. While all Christians reject ATR cult, its deities and rituals, they recognize the creative, active and healing presence of the Holy Spirit. This recognition is, in my view, a successful retrieval and transformation of the dynamic dimension of Spirit in West African ATR. The Holy Spirit energizes the community and empowers members with diverse gifts to render services to the community (cf. 1 Cor 12).

The West African Christian recapture of Spirit—through merging and transforming the economy of spirit (deities) familiar to their ancestral religion—can be successfully aligned with faith in one and only God of Jesus Christ through drawing from the process of Jewish monotheism described above. It can be successfully aligned with the Trinitarian imagination of the great Christian tradition through learning from the pneumatological creativity of Origen. Despite the weaknesses in Origen's theology (aspects of which have been condemned as heterodox—e.g., the mythological speculations on pre-existence) one must acknowledge the enormous impact the Alexandrian "man of steel" had on the Fathers and on the development of the Christian tradition. His enormous insight into God-Word-Spirit that gave direction to his disciples and the Fathers is relevant for exploration into Christian practice in West Africa. For example, his anthropology of ascent to God is palpable in the Patristic tradition. Balthasar insists, "Not only did all the Alexandrians after him, not only did Pamphilius, Gregory the Wonder-Worker, Didymus,

2. See commentary of O'Day, "Gospel of John," 565.

3. Okure, *Johannine Approach to Mission,* 116.

Eusebius and the Cappadocians, Jerome, Hilary, Ambrose and, through all these, Augustine accept his model of the *ascensiones in corde*, but also, mediated through these dominant figures, the little thinkers, the preachers, the people."[4] Origen's carefully systematized pneumatology and religious anthropology focused on the human journey to holiness. I find them attractive for discussing the *spirit-oriented* and *spirit-embedded* West African Christianity. I first explore Origen's anthropology where *spirit* plays a fundamental role, and then proceed to discuss its impact in elucidating the West African contribution to Christian pneumatology.

THE RELIGIOUS ANTHROPOLOGY OF ORIGEN— A DYNAMIC ACCESS TO THE TRIUNE GOD

Origen of Alexandria developed a pneumatology that is suffused with the teaching of the Fourth Gospel and Paul on the Spirit. The *spirit* is ground for revelation of the full individual.[5] But Origen's commentary on Pauline and Johannine texts was embedded in Greek mythology. The pre-existent self (*nous*—the basis of the individuality of the human person) was capital to his development of access to the Trinitarian God. His point of departure and the atmosphere or philosophical culture that he breathed are different from our West African context. However, the content of the myth of pre-existence is not very distant from West African myths of the pre-existent self, as I will show below. The myth of pre-existence was considered heterodox after Origen. Though one does not have to agree with it, it forms part of the thought processes that configured the doctrinal elaborations of Origen. Balthasar argues that the Platonic speculations are separate and separable from the "purely formal influence on the whole of his thought" of "the whole philosophical culture" that the "age of the waning antiquity breathed." It was an attitude or "a common atmosphere" that is difficult to name but whose influence on Origen, his pupils, Eastern and Western Fathers, from his critics who copied him like Jerome, to admirers who transmitted his texts and pattern of thought like Gregory of Nyssa.[6] "Platonism," accord-

---

4. Balthasar, *Origen: Spirit and Fire*, 9.

5. In what follows I depend on commentaries and treatises of Origen and on the works of Henri Crouzel and Jacques Dupuis. Crouzel, *Origène*; Dupuis, "*L'esprit De L'homme*."

6. Balthasar, *Origen: Spirit and Fire*, 6–10.

ing to Balthasar, hardly describes this attitude or common atmosphere that includes the Stoa and Aristotle.

The religious anthropology of Origen is trichotomist (three dimensional)—based on spirit-intellect-body. Though his discourse is suffused with Platonic speculation, the fundament of this trichotomist anthropology is the Bible. It is characteristic of Origen to begin all theological meditation from the Jewish Christian Scriptures. He discovered in Paul's letter to the Thessalonians (1 Thess 5:23) the anchor for his anthropology:

> May the God of peace himself sanctify you entirely; and may your spirit and soul and body be kept sound and blameless at the coming of our Lord Jesus Christ.

Origen transformed the biblical concept—"spirit and soul and body"—into a coherent synthesis that remained unchanged throughout his lifetime. It is however curious, according to Crouzel, that "it rapidly disappeared after him, even among his key disciples."[7] In this anthropology, the self in pre-existence, the self struggling for perfection in the course of life on earth and the self enjoying the glory of the saints are neither described in monistic nor dualistic (oppositional, body-soul) terms. Rather the life of the self is defined in composite, flexible, relational triadic terms of *pneuma-nous-soma pneumatikon* (spirit-intellect-spiritual body).

The *Nous* in pre-existence lived a pneumatic or spiritual life. In other words the human *pneuma* (spirit), fully alive, ensured that life is lived in total bliss; the body (*soma)* that was not of this world was also pneumatic—ethereal, scintillating spiritual body. After the *Fall* (of Adam) as recorded in the Jewish Bible, human life changed dramatically; nevertheless, the relational process in the self remained the same. The human person remained a relational trichotomist or three-dimensional composite. The *pneuma* remained the director of the journey on earth towards spiritual progress; however, in this fallen state the *pneuma* (spirit) is more or less asleep. The *nous*—the basis of the individuality of the human person—is no longer under the total direction of the *pneuma*, but rather becomes the intellectual part of the *psyche* (soul) that has also a sensible dimension. This helps one to appreciate the dimensions of intellect and sensibility in the human person. Finally, *sôma gêïnon* (earthly

7. Crouzel, *Origène*, 124.

body) is ambivalent—it could lead the soul either to good or to evil.[8] Sometimes Origen distinguishes between body (*soma*) and flesh (*sarx*) to draw attention to the ambivalent orientation of the earthly body that could lead either to good or to evil. But these distinctions are not always strictly maintained. The world becomes a theatre for spiritual combat.

The intent of Origen's anthropology is to display the ascent of the human person to sanctity drawn by the Spirit; a mysticism of ascent—an experience that Greek philosophers call *homoiôsis*—the imitation or the "following" of God. Imitating or following God is of the very nature of humans; Christian spirituality of "imitation" introduces a qualitative and not a quantitative difference.[9] I will show later the similarities and dissimilarities between Origen's mysticism of ascent and West African mysticism of descent.

The *human pneuma* is strategic to the Christian religious anthropology of Origen. The *human pneuma* is the divine element (totally immaterial) present in each human person—equivalent to the *ruah* (breath) of Hebrew Scriptures. I argue that it is also not dissimilar to the West African *personal spirit* that is bearer of destiny: *chi* (Igbo), *ori* (Yoruba), *kra* or *okra* (Asante), *aklama* (Ewe), *se* (Adja-Fon); God's gift that humanizes. It cannot be called a quality of the person because the *pneuma* does not assume responsibility or guilt for one's sins. *Pneuma* is rather the tutor of the soul (*psyche*) or rather of the intellect (*nous*). Conscience, knowledge of God and motion towards prayer reside in the *human pneuma*. In Origen's anthropology the *human pneuma* is totally grounded in the Holy Spirit poured out on the faithful; it is a created participation in God's Spirit. First of all, no life is possible apart from the Spirit of God who is life. For Christians, the human *pneuma*, as the created participation in the Holy Spirit, becomes the privileged point of contact between the human person and the divine *Pneuma* that indwells the Christian person. Therefore the *human pneuma* is the point of contact or relationship between the human person and the Trinity. This connection with the Triune God arises from the relational flow of the mystical ascent of the person (or soul) to the Trinity (through participation) that follows the line or order of descent of the Trinity toward humans.[10] In West African terms, that I argue can be aligned with

8. Dupuis, "*L'esprit De L'homme*," 33–40.

9. See Crouzel, *Origène*, 136.

10. Dupuis, "*L'esprit De L'homme*," 256–57; Crouzel, *Origène*, 124–25.

Christian anthropology, *chi, ori, kra* or *okra, aklama, se, etc.,* mediates the Christian participation in divine life (grace) and links each Christian, originally endowed with destiny by the transcendent One God, to life in the Trinity. The *pneuma* as spirit, and therefore as life belongs to God; it is taken back by God in the event of one being condemned to Gehenna.

In his study of Origen, Jacques Dupuis came to the conclusion that the *human pneuma* rather than being a spiritual quality of the rational creature (a quality of the created intellect), is indeed divine life itself.

> In Origen's religious anthropology the *pneuma* is the corner-stone. And the order in which it functions is the order of the true life. It occupies a central position in this order. On the one hand, it is the divine element present to a human being. On the other hand, it is the superior trichotomist element, as it should be. The *pneuma* is thus the link between the divine and the human. Better still: the *pneuma* plays a primordial role in the divine life in the human person. It is passive with regard to God because it is received from him; it is active on the part of humans. It is to it (*pneuma*) that it pertains to transmit to the totality of the human person what is peculiarly human[11]

Pneuma, conceived by Origen in dynamic or relational terms, is life. God is *Pneuma* (Spirit) because God is and gives life. The creature is *pneuma* to the degree that it possesses life. Drawing from Paul, Origen notes that the God of the "new covenant" guaranteed the gift and ministry of this covenant in the *spirit:* it is a covenant "not of letter but of *spirit*; for the letter kills, but the *Spirit* gives life" (2 Cor 3:6). Origen's anthropology is thus anchored on Pauline and Johannine pneumatology. God as Spirit "defines not the nature of God as such but the mode of his creative, life-giving action in human beings . . ."[12] This resonates with West African religious anthropology. In Book XIII of his commentary on the Gospel of John, Origen's reflection on the nature of God who is light, fire, and spirit grounds human life (*spirit*) in God's Spirit because "God is *pneuma*":

> Such also is my impression on the issue of the expression "God is pneuma": since we are made participants of this ordinary life that is generally called "life" when the *pneuma* that is in us breathes in what is called, when it concerns the body, the "breath of life,"

---

11. Dupuis, *"L'esprit De L'homme,"* 256.

12. Okure, *Johannine Approach to Mission,* 116.

similarly God, who leads us to the authentic life, is called *pneu-ma*, I suppose after that *pneuma* (i.e., breath of life). Indeed, according to Scripture it is said that the *pneuma* gives life, certainly not the ordinary life but the divine life. For the letter kills and brings death not that which is produced during the separation of the soul and body, but that which occurs during the separation of the soul from God, from its Lord and from the Holy Spirit (*Pneuma*).[13]

The position of Origen on *Pneuma*, the grounding or embedding of the human spirit in divine life, is fully Christian and fully consonant with West African anthropology. Many West African narratives have a corresponding *spirit* bestowed on each human by the creator, embodying the individual's destiny—a providential indwelling *spirit* testifying to the accompaniment of the individual by God. No wonder the Akan refer to *okra* as "spark of God." The conceptual dimensions of the West African *spirit* are recaptured by AICs and Charismatic movements. The West African Christian practice finds echo in Pauline and Johannine theology as well as in the pneumatology of Origen.

The *Psyche (anima—soul)* is also important for the appreciation of Origen's mystical approach to God that is the overriding preoccupation of his anthropology. *Psyche* is the seat of freedom, choice and personality embedded originally in each human: "every rational soul is possessed of free-will and volition; that it has a struggle to maintain with the devil and his angels, and opposing influences."[14] The superior element is the mind (*mens—nous* or intellect of Platonists), which is the hegemonic or coordinating faculty. But *psyche* has an inferior dimension as a result of the *Fall*—the principle of instincts and passions. This makes life a spiritual combat. If the *psyche* (soul) allows itself to be drawn towards the *pneuma*, a person becomes totally spiritual—the spirit consumes the inferior dimensions of the soul. But if *psyche* rejects the spirit and turns towards the flesh, the inferior dimension (instincts and passions) robs the superior (intellect) of its control; the soul becomes carnal. Origen illustrates how *psyche* is pulled by *pneuma* in the union of the soul of Jesus to the Word from pre-existence: "that soul which, like an iron in the fire, has been perpetually placed in the Word, and perpetually in the Wisdom, and perpetually in God, is God in all that it does, feels, and un-

13. Origène, *Commentaire sur Saint Jean,* tome III, XIII: xxiii, 140.
14. Origen, "De Principiis," Pref. 5; see also Crouzel, *Origène,* 271.

derstands, and therefore can be called neither convertible nor mutable, inasmuch as, being incessantly heated, it possessed immutability from its union with the Word of God."[15] Nevertheless, by the incarnation of the Word the inferior dimension of the soul was necessarily present in Jesus making Him totally like us in everything except sin. This inferior part of the soul, as the Gospels show, was the source of temptation, distress, sadness and suffering.[16]

The third element in Origen's trichotomist conception of the human person is the *Soma* (*body*). This is not to be confused with *flesh* understood in a pejorative sense. The body is created good, by God! True, human participation in *image of God* is in the soul not in the body. Nevertheless, the body is the sanctuary that contains the image—sin is profanation (1 Cor 6:13–20). According to Crouzel, in the three moments where the body figures in Origen's anthropology—pre-existence (ethereal body), Fall (terrestrial body), and glorification (celestial body)—the "substance" of the body remains the same; only the quality changes. In other words the ethereal body subsists in the form of "seeds of the word" during the terrestrial fallen existence from which it will germinate into a glorious body.[17] This dynamic perception of the body ensures that Origen is not locked up in the Platonic perception of body as prison for the soul.

VERSATILITY OF THE SPIRIT AND HUMAN PARTICIPATION IN TRINITARIAN LIFE

The *Spirit* as anchor to Origen's religious anthropology makes dialogue with the Alexandrian Father easy for West African Christianity. The Spirit that is life is the mediator of sanctification. Origen's Trinitarian theology is not interested in just defining the life of God, but rather the *life of God in relation to us*. The human ascent to God, holiness, is locked onto the descending order of the relational or dynamic Trinity. Dynamism in the Trinity (God is Spirit) is replicated in dynamism in human life, embedded in the human *pneuma*.

In Origen's Trinitarian thinking, the *Spirit* that gives holiness is not presented as dominating the Trinitarian relationship. True, the sanctify-

---

15. Origen, "De Principiis," II, 6, 6.

16. Crouzel, *Origène*, 124–26.

17. Ibid., 128.

ing power of the Spirit is given only to the just while operations of God the Father and the Son extend to both the just and unjust. However, this does not imply the superiority of the Spirit:

> Let no one indeed suppose that we, from having said that the Holy Spirit is conferred upon the saints alone, but that the benefits or operations of the Father and of the Son extend to good and bad, to just and unjust, by so doing give a preference to the Holy Spirit over the Father and the Son, or assert that His dignity is greater, which certainly would be a very illogical conclusion. For it is the peculiarity of His grace and operations that we have been describing. Moreover, nothing in the Trinity can be called greater or less, since the fountain of divinity alone contains all things by His word and reason, and by the Spirit of His mouth sanctifies all things which are worthy of sanctification, as it is written in the Psalm: "By the word of the Lord were the heavens strengthened, and all their power by the Spirit of His mouth." (Ps 33:6)[18]

In his *Commentary on John* Origen states that the Holy Spirit comes from the Father through the Son. Though the Holy Spirit is not a creature he has existence through the Son. The Holy Spirit, the first of all that has existence from the Father through the Son, is highest in dignity. Only the Son is son by nature, and the Holy Spirit needs the mediation of the Son to subsist individually, and participates in all the denominations (or virtues) of the Son. Charisms are dimensions of the Holy Spirit; they are produced by God, procured by Christ, and subsist in the Holy Spirit. *Charisms are the Holy Spirit in person.*[19] Cécile Blanc points out that Origen's Trinitarian theology clearly underlines *ex Ipso* as economy of the Father (*from whom* all derive existence), *per Ipsum* as economy of the Son (*through whom* all including the Holy Spirit derive existence) and *in Ipso* as economy of the Spirit (*in whom* those whose life is transformed find subsistence and consistence in God's perfection).[20]

The *Son* according to Origen, as minister and collaborator of God, i.e. as demiurge, helped the Father in creation, since all things are made through him. Indeed the Son alone in his divinity is *image of God*. Incarnate, died and raised from the dead, He is always Son because the

18. Origen, "De Principiis," I, 3,7.

19. Origène, *Commentaire sur Saint Jean,* Book II, 75–77, esp. art. 77 ; Crouzel, *Origène,* 262.

20. Comments in her translation and notes, Origène, *Commentaire Sur Saint Jean— Tome 1.* 252 n. 1, 256 n. 2.

Father never at any time began to be Father. Furthermore, the Father begets his Word every instant like the light that transmits always its luminosity. The Father sends, and the Son and the Spirit are sent. The Father is absolutely One! The Son is one in his person (*hypostasis*) but multiple in his denominations (*epinoiai*). Chief among the denominations are first, Wisdom; second, Word. And then there are many others like Light, Life, Resurrection, First born from the dead, etc. The Son is the sum total of all virtues.

The relationship between the Son of God and humans, and the whole of creation, is conceived in two ways. First, as Word, Christ is the one unique *image of God*. Creatures are created according to this image. Human life, orientated towards holiness, is imitation of God in order to resemble God or Christ, the image. As Crouzel says, the "according to the image" is for Origen "our principal substance," the essence of our nature. At the depth of our being, we are defined by our relationship to God. By God's action and through the operation of human freedom we are in motion towards the resemblance of the model.[21] Second, there is the action of being formed in the image of the Word. The Word forms the Christian into his image, similar to the way the Word acted on John the Baptist in his mother's womb. Through the practice of virtue the Word forms himself in the Christian. Each virtue and the totality of the virtues are the Son of God in person. Resemblance to the image reaches perfection at the *eschaton*. Then all will become sons in the unique Son. The saints become transformed into one sun within the Sun of Justice. Only within the interior of the Son would the saints (transformed into *sun* or the *son)* see the Father as the Son and shine with the Son's glory.[22] The above shows that despite the indwelling of God in the saints through the Spirit, the Son is the foundation of this life in the Spirit.

God the *Father,* One and transcendent, is not utterly distant from humans. By nature God is incomprehensible, invisible, but always inseparable from his Son. He is the one true God—not "a god" but "the God" (*ho theos*—with the definite article.) He is Father of the Logos or of the Wisdom. The Son is the image of his Father. The Father has the gift of existence, "the one who is," the source of all being. He derives existence

21. Crouzel, *Origène*, 134.

22. Ibid., 136–37. Origène, *Commentaire Sur Saint Jean—Tome1 (Livres I–V)*. Book I, XVI, 92; I, XX. Crouzel summarises Origen's commentaries in John (I) and Matthew (X, 2).

from no other, while every other derives existence from him.[23] Origen insists that this transcendence does not imply a *Deus otiosus* (an otiose or lazy inactive God) because the *Father* is the one acting in the activity of his Son, who is his minister. The Father is also acting in the sanctifying economy of the Holy Spirit. But Origen insisted that the material of all charisms come from the Holy Spirit:

> And I consider that the Holy Spirit supplies to those who, through Him and through participation in Him, are called saints, the material of the gifts, which come from God; so that the said material of the gifts is made powerful by God, is ministered by Christ, and owes its actual existence in men to the Holy Spirit. I am led to this view of the charisms by the words of Paul which he writes somewhere, "There are diversities of gifts but the same Spirit, and diversities of ministrations, and the same Lord. And there are diversities of workings, but it is the same God that worketh all in all."[24]

The Trinitarian relational order commands God's action *towards us humans*, God's solidarity or suffering with us. *God is not impassible!* His distance does not mean absence. In *Homily in Ezekiel* Origen underlines the type of *passion* or feeling of love that God has for us. First, the Son, the *image of God,* our savior, had pity for the human race. The divine pity made him descend to the earth to save us. He really suffered like us even before the incarnation and the cross. Suffering like us explains his sharing our human life. The *passion* the Son endured, which made him come down, is the "passion of love." Going a step further, Origen demonstrates the *passion* or *suffering* of the *Father*:

> And the Father himself, God of the universe, "full of indulgence, mercy and pity," is it not true that he suffers in some way? Or, do you forget that when he is preoccupied with human affairs, he feels human sentiment? For "he, the Lord your God, took on himself your ways of being, as a man takes on himself his son." God takes therefore on himself our ways of being, as the Son of God takes our feelings. *The Father himself is not impassible* [my emphasis]. If we pray to him, he has pity, he suffers with us, he has a feeling of love, and he places himself in a condition that is

---

23. Origène, *Commentaire Sur Saint Jean—Tome1 (Livres I–V)*. Book II, 14–17.

24. See Roberts and Donaldson, *Ante-Nicene Fathers*: Volume X, Book II, 6.

incompatible with the grandeur of his nature; and for our sake takes upon himself human passions.[25]

In Origen the emphasis on God's transcendence is not decoupled from relationality. Origen could thus challenge those who think that transcendence implies utter otherness and distance that would render God inactive or shielded from "human passions". Transcendence is affirmed in very strong terms by Origen. But transcendence is not the "departure" or "eclipse" of God. Rather transcendence of the relational Trinity paradoxically entrenches divine pity and presence. This echoes Yahweh who assimilates the epithets of West Semitic deities; it also echoes the qualities of *Mawu, Onyame, Amma, Chukwu, Olodumare* etc., of West African experience that have been integrated into the Christian faith.

The position of Origen illustrates a successful deployment and transformation of Greek categories. The atmosphere or philosophical culture that he breathed was subjected to Biblical revelation. The transcendence of the Trinitarian God has nothing in common with the distance of the rationally deduced God of Greek philosophical monotheism. Origen and other Fathers in the Catholic tradition opened up the Jewish-Christian tradition to Greek reality. But in contradistinction from Greek philosophical speculation God is not enclosed within a death dealing "dangerous purity"—the philosophical purity of exclusive monotheism. Rather as I noted in discussing the forging and maturing of Jewish-Christian monotheism—from monolatry to absolute monotheism of exilic and postexilic period, received into Christianity—Trinitarian relationality ensures the active presence and conjugal love relationship of the God of the covenant.[26] The God of the Bible who is Spirit-Life, whose Wisdom was "delighting in the human race," "places himself," for our sake, "in a condition that is incompatible with the grandeur of his nature."

Relationality is the core of Christian Trinitarian discourse. God's concern for us peaked in the Cross of Jesus Christ—a cross without a handle, the opposite of a briefcase, that Jesus the cross-bearer did not really know how to carry![27] Interpreting God's *passion* (Origen) or God's solidarity with us in the Cross has produced controversy over the *suffer-*

---

25. Origène, *Homélies Sur Ezéchiel*, VI, 6.

26. See Gesché, "Le Christianisme Comme Athéisme Suspensif," 206–8.

27. Koyama, *No Handle on the Cross*, 7.

ing of God. Greek Fathers like Gregory the Wonder-Worker who had Origen as teacher agree that the "unsuffering God suffers."[28] Thomas Weinandy, in *Does God Suffer?*, presents a good literature survey of the debate. Does God suffer in Jesus Christ? Is God's humanity manifest in Jesus? Is the impassibility of God possible? What does one make of the Son's fatherlessness (dereliction on the cross) and the Father's sonlessness? How does one come to terms with the God of OT and NT, very close to suffering people, a "Crucified God," and continue to claim that God does not suffer? Does love in God imply emotion? Does the experience of emotion implicate corporeality and must God be corporeal to feel love? The distressing human condition of suffering, which for Western philosophical theology peaked in the *Sho'ah* (Auschwitz), keeps alive this discussion in Trinitarian theology. The Rwandan genocide and the increased suffering and human helplessness in our world challenge the perception of God in Christianity and other religions. Can suffering be understandable alongside faith in a loving God? Moltmann, Jüngel, Whitehead, Hartshorne, Barth, and Bonhoeffer, contribute to the debate. Process theism affirms God's presence in events of human history and nature. Therefore, God suffers "the experiences of violence and pain of the earthly creatures."[29]

Origen while affirming that God suffers will not admit corporeality in God. Corporeality is the quality of creaturehood—human or angelic, before or after the Fall. That explains why the unique, authentic and only image of God is the Son of God, the Christ. He is the perfect image of God through his divinity—the invisible image of the invisible God. God who is invisible and incorporeal can only have an image that is invisible and incorporeal.[30] But Origen's closeness to Scripture led him to assert that "*God is not impassible.*" The views of J. Y. Lee is close to the Alexandrian Father: "Divine passibility was not the consequence of incarnation but the Incarnation was the consequence of divine passibility . . . The Incarnation is certainly not the beginning of divine passibility but the continuation of it with an intensification in time and space."[31] This sums up the position of partisans of the God who suffers in contemporary Western theology.

28. See the study of Figura, "Suffering of God in Patristic Theology."

29. Gnuse, *No Other Gods*, 305.

30. Crouzel, *Origène*, 130.

31. Lee, *God Suffers for Us*, 56. Cited by Weinandy, *Does God Suffer?* 14.

A few years ago, Adolphe Gesché revisited the issue of the Christian monotheistic faith, and took to task Aristotelian philosophical mono-theism that projects One God—abstract, absolute and insular. He opted for "relational" or even "relative" monotheism, judging the abstract and absolute philosophical monotheism heretical! Christians should practice "suspended atheism" with respect to such deity. Gesché even considers atheism as structural or internal to the Jewish-Christian tra-dition. Christian monotheism, rather than being the affirmation of the existence of only one God, is indeed the choice of only one God. Since choice embodies freedom to accept or to reject, Gesché argued, the Jewish and Christian traditions internally carry "suspended atheism." Relationality is therefore understandably structural to the Christian no-tion of God. The Jewish-Christian God is one and true only because God is relational. Gesché prefers "relative monotheism" to "relational monotheism" in order to confront head on the concept of "absolute." The Christian confessional (kerygmatic) monotheism rooted in the in-carnation and the divine economy affirms or confesses "God" and the "Human" in the same breath! Never one without the other! God's exis-tence is denied where the human is denied. Gesché concludes, "there is no God where the human is denied." Therefore, no abstract or absolute God, isolated and unrelated, exists![32]

Gesché's position is rooted in aspects of Biblical theology and at the same time grounded in dynamic Western philosophical traditions of phenomenology and existentialism. He appropriates Thomistic Trinitarian theology, but dissociates himself from Thomistic philosophy anchored on Aristotle. Gesché does not engage with Origen but he does plunge into Patristic memory to evoke Tertullian's use of Stoic categories to think God in the plural, to keep alive the dialectical tension God-Man, God for us, in the conception of the One True God of Christianity. God is True within this dialectical tension and false when the Human side of the dialectics is denied. From the perspective of West African Christian appropriation of the transcendent One God encountered in ATR, I find Gesché's position helpful to realign West African Christianity with the great Christian tradition following the insight of Origen. His emphasis on relationality is unimpeachable; but his choice of "relative" in opposi-tion to "absolute" monotheism leaves him open to criticism. His biblical

---

32. See Gesché, "Le Christianisme Comme Athéisme Suspensif," 204–5. See also Gesché, "Le Christianisme Comme Monothéisme Relatif."

theology represents more the OT period of increasing monolatry and propaganda for mono-Yahwism that characterized the Elijah circle, Hosea and Deuteronomistic history and reforms. It ignores the radical position of Deutero-Isaiah who, in the absolute weakness of the exile proclaimed Yahweh as the One and Only God and Israel as witness. I think the evocation of Origen who insists that the relational divine economy is *for us,* and the appropriation of Gesché's insight that "there is no God where the human is denied" represent interesting molding blocks for interpreting the Spirit-focused or Spirit-embedded West African Christianity.

Western philosophy and theology claim continuity with Graeco-Roman philosophical tradition. But in the West, Origen's trichotomist religious anthropology and contribution to Trinitarian contemplation, the human ascent to God through the Spirit, have not been valorized. His speculations on pre-existence based on Platonism were rejected by the Church Fathers. This should not diminish his contribution to the Christian tradition. Balthasar rightly stressed the enormous impact of Origen on his disciples and on the Patristic tradition, especially the general Patristic dependence on Origen's *ascensiones in corde.* To situate my appropriation of Origen's Trinitarian insight—by way of his trichotomist anthropology—I describe in the next chapter the multidimensional perception of the human person in West Africa and the crucial position of *spirit* in this anthropology. Then I analyze critically the West African Christian practice of life in the Spirit, who *descends upon* (possesses) the Christian, as entry into Trinitarian life, guided by Origen's analysis of the economy of the Spirit.

6

The Primacy of Spirit in the West African Access to the God of Jesus Christ

A Conversation with Origen of Alexandria

WEST AFRICAN ANTHROPOLOGY DISPLAYS a complex notion of the human person. This is the interpretive prism through which the experience and realization of the human individual's course in life, providentially bestowed by God, the Origin of origins, is grasped. While discussing five models of the West African worldview and the dynamic relationship between the transcendent One God, the deities, ancestors and humans (chapter 3), I alluded to the notion of person dominant in this region. To explore and critique the recapture or fusion into Christianity of the West African world vision by West African Christians, practicing and theoretically restructuring their faith in Jesus Christ, it is important to highlight the key elements of West African anthropology. This reveals amazing similarities with the religious anthropology of Origen, ranging from views on pre-existence to ubiquitous spirit-embedding in divine-human relations in the human world. These similarities aroused my interest in Origen's thought in a search for ways of realigning Christian belief and practice in West Africa with the Trinitarian tradition of the Great Church.

HUMAN PERSON AS COMPLEXITY OF RELATIONSHIP— PRESUPPOSITION FOR LIFE IN THE SPIRIT

The overriding characteristic in the way humans are perceived in West African societies is "relatedness". This is in harmony with the fundamental relationality (duality or multiplicity) that is the grand norm of *being* in the world. (I draw my examples from peoples living in Nigeria, Benin Republic, Togo, Ghana, and Cote d'Ivoire).

Sacred narratives recount the pre-existence of each human in the land of the dead, the land of spirits. Each human is indeed a "re-incarnation" into the human world through the creative act of a guardian personal *spirit* that embodies individual destiny. Destiny is assigned to each person by God or involves a choice by each pre-existent self. Asante, Ewe and Igbo mythologies therefore imply that humans are not pawns in the hands of fate or deities. The language of reincarnation is to be understood in West African rather than in Hindu terms. In West Africa reincarnation projects images of the "return" of aspects or qualities of the cherished dead. The personal *spirit—chi* (Igbo), *ori* (Yoruba), *kra* or *okra* (Asante), *se* (Adja-Fon) a*klama or kla* (Ewe)—specially assigned to each person "incarnating" into the human world, is crucial for the definition of the human person. *Chi* of the Igbo is a complex *spirit* dynamically related to individual destiny, and to the "returning" dead and to God himself. *Ori* of the Yoruba is highly symbolic and evokes a multiplicity of images. It is the human head and more than that! A profound spiritual reality that functions as the emplacement of the head, it is described as the interior, invisible, essential head, around which is focalized (fixed) the individual's destined and successful course in life. *Se* of the Fon is structurally related to prenatal "democratic" choice that each existent must follow in life; the choice is made before *Mawu,* also called *Segbo* (the Great *Se).* Similarly *aklama* (Ewe) determines a person's character, sees to one's wellbeing, can punish one who deviates from the character or destiny, and departs after death. Finally, *kra* or *okra* (Asante) is a personal spirit or spark coming from God, the "divine spark" inhabiting each person; it returns to God after death.[1]

1. The literature is abundant. See my summary in Uzukwu, *Listening Church,* ch. 3. For the Igbo, see Uzukwu, "Igbo World and Ultimate Reality and Meaning"; for Asante and Ewe, see Sarpong, "Individual, Community, Health and Medicine in African Traditional Religion"; and Fisher, *West African Religious Traditions,* 139–41; Eggen, "Parenté Du Dieu Qui Ne Tue Pas," 128–30; Meyer, *Translating the Devil,* 63–64; and Yoruba see, Laléyé, "Les Religion De L'afrique Noire," 666. The collective work on the notion of person in Africa contains entries on many West African peoples—*La Notion De La Personne En Afrique Noire*; See also Metuh, *African Religions in Western Conceptual Schemes,* ch. 7; Uchendu, *Igbo of South-Eastern Nigeria.*

The above fundamental spiritual linkage from pre-existence illustrates a key molding block for apprehending the human person in West Africa. The spirit dimension of the person linking the individual from pre-existence into life in this world is strategic to the notion of person. This *spirit* carries or reflects individual destiny providentially assigned by God, the origin of origins, and/or democratically chosen by each pre-existent. It constitutes the acknowledged and unacknowledged link with God in the evolving destiny of the individual or in questions asked about fortunes and misfortunes by the individual and community. One should not underestimate the cosmological and anthropological position of this structural determinant of destiny, the embedded spirit, the original gift and guardian from God that humanizes the person. The description of the human *pneuma* by Origen as life coming from God puts the West African principle on the same pedestal as the Greek *pneuma*—both are humanizing principles that come from and return to God: God is Spirit, "breath of Life." The ontological truth about this reality expressed in the language of myth is that each person is a unique creation, a unique concern of God, and an intimate of God the creator! This truth is generally internalized whether one believes or does not believe in pre-existence. The embedded *personal spirit* embodying goals (destiny) comes from God and confirms the fundamental goodness of created humans and of creation: "God saw everything that he had made, and indeed, it was very good" (Gen 1:31). Each human is accompanied by God from pre-existence, is provided with providential care to ensure the realization of the destined course in life. Achebe's comment is apposite,

> The idea of individualism is sometimes traced to the Christian principle that God created all men and consequently every one of them is presumed worthy in His sight. The Igbo do better than that. They postulate the concept of every man as both a unique creation and the work of a unique creator (*Chi*) which is as far as individualism and uniqueness can possibly go.[2]

The following Igbo aphorism neatly captures the situation: *otu nne na amu ma otu chi adi eke*—"people may be born of the same mother but are not created by the same *personal chi*." In other words the creative *personal spirit* assigned to each self by God, to humanize the person, differs from person to person. Consequently, destinies, or what God has

2. Achebe, "Chi in Igbo Cosmology" in Achebe, *Morning yet on Creation Day: Essays*, 98.

in store for humans, differ. Diversity or multiplicity is the rule; yet, all humans are at equal distance from God no matter the differences in parentage or genealogy. We shall have cause to refer to this as a fundament or presupposition for contextually appropriating Paul's and Origen's doctrine of the Holy Spirit linked to the human spirit: "When we cry, 'Abba! Father!' it is that very Spirit bearing witness with our spirit that we are children of God" (Rom 8:15b–16).

But there are other dimensions that should be mentioned before assessing the rational basis of the West African notion of person. These dimensions are oftentimes expressed as multiplicity of souls or life principles. For example, the Bambara of Mali have eight principles that are paired making up the human person. Pairing or twinning is basic to identity and definition of existence in the world. To be is to be multiple. The Asante reduce to seven the elements that converge for the emergence of a person. First, *mogya* (blood) is the fundament of the clan system in a matrilineal society. This matrilineal part of the person dies; i.e., disappears after death. Second, *okra* (the guardian personal spirit) is the humanizing and undying part of the person. It is similar to the Greek *pneuma*. Third, *sunsum* is a spiritual pre-existent principle that can be trained to be "heavy" instead of being "light" to resist malevolent witches. It is the individualizing principle in the human person, and is similar to the Greek *Nous*. Fourth, *honhon,* is the person considered as shadow that enables motion even when one is asleep. Fifth, *sasa* is an ethical component, a kind of underlying conscience. It is the avenging part of the person that prompts the confession of wrongs committed against others. Sixth, *ntoro* is a spiritual element transmitted by the father; it guides one until puberty. At puberty one reaches socially defined maturity and one's personal *ntoro* becomes dominant and displaces the father's spiritual element. Finally, *saman* is the form one assumes after death.[3] How rationally defensible is this anthropology in intercultural encounter?

RATIONAL BASIS OF WEST AFRICAN ANTHROPOLOGY

The late Meinrad Hebga, an informed student of the paranormal and a pastor involved in prayers of deliverance in Cameroon, Cote d'Ivoire

---

3. Sarpong, "Individual, Community, Health and Medicine in African Traditional Religion."

and elsewhere in Africa, attempted to demonstrate the rational basis of the underlying anthropology and psychology of person related to the paranormal phenomena common all over Africa. This involved explorations into the language, discourse and experience of possession, metamorphosis, and behavior generally classified as witchcraft. Elements that are crucial to his analysis include *body, breath, shadow, spirit, heart,* or any other variant concept. Fourteen ethnic groups from Central, South, East and West Africa are included in his survey. Hebga distanced himself from and at the same time positioned himself to dialogue with Thomistic-Aristotelian and other Western philosophical systems.[4]

First, Hebga noted the importance of *body* as the epiphany of the person—*nyuu* (Basaa), *nyolo* (Duala), or *nyol* (Ewondo) of Cameroon as well as *ñutila* (Ewe) of Ghana and Togo. *Body* is the living expression of the person—*eduwulu* of the Alladian of Cote d'Ivoire, *ara* and *aru* of Yoruba and Igbo of Nigeria. *Body* is the living person made visible as opposed to the non-visible aspects of the person.

Second, *breath* is the spirit or soul. This is not to be confused with sensible breath that is only the sign of *breath*. *Breath* is the person acting—the element responsible for autonomous motion; the subsisting subject to which actions are attributed. *Breath* is equivalent of *psyche* and *pneuma* (Greek), *anima* and *spiritus* (Latin—Hebga echoes Thomistic-Aristotelian psychology). Hebga did not extend his survey to Origen. Origen's trichotomist anthropology did not merge *psyche* and *pneuma*, rather he distinguished between *pneuma* (*spirit*), *nous* (*intellect*), and *psyche* (soul). After the Fall of Adam the *nous* merged with the human soul yielding dimensions of intellect and sensibility. Hebga also missed the subtlety of West African anthropology and psychology that distinguish between *spirit* as gift of God bearing destiny and the *soul* (responsible for individualization). Rather he merged the two. While the *spirit* as gift of God bearing destiny is not mentioned as a component of the person in Tempels' *Bantu Philosophy*, Middleton's study of the Lugbara of Uganda (Bantu or semi-Bantu ethnic nationality) recognized the "guardian spirit" (*adro*) and "personality" (*tali*) given by God at birth and associated with divine power; both entities go back to God after

---

4. Hebga, *La Rationalité D'un Discours Africain Sur Les Phénomènes Paranormaux,* 90. See other works of Hebga, *Sorcellerie, Chimère Dangereuse ?*; Hebga, *Sorcellerie Et Prière De Délivrance.*

death.[5] West Africans and Origen consider it foundational to distinguish between *spirit* and *soul*. It is interesting how in Bible translation and liturgy, nineteenth-century German Pietist missionaries to the Ewe of Ghana and Togo were struck with the subtle theology, anthropology and psychology embedded in traditional religion. They adopted *luvo*, which originally referred to "shadow," for "soul"; but they rejected *aklama*—the personal creative deity that embodies destinies, designated by divination on the day one is born, and materialised in figurines and worshipped. The connection of *aklama* with ritual and cult made its rejection by missionary Christianity imperative; this eliminated the confusion between Christian worship of God (*Mawu*) and Ewe worship of deities (*trowọ*). The guardian deity *aklama* was diabolized.[6] But Ewe Christians reinvented *aklama* in *gbọgbọ* (breath, a secular term acceptable to missionary Christianity), by extending its semantic range as we shall see below.

Third, *shadow*, not to be confused with the silhouette of the human body that is only the sign of *shadow*! *Shadow* is the being or person as invisible, as spiritual being. *Internal shadow* or *shadow-soul* is strategic to Hebga's analysis. It is characterized by mobility, agility, and mastery of space. It is immaterial or spiritual because freed from weight, grasp or constriction by the senses. Consequently, the *shadow-soul* could leave the sleeping body and wander off, as in dreams, manifesting subsistence or existential autonomy. According to Hebga "the presence and action of a person are not circumscribed by his body, by the surrounding space, by his voice or even by the range of his sight."[7] Depending on one's force or power one can always overcome spatial limitations and spread out. If "soul contains the body to effect the union" (Thomas Aquinas), Hebga insists that *soul-shadow* is the principle of empowerment for self-deployment beyond the body, enabling the person to act beyond corporeal spatial constriction. However, this component of person that is crucial to the language of witchcraft remains a capacity, a virtuality that can be actualized or activated for ill or for good. The negative activation of *shadow-soul* will be further explored below.

---

5. See the discussion of Tempels and Middleton in Metuh, *Comparative Studies of African Traditional Religions*, 172–73.

6. See Meyer, *Translating the Devil*, 79.

7. Hebga, *La Rationalité D'un Discours Africain Sur Les Phénomènes Paranormaux*, 114; the detailed explanation of these elements of the person is on 95–116.

The above are the principal, most common, constituents of the human person, the basis of African anthropology and psychology as presented by Hebga. West Africans will be generally at home with Hebga's analysis of *Shadow*. His insistence on *shadow-soul*, a component of the individual with *breath*, is an interesting presupposition to appreciate not only the language of witchcraft, but also the language of the *Holy Spirit's* manifestation, indwelling or embedding through "possession" or "seizure," enabling those gifted or chosen to receive revelation through dreams, visions and auditions. The missionary impact on Ewe (Ghana and Togo) led to the adoption of *luvo* (shadow) as "soul." This did not eliminate its meaning as *shadow* that has the power to move about in dreams—to attain invisible realms accessible only during sleep. Its activation for good and for evil enables the Ewe to distinguish between *luvoagbeto* (soul or shadow of life) and *luvokuto* (soul or shadow of death). Hebga's choice of the dynamic elements, *breath* and *shadow*, as key to African psychology is convincing. He rejects the adoption of *soul-spirit* by African Thomist-Aristotelians like Kagamé, Nimisi or Guissimana. He argues convincingly that *Shadow* explains sufficiently what these authors classify under *spirit* (ghost) in some Bantu traditions. These authors hold that the personality of *soul-spirit* is fully activated after the separation from the body. Their dualistic perception of person, body-soul, heavily influenced by the Thomistic-Aristotelian system, fails to account for the flexibility that underlies possession, metamorphosis, bewitching, etc., which dominates the discourse on witchcraft and mysticism. Furthermore, African Thomist-Aristotelians are inconsistent. When it suits them they abandon dualism and fall back, without apologies, into a pluralistic (African) psychology of the person.[8]

On the other hand, Hebga's rejection of the term "double," as in the Egyptian *ka*, is less convincing from a West African standpoint. According to him the term is used only by non-Africans in describing African psychology. His analysis does not scrutinize the pre-existent self and the guardian *spirit* embodying one's destined course in life. Destiny dominates the concept and experience of life in West Africa. The guardian *spirit* is independent of, and yet intimately related to the person. This

---

8. Ibid., chapter VI. The works cited by Hebga are Kagamé, *La Philosophie Bantu Rwandaise De L'etre*; Kagamé, *La Philosophie Bantu Comparée*; also Nimisi, *L'homme Dans L'univers Bantu*; and Guisimana, «L'homme Selon La Philosophie Pende.» For the Ewe, see Meyer, *Translating the Devil*, 64.

personal spirit is certainly close to the Egyptian *ka*. The radical rejection of *aklama* by the German Pietist mission had enormous impact on the Ewe and presents a major example of imaginative creativity in pneumatology. *Aklama*—the personal guardian spirit—determines one's character, wellbeing, fortunes and misfortunes. It cannot be wished away. The Protestants imbued a secular term *gbɔgbɔ* (breath) with the characteristics of a spiritual reality to represent the human spirit, Holy Spirit and evil spirit. The resultant trichotomist anthropology was acceptable to Christians—*ñutila* (body), *luvo* (soul—originally shadow), and *gbɔgbɔ* (breath and also a person's spirit). Meyer comments, "Many historical documents of discussions between Ewe evangelists and non-Christians reveal how important the *aklama* was for the latter, who, taking up the Christian terminology, even called them their personal *mawu* [personal God]."[9] This is not surprising. The neighbouring Akan call *okra* or *kra* the "spark of God." The rejection and diabolisation of *aklama* ended in a reinvention of *aklama* as *gbɔgbɔ* by Ewe Christians through the expansion of the semantic range of *gbɔgbɔ* (breath, spirit). "For Ewe Christians, *gbɔgbɔ*, instead of aklama, became responsible for a person's fate. Like *aklama*, *gbɔgbɔ* is considered to have a decisive influence on one's life. But unlike *aklama*, one's *gbɔgbɔ* is not conceived as a separate, independent entity, but rather as an open space in the mind which can be filled by Mawu's spirit or an evil one."[10] The split within the Evangelical Presbyterian Church in Peki (Ghana and Togo) while arising from no clear doctrinal reasons had clear ritual reasons. Both the parent missionary church and the independent churches recognized the presence of the Devil, transformed into the prince of Ewe deities (this is similar to the transformation of Baal to Beelzebub in the prophetic struggle with Canaanite deities).[11] But while the parent missionary churches simply named and then ignored the devils, the splinter ones claimed the experience of actual possession and invested energy in exorcisms—dislodging the devil dwelling in the person.

Having sketched the West African anthropology and psychology, I focus on the procedure for living in God or living in holiness among West African Christians and its Trinitarian dimensions. Life in God is through the Holy Spirit: God is Spirit, is (breath of) Life. This is dis-

9. Meyer, *Translating the Devil*, 79.

10. Ibid., 145.

11. Gnuse, *No Other Gods*, 77ff.

played in the practice and discourse of AICs and Charismatic movements; and it is intimately related to the ATR conceptual framework. In the ATR pattern of mystical experience the initiate is *possessed* and *empowered* by a deity for the common good; in AICs and Charismatic movements the Holy Spirit takes *possession* of Christians for the common good. The strategic position of deities and the Holy Spirit helps one to appreciate that pneumatology is the privileged entry point into Trinitarian theology. Since the air that AICs and Charismatic movements breathe is suffused with the ATR and Biblical universe, I argue that deities are radically transformed into the dimensions of the One Holy Spirit of God. This has happened before! In the process of the evolution of Yahweh, the Jewish religious imagination creatively realigned the Canaanite deities, *deber* (plague) and *resep* (pestilence) into Yahweh's bodyguards (Hab 3:5), and converted *tôb* and *hesed* ("goodness" and "loyalty"—Ps 23:6) into virtues. Even the image of Dame Wisdom in Proverbs 8 could be a strategic reduction of the powerful Asherah and/ or "Queen of Heaven" into subordinates of Yahweh, primordial creatures of Yahweh. Furthermore, in Origen the Word/Son is the sum total of all virtues, and the Holy Spirit is the sum total of charisms. I believe the heart of West African Christianity is going in the right direction; it only needs realignment.

MYSTIC EMPOWERMENT BY THE HOLY SPIRIT: FACILITATING ACCESS TO THE TRIUNE GOD

What is inescapable in Origen's Trinitarian theology, in accord with the Catholic tradition, is that the transcendent God is fundamentally relational. The *Father,* origin of origins, who sends the *Son* and the *Holy Spirit* are intimately related. This relational divine economy according to Origen is *for us.* The Trinity is in relation to us in the descending order of persons—Father-Son-Spirit. We connect with or ascend to God (holiness—*ascensiones in corde*) by being drawn into the Holy Spirit through the *spirit,* the human *pneuma,* embedded in each and every one of us.

The Christian recapture of this Trinitarian life in West Africa, as recorded and lived in communities outside the control or scrutiny of the mainline missionary churches, demonstrate an access to God enjoyed pre-eminently through the Holy Spirit for the overall good (health-wholeness) of the community. AICs, new African Pentecostalism, Catholic and Protestant Charismatic movements overtly display life in

God as life in the Spirit. Trinitarian theology, discourse, and practice of the mainline churches do not overtly depart from the received tradition transmitted by missionary Christianity. AICs and Charismatic movements presuppose the Trinitarian faith of mainline Christianity, but they fundamentally link the process of experiencing God with the pattern of access to God in West African religion. Their viewpoint of living the Christian faith, of being drawn into the life of the relational Trinity, displays a creative engagement of Biblical narrative with the typical West African anthropology and psychology.

The common element that researchers have highlighted about AICs, an element shared by the new African Pentecostalism and the Charismatic movements of the mainline churches, is the experience of the *overwhelming power* of the Holy Spirit. The emphasis on *power,* very attractive to sociologists of the Weberian school, explains the exaggerations and errors in AICs. Some are even accused of sorcery and possessing charms in search of power. This emphasis on power also led to the confusion of AICs with the new African Pentecostalism of American inspiration, ruled by "powerful" men and women and proclaiming "prosperity message" or "power Christianity." One cannot accept the errors nor condone the exaggerations of AICs. But it is important to underline their positive experience of the *overwhelming power of the Holy Spirit.* AICs are "Spirit-churches": "With regard to spiritual beings other than God, the Holy Spirit is the most powerful of all existing spirits with an enormous capability to cure, heal, provide fortune, good health and insure victory over malignant enemies and evil forces."[12] The pre-eminence of the Holy Spirit is stated in the 1996 AICs' manifesto: "*The renewal of the Holy Spirit* is continuous with and greater than the spirits around us. Our dependence on the Holy Spirit for protection from evil forces has liberated us to share with others our freedom from fear, a very enticing proposition in the African context, as well as in the rest of the world."[13] The strategic economy of the Holy Spirit is for the "common good." Those "possessed" or "seized" by the Holy Spirit in the *Aladura* (prayer) Churches of Nigeria act with the Spirit's "secret and sacred power" (*ase*

---

12. See Mbiti, *Bible and Theology in African Christianity*, 142, citing the work of Kenneth Ennang among the Annang (Nigeria).

13. The manifesto is recorded in Pobee and Ositelu II, *African Initiatives in Christianity*, 71. Anderson develops AICs' theology in Anderson, *African Reformation*.

in Yoruba ancestral religious parlance). They are *elemi* (mediums), the Holy Spirit's "mouth." According to Olayiwola,

> The fact that the *elemi* attribute their "power" to the Holy Spirit suggests that they believe in the Trinity. None of them mentioned explicitly the name of Jesus Christ. This, however, does not imply that Jesus is unimportant to them, but that in their calling the Spirit predominates.[14]

The term 'medium' is an approximation. Roger Bastide rightly insists that African mysticism is not to be confused with spiritualism; it is a distinctive contextual approach to the sacred that is the domain of religion.[15] (I shall return to this later when discussing West African mysticism of descent.) Possessed of the power of the Holy Spirit, the *elemi* predict or identify sickness in people through dreams, vision and audition; they accomplish faith healing, solve human existential problems, and bring success to the business of clients. The AICs manifesto is clear: "*Spiritual healing*, in most of the AICs, is in a literal sense, the principal focus of our worship and liturgical practices, being the main cause of our impressive growth."[16]

The "implicit" Trinitarian theology underlying AICs' focus on the Holy Spirit can be supported or clarified by resorting to Origen's argumentation on the immediacy and importance of the Holy Spirit to the saints. In Origen, the Spirit's operation, which does not displace God the Father or the Christ, follows the descending order of Trinitarian activity towards us. In the AICs, empowerment is from the Holy Spirit, but the sacred names of Jesus and the diverse epithets of God (drawn especially from the OT) are uttered during ecstatic experience.

My *provisional* probing of the experience of being drawn into the life of the Triune God through the economy of the Holy Spirit will follow two channels of theological reasoning. First, in the rest of this chapter, I shall discuss or probe the identity of the Holy Spirit experienced in West African Christianity and its relation to the multiple ATR deities. This is

14. Olayiwola, "Aladura Christianity in Dialogue with African Traditional Religion," 354; see also Olayiwola, "Interaction of African Independent Churches with Traditional Religions in Nigeria."

15. Bastide and Parrinder expressed similar views on the issue in discussion following the paper of Parrinder, "Le Mysticisme Des Médiums En Afrique Occidentale," esp. 138–42.

16. Pobee and Ositelu II, *African Initiatives in Christianity*, 71.

important for appreciating the operation of the Holy Spirit for individual holiness and the bestowal of the Spirit for community tasks. Second, in the next chapter, I focus on the better-known and better-discussed public or overt empowerment by the Spirit for the "common good". This naturally includes the mystical experience of "possession" by the Holy Spirit through trance, for the common good. But it will also include forays into the shadow side of mystical possession—the dangerous possession by/of mystical power (witchcraft and sorcery) that must be exorcised through the ministry of those powerfully gifted by the Holy Spirit. In my discussion of both the implicit and explicit Trinitarian theology circulating among Christians in West Africa, I affirm consonance between Origen's language and West African practice and highlight where Origen helps theological discussion to move forward in the region.

"THE HOLY SPIRIT IS CONTINUOUS WITH AND GREATER THAN THE SPIRITS"— TRINITARIAN ECONOMY OR PROVIDENCE

AICs serenely declare, "*The renewal of the Holy Spirit* is continuous with and greater than the spirits around us." Here I concern myself with two issues, (1) the relationship between the *personal spirit* (gift of God, guardian and embodiment of destiny), and the Christian Holy Spirit, and (2) the relationship between the Holy Spirit and multiplicity of deities responsible for orientating, governing and directing human destiny as well as administering the world for the overall good (health-wholeness) of human society.

Personal Spirit, Holy Spirit and the Realization of Individual Destiny

Each individual's uniquely destined course in life, embodied or transmitted through the *personal spirit* specially assigned by God to the individual at creation (called *chi, ori, okra, se,* or *aklama)*, makes the Holy Spirit-focus of AICs understandable and theologically defensible. In the language of Origen the Holy Spirit connects with us and we are drawn to the Holy Spirit and the Triune God through the personal *pneuma*—the personal spirit (*chi, ori, okra, se,* or *aklama*)—that is independent of the person and returns to God in the unfortunate situation of the person going to Gehenna. The Holy Spirit is attracted to our *spirit* and attracts us like magnet; this explains the embedding of the Holy Spirit in the

Christian. But can we possibly say that the Holy Spirit is close to our *chi, ori, okra, se,* or *aklama*—the embedded *personal spirit* that embodies individual destiny, materialized in icons or figurines, and recognized through ritual and cult? Is this theologically defensible? No, and yes! I argue that the understanding of *personal spirit* (*chi, ori, okra, se,* or *aklama*) characteristic of ATR cosmology and West African anthropology, and presupposed by West African Christianity, has gone through a radical transformation precisely because of the impact of Christianity.

The decision taken by Pietist missionaries in Togo and Ghana to diabolize the deities is replicated in other missionary denominational churches. Only God, the "Supreme Being," clothed with the characteristics of the God that Jesus Christ called *Abba*—*Chukwu, Olodumare, Onyame, Mawu, Amma*—is adopted. But since the air that West African Christians breathe is suffused with ATR and Biblical cosmology, Christians must come to terms with and make sense of the new faith in their context. The dimension of the ancestral cosmology that refuses to go away hinges on destiny—the economy of the *personal spirit.* The emphasis of Christianity on the One and Only God put pressure on Ewe ATR experts; they transformed the *personal spirit* (*aklama*) into the Spirit of *Mawu* (God)—while of course worshipping other deities (*trowo*). Ewe Christians, on their part, adopted the semantic evolution of a secular term *gbogbo* that missionary Christianity imbued with a spiritual meaning—it meant mere breath, but also the human spirit, and is applied to the Spirit of God (*Mawu*). But in response to the contextual pressure around destiny, that falls within the economy of the ATR *personal spirit* (*aklama*), Ewe Christians expanded the semantic range of the Christian *gbogbo* (*breath,* human spirit and God's Spirit) to embrace destiny. *Breath* however is not an independent entity like the *personal spirit* (*aklama*). It is conceived "as an open space in the mind," fundamentally oriented to be filled by God's Holy Spirit (*Gbogbo Kokoe*) or by Satan's evil spirit (*gbogbo vowo*). "Through introduction of the term *gbogbo* in a suprasensory sense the linguistic base was laid for a theory of spirit possession which integrated both non-Christian spiritual beings and the Spirit of the Christian *Mawu* as comparable, though conflicting, entities, thereby opposing them on a single, spiritual battlefield."[17]

The imaginative creativity of Ewe Christianity avoids syncretism; it accords no independent existence to the *personal spirit* and puts an

17. Meyer, *Translating the Devil,* 146.

end to sacrifices made to *aklama*. At the same time, Ewe Christianity assimilates the characteristics of this transformed ancestral religion and cosmology. The level of creativity involved in forging convergence between Ewe Christianity and ancestral cosmology could be appreciated when one reflects on the choice of the expression "open space in the mind" to transform *aklama* into a Christian quality. It is more interesting when links with Yoruba cosmology are indicated. Ewe and Yoruba, despite the distance between Nigeria and Togo/Ghana, are close cousins. Historically the Ewe migrated from Abeokuta, Yoruba territory of Nigeria. The Yoruba equivalent for *aklama* is *ori*—the *personal spirit* that has dual residence—partly in God's house and partly fixed in the head of the individual. *Ori* is the head and more than the head; it is the space for the head. It is correctly called the "emplacement of the head"; the interior, invisible, essential head where possession by a particular deity, *orisa*, is localized. Ewe Christianity denied a separate existence to *aklama/ori* but endowed *breath* (*gbogbo*, as human spirit) with additional quality—"open space in the mind"—comparable to the Yoruba *ori* that creates space for the emplacement of the spiritual head that is "mounted" or "entered" by the possessing spirit.

This space, which can be filled by God's Spirit, as well as by an evil spirit, assimilates qualities of ATR into Christianity but denies ATR deities "air time." Negatively, figurines and particular cults are eliminated. Positively, God's predetermined plan for each human, God's endowment of each human with "creative space," with the palace of freedom "in the mind" for the indwelling of God's Holy Spirit that descends, ensures the realization of one's destined course in life. This "open space in the mind," which radically replaces the "spark of God" as an *entity* with independent existence, retains the *quality* of "spark of God" and attracts the descending Spirit of God that magnetizes the person. One's intellectual soul (*nous*), the hegemonic principle (Origen), has the added advantage of being drawn, thanks to the "spark of God", towards the Holy Spirit, enabling the person to become totally spiritual. Through the mediation of the "open space in the mind," the soul groans "with eager longing" (cf. Rom 8:19, 22) for the indwelling Holy Spirit; the inferior dimensions of the soul (the seat of passions) are effectively consumed by the *personal spirit* quality under the magnet of the Holy Spirit that makes Christians adopted children of God. Helped by Origen and Paul, one is able to identify the full effect of the impact of the indwelling Holy Spirit on humans through the *personal spirit*:

> For all who are led by the Spirit of God are children of God. For you did not receive a spirit of slavery to fall back into fear, but you have received a spirit of adoption. When we cry, "Abba! Father"! it is that very Spirit bearing witness with our spirit that we are children of God, and if children, then heirs, heirs of God and joint heirs with Christ—if, in fact, we suffer with him so that we may also be glorified with him. (Rom 8:14–17)

The above description of the novelty or qualitatively different approach to the experience of Trinitarian providential economy, founded on the anthropology of the *personal spirit,* is theologically defensible. The *pneuma* that is structural to Origen's religious anthropology is displayed in a mysticism of ascent, the imitation (*homoiôsis*) or the "following" of God that is of the very nature of humans. Christianity introduces a qualitative and not a quantitative difference to this mysticism.[18] Similarly, the active realization of one's destined course in life in West Africa is through the *personal spirit*, the humanizing guardian, companion and indwelling protective Gift. This *personal spirit* ensures communion with God who is Life or Spirit. This *spirit* that is unique in each individual is the bedrock of divine companionship, the indwelling Providence in each person whether the person is Christian or not.[19] The radical Christian reinterpretation of the *personal spirit,* which passed through a process of demonization followed by the assimilation of its characteristics, introduces a qualitative difference and creates an acceptable Christian enabling condition or environment for life in God.

What Ewe Christianity calls "open space in the mind" is God's providential care for each human that dates from all eternity. To adapt Origen—the Eternal Father who never at any time began to be Father, knew eternally that humans will be created and carefully provided for. One does not have to affirm pre-existence to realize the wonder of our being and the eternity of God's plan for us. Astonishing indeed is this creative and providential care that one chants in Ps 139!

> O LORD, you have searched me and known me. . . . For it was you who formed my inward parts; you knit me together in my

18. See Crouzel, *Origène*, 136.

19. See Uzukwu, "Le Destin De La Personne Humaine Dans Une Religion Africaine."

> mother's womb. I praise you, for I am fearfully and wonder-
> fully made. Wonderful are your works; that I know very well.
> My frame was not hidden from you, when I was being made in
> secret, intricately woven in the depths of the earth. Your eyes be-
> held my unformed substance. In your book were written all the
> days that were formed for me, when none of them as yet existed.
> (Ps 139:1, 13–16)

Olaudah Equiano, the first Igbo and one of the first African slaves to write on antislavery (1789), narrated his childhood experience in a language suffused with Biblical as well as Nigerian cosmology captured by the term "providence." His frequent use of "Providence" (always capitalized), destiny and fate, the "kind and unknown hand of the Creator (who in every deed leads the blind in a way they know not)," captures the Igbo cosmo-vision that is very close and not antithetical to the Biblical imagery.[20] Equiano's language contains an implicit theology of the Trinity that is hard to understand outside the experience of the *personal spirit, chi* in Igbo cosmology. Edwards and Shaw insist that although *chi* is "invisible" in Equiano's narrative, "it would have formed an integral part of the conceptual framework through which he gave meaning to his later experiences." These experiences are dressed in the following or similar language, "the awful interposition of Providence," "a singular act of Providence," "the particular interposition of Heaven," "what all powerful fate had determined for me," etc.[21] In the opening chapter of his *Narrative* Equiano stated the *personal chi* conviction, expressed and interpreted from the Christian perspective:

> I believe there are few events in my life which have not happened
> to many; it is true the incidents of it are numerous, and, did I con-
> sider myself an European, I might say my sufferings were great;
> but when I compare my lot with that of most of my country-
> men, I regard myself as a *particular favorite of heaven*, [Equiano's
> emphasis] and acknowledge the mercies of Providence in every
> occurrence of my life.[22]

---

20. Equiano, *Interesting Narrative of the Life of Olaudah Equiano*, 60. Paul Edwards and Rosalind Shaw were struck by the frequent evocation of Providence in Equiano and they related it to *chi* in Igbo cosmology—Edwards and Shaw, "Invisible *Chi* in Equiano's *Interesting Narrative*."

21. Edwards and Shaw, "Invisible *Chi* in Equiano's *Interesting Narrative*," 148.

22. Equiano, *Interesting Narrative of the Life of Olaudah Equiano*, 33.

West Africans take religion, communication with Spirit or life in the Spirit as a given. For Christians, the indwelling *personal spirit* (*chi, ori, okra, aklama,* or *human pneuma* that is *life,* according to Origen), the open space in the mind that is now denied independent existence, attracts and is attracted to God's Spirit. One receives the revelation of God in Jesus Christ through this providential predisposition, the "open space in the mind," the indwelling gift or the *personal spirit* through which the economy of the Holy Spirit radiates. This experience is accessible to every Christian, just as it is accessible in ATR to every human coming from pre-existence into this world in the power of the *personal spirit.*

The attention drawn to the *human pneuma* by Origen and to the *personal spirit* by West Africans describes the same reality in/from different anthropological perspectives. In Trinitarian theological discourse the intimacy with God's Spirit accessed through the providential *personal spirit* shows that the Christian faith introduces a qualitative modification of the traditional beliefs and anthropology instead of introducing quantitatively something totally new. Of course the fundamental quantitative and qualitative novelty is Jesus, the Crucified-Risen Christ. The fundamental qualitative modification is the conversion and assimilation of the *personal spirit* into God's providential indwelling that guides each Christian. There is no question of a special cult of the *personal spirit* (*chi, ori, okra, aklama, se*) as was the case in ATR. Rather God who gives life through the indwelling *personal spirit* enables (sanctifies) each human, through the economy of the Holy Spirit, to realise his/her destined course in life embedded in the *human pneuma* or *personal spirit.* Ewe Christianity and AICs insist on "prayer" as constant nourishment of the indwelling of the Holy Spirit to keep evil spirits at bay. Without Prayer one's "open space in the mind" becomes a "waterless" region, a good "resting place" for an evil spirit that could bring "along seven other spirits more evil than itself" (Matt 12:43, 45). Origen and West Africans chant: Life is a spiritual combat. AICs could justifiably affirm, "*The renewal of the Holy Spirit* is continuous with and greater than the spirits around us." What is the relationship between the Holy Spirit and the "spirits around us"?

THE HOLY SPIRIT AS THE SUM TOTAL OF CHARISMS (ORIGEN) INDENTIFIED WITH GENERALIZED ONE HOLY SPIRIT IN WEST AFRICAN CHRISTIANITY

The multiple deities in West African religion, each with given areas of competence, have therapeutic impact on the community. The therapeutic principle is assumed and transformed in the AICs that invest in rituals "to cure, heal, provide fortune, good health and insure victory over malignant enemies and evil forces."[23] One needs to repeat that the adoption of the Biblical and West African worldview was the practice of the missionary churches as well as all other Christian churches in this region; of course with varying degrees of caution if not suspicion. Mbiti and Sanneh have argued that the assumption of the "indigenous name of God"—e.g., *Olodumare, Amma, Onyame, Chukwu,* and even the dual-gendered *Mawu-Lisa*—with the underlying philosophical, economic, and socio-political implications "represented the indigenous theological advantage vis-à-vis missionary initiative" (Sanneh): "Western missionaries did not introduce God to Africa—rather, it was God who brought them to Africa, as carriers of news about Jesus Christ" (Mbiti).[24] No one will dispute that Bible translation stamped this appropriation with its authority.

The matter is viewed with greater reserve, suspicion and antagonism when one comes to consider the deities. They were generally demonized by missionary Christianity, and this procedure is more or less followed by their successors. Missionary Catholicism had the advantage of being ritualistic, bringing it closer to West African ritual attitude. At the opposite end of the spectrum, the new African Pentecostalism is intolerant of anything related to ancestral culture. They denounce any "covenanting with ancestral spirits" radically opposed to "covenanting with Christ," this covers whatever has anything to do with extended family structures, ancestors and deities. They also reject ritual objects like candles and holy water associated with some mainline missionary churches. But they indulge in exorcisms and faith healing.

---

23. See Mbiti, *Bible and Theology in African Christianity*, 142, citing the work of Kenneth Ennang among the Annang (Nigeria).

24 Sanneh, *Whose Religion Is Christianity?* 31–32. Mbiti, *Bible and Theology in African Christianity*, 11. See also Mbiti, "Encounter of Christian Faith and African Religion."

Charismatic movements that recognize the ministry of gifted members of the Christian community—revealed especially through speaking in tongues and other charisms that show the power of the Holy Spirit for the common good—reject the deities, but they use rituals. The AICs are closest to the ground in assimilating but transforming the ministries that are connected with the deities. They reinterpret the services (e.g., healing) rendered by the elect of the deities as the sphere or the economy of the Holy Spirit. Consciously or unconsciously they clothe the Holy Spirit with the qualities of the deities. Canaanite deities, as noted above, were radically reinterpreted in a similar way and integrated into the personality of the One and Only Yahweh. Can we justify AICs' reinterpretation and integration of deities as dimensions of God's Holy Spirit, while eliminating the ambivalent and evil aspects associated with the deities? Is the teaching of Origen on charisms as the sum total of the Holy Spirit helpful here? I first focus on the advantages and pitfalls of the integration of the characteristics of the deities into the Holy Spirit. Then I explore the actual practice of ministry of those "possessed" by God's Holy Spirit that is anchored both on the model handed down by the Bible and the ancestral cult of the deities.

Forging the Image of God's Holy Spirit— Assimilating Qualities of Deities

The West African context poses serious problems because it is rooted in a worldview that is suffused with, and related to, a multiplicity of divine beings that are still active in the world where Christians live. (Togo is dominantly ATR inclined.) The deities are ambivalent—they have both positive and negative attributes. How does one theologically defend the affirmation contained in the AICs' manifesto, "*The renewal of the Holy Spirit* is continuous with and greater than the spirits around us"? While the indwelling Holy Spirit protects Christians "from evil forces," the status of "spirits around us" is not clear. Have these been reduced to angels and demons?[25]

25. See Sarpong, "Libation and Inculturation in Africa," 334–35. Peter K. Sarpong, the Archbishop of Kumasi Diocese (Ghana), clarified his position on the thorny ritual of libation that involved on the one hand the invocation of God, deities and ancestors to bless the community and on the other curses against enemies as is common in African and biblical prayers. In Sarpong's view, "libation is an institution of our fore-fathers that should not be condemned." Nothing in the prayer of libation indicates diminishing the power of God. However if "some people object to parts of it, then the simplest thing is

The AICs' assumptions and responses are so close to ancestral cosmology that they arouse suspicion of mainline churches and lead to outright condemnation as paganism and superstition by neo-Pentecostalism. For example, the *Celestial Church* in the Republic of Benin demonizes *vodhun* (ATR spirits), but at the same time proceeds to assume the discourse and practice patterns of *vodhun* in the name of the Christian Holy Spirit. The AIC position could be justified theologically. There is an interesting similarity between AICs' logic and the procedure adopted by the Fathers of the Church in the development of sacramental theology. (I will turn to this later as a prop for probing the theology that is emerging from the AICs' assumptions and theories.)

The *Celestial Church of Christ* denounces *vodhun* or the cult of ancestral deities as diabolical. It states that ancestral worship has no effect for Christians and rejects the pertinence of the theology of *vodhun* for Christians. Furthermore, the initiation ritual of those called into the therapeutically oriented Christian ministry of vision/audition is embedded in the language and practice of the Jewish-Christian Scriptures. Up to this point the boundaries with *vodhun* are clear; there are no camouflages. However, in detailing its church ministries, the *Celestials* adopt *vodhun* ritual architecture; and in interpreting the Jewish-Christian Scriptures and tradition, they assume *vodhun* ritology and co-opt the universe of *vodhun*. This is denounced by neo-Pentecostalism as "covenanting with ancestral spirits"! Mainline churches highly reserved over experiences of "possession," trance, and the use of ritual objects like multicolored candles, fruits, oils, water, the use of beaches, sea-sand etc., are suspicious of these practices. However, I do not see any clear theological error in *Celestials'* approach. The exaggerations on details need only be realigned by stronger theological education. It cannot be compared to the recent Kimbanguist error of interfering with the persons of the Trinity.

The advantage *Celestials* have in being rooted in the Bible is that only one Holy Spirit descends on the elect and endows the community with gifts or charisms hitherto refracted in individualized *vodhun* or

---

to leave out those parts." On the question of deities that are mentioned while pouring the libation, to which Christians raise serious objections he says, "In place of the gods and the divinities, we might also substitute the Saints and the Angels in globo, specifically or individually, by mentioning names as we do in libation." Sarpong will therefore approve of the reduction of the divinities into saints and angels, or even converting the divinities into epithets or qualities of God.

deities. Scripture as rule of faith protects the *Celestials* from error with regard to key referents of the Christian revelation. Denying space to individual *vodhun* puts them alongside Paul's pattern of resolving the conflict at Colossae: "See to it that no one takes you captive through philosophy and empty deceit, according to human tradition, according to the elemental spirits of the universe, and not according to Christ" (Col 2:8). *Celestials* therefore demonize *vodhun* and denounce any of their members who continue to participate in any way at all in the cult of *vodhun* as being gravely in error. Ewe Christians did the same in respect to *aklama* (*personal spirit*) as an independent deity; they absorbed the concept and characteristics of *aklama* into the new Christian definition of the human *personal spirit* (*gbọgbọ*), that enables "the open space in the mind" for the indwelling of the Holy Spirit.

The denunciation of *vodhun* or *aklama* is a new element in West African religious practice introduced by exclusivist and militant Christianity. It is foreign to ATR. The familiar West African procedure is to withdraw support for and services from a deity that no longer per- forms, or to expel and set ablaze the symbols of a deity that leaves "what he was called to do and did other things" like killing the members of the community.[26] There is no doubt that Christians, by the nature of con- stituting an alternative community with an alternative narrative, must set boundaries with the ATR cult. Not only evangelicalism but also all Christian churches practice this. Nevertheless, the existence of *vodhun* and their independent operations are not in doubt. *Vodhun,* far from being "fetish," is rather a genuine experience of the sacred at the heart of every Beninois and Togolese, while magic and witchcraft are only de- generate aspects of this religion.[27]

Celestials and other Christians are theologically correct in deny- ing *vodhun* "airtime." *Celestials* thereby are not syncretistic. But there are slippery areas of practice that call for caution. In a pictorial and journalistic narrative of the practice of religion in Benin Republic, Henning Christoph and Hans Oberländer drew attention to the homol- ogy between the maps of the universe utilised by the competing *vodhun* practitioners and the *Celestial Church of Christ*. White robed *Celestials* with blaring loudspeakers denounce *vodhun* as satanic; they instruct the populace to abandon *vodhun* for salvation in Christ. On the other

26. Cf. Achebe, *Arrow of God*, 180.

27. Cf. Agossou, *Christianisme Africain*, 82–83.

hand the white robed *vodhun* clergy are discrete. They attack neither Moslems nor Christians! They know too well that both groups come back to them, if only at nightfall. Christoph and Oberländer were struck by the similarity between *vodhun* clergy and the *Celestials—white robes* as dress, imposition of severe taboos and laws regulating details of all aspects of life, and the assumption that divine message is transmitted to the faithful through trance.[28] Both are drawing from the same well. This explains the dismay of Yoruba *orisa* worshippers over the "harsh polemics" of nineteenth-century missionary Christianity. In Abeokuta (1853), Christian evangelists were warned to desist from castigating traditional religion—"Everyone should abide in whatever religion he chooses to follow."[29] They all presuppose the same universe even if they color it differently.

The negative evaluation of AICs by neo-Pentecostals who accuse them of superstition, syncretism and paganism is certainly exaggerated. Pentecostalism also presupposes the ancestral map of the universe but colors it in absolute negative terms.[30] Neo-Pentecostal membership is drawn from the educated youth (university graduates). They share the bias of missionary churches with regard to AICs but also prefer the modern international style "inspired by marketing techniques." They insist that members should be exorcised from both AICs and "dead orthodox churches" (e.g., Roman Catholicism).[31] But the truth is that between *vodhun* and AICs there is a major difference—while *vodhun* embrace and expand the ancestral cosmology, AICs like other Christian groups combine the Biblical and ancestral cosmologies. The *Celestials* adopt openness in reference to the experience of faith in Christ; this experience is accessible to all. They boldly and radically convert the ancestral world of *vodhun* into the domain of the Holy Spirit who is active amongst them in the prophetic ministry of visionaries. On the other hand, the *vodhun* religious structure is couched in secrecy and is accessible only to initiates and those specially called to minister for the good of the community. For AICs, dying with Christ necessarily im-

28. Christoph and Oberländer, *Vaudou: Les Forces Secrètes De L'afrique,* esp. 83–95.

29. McKenzie, *Hail Orisha!,* 558.

30. See Kalu, "Estranged Bedfellows?" 126 quoting C. Fyfe and A. F. Walls, *Christianity in Africa in the 1990s* (Edinburgh: Centre for African Studies, University of Edinburgh, 1996).

31. See Ojo, *End-Time Army,* 203.

plies denying airtime to the deities and subsuming their existence and benevolent gifts under the Holy Spirit: "If with Christ you died to the elemental spirits of the universe, why do you live as if you still belonged to the world? Why do you submit to regulations, 'Do not handle, Do not taste, Do not touch'"? (Col 2:20–21) One is not wrong to evoke pre-exilic and exilic forging of mono-Yahwism, and to counsel patience in order to give room for maturity of doctrine.

This is where one may gain theological mileage by sitting at the feet of the Fathers of the Church to learn from their assimilation of the ritual and linguistic symbolism of the Greco-Roman mysteries in developing Christian sacramentology. From Patristic theology and practice the procedure of the *Celestials* cannot be faulted, even though there may be errors of detail. Christian apologists employed with the greatest reserve and even with reluctance, mystery language to explain the Christian rites, or even to refer to Christianity as a mystery religion. Clement of Alexandria was an exception. He took the initial (and bold) step of making the Christian rites meaningful to Alexandrians in terms of mystery concepts. Tertullian did so grudgingly; he castigated the mysteries that had rituals which equaled those of Christians. Later, inculturation was undertaken by the Fathers with deliberate vigor after the peace of Constantine. By then Christians had defeated the oriental mysteries rhetorically and militarily. Sacramentology thereafter developed confidently around mystery rhetoric and practice. Terms like initiates (*memnemenoi*), teachers of the mysteries (*mystagogoi*), mystery teachings (*mystagogia*) were assimilated into Christian practice and discourse. Baptism became *photismos* (illumination) or *sphragis* (seal) or simply *mysterion* (mystery—used also for the Eucharist). The presiding bishop was *protomystes* (first initiate), and the clerical tonsure was adopted from the practice of priests of Isis. There were far-reaching reforms in Christian practice to respond to the ritual procedure of the mysteries. Baptism did not follow conversion (*metanoia*) as in the New Testament. Rather a preparatory period of between three to five years (catechumenate) was developed. The boundary between the baptized (initiates) and the non-baptized catechumens and enquirers (non-initiates) was firm. The discipline of silence (*disciplina arcani*) was imposed with rigor; initiates said nothing to the catechumens if they enquired about the mysteries. Veiled language was often employed by Cyril of Jerusalem, John Chrysostom, Theodore of Mopsuestia, and Augustine in order to guard the secret of the mysteries. But today we accuse *vodhun* ritual procedure of secrecy. The major difference between the social context of *vodhun* and the Patristic mysteries is that West Africa is tolerant and flexible while post-Constantinian Christianity did not tolerate alternative viewpoints on the question of God and practice. Excessive violence was used in Rome against Mithraic worshipers—their priests were killed and buried under the rubble of their places of worship.[32] West Africa prefers rhetoric and propaganda.

African slaves in the diaspora were as creative as the Fathers of the Church, but to the benefit of ATR following the Yoruba model. They radically adapted the catholic martyrology and angelology and converted them into fronts to camouflage referents of their world of spirits. This creativity, in conditions of utter weakness, argues for the resilience of African religious universe. It also anticipated the dynamism and creativity of West African Christianity. I already drew attention to the ambivalent interpretation of *Eshu* (*Legba*) as devil, guardian angel, angel Gabriel, or St Peter depending on which Candomblé (meeting) one attended. Similarly, the weekly and annual calendars were radically adapted by Candomblé, creating parallels between the *orisa* and Christian cult: Friday was reserved to the cult of *Obatala* (the son of God, *Olorun* or *Olodumare*—the demiurge through whom all things were made), because Jesus Christ died on Friday; 24th June is the festival of *Shango* (the *orisa* of thunder who sleeps in on that day) to correspond with Medieval myths that John Baptist (who spits fire) mercifully slept in on June 24 (the summer solstice). The female deities of the ocean (*Yemanjà*) and rivers (*Osun*) are celebrated on key festivals of the Blessed Virgin Mary (2nd February, Purification; 8th December, Immaculate Conception.)[33] The creativity of the *Candomblé* displays a retrieval of African religious resources by the oppressed as a symbol of identity and liberation. However, *Candomblé* and its cousins, *vodun* and *santeria* are not Christian. They are creative ways that captive Africans radically adapted to change in a difficult world through their religion. Today in West Africa (e.g., in Nigeria) adaptations within groups like Sabbath healing homes and vitalistic or nativistic assemblies, which focus on healing with no reference to Christ, are also not Christian

32. Lease, "Mithraism and Christianity," esp. 1308–309. See Uzukwu, *Worship as Body Language*, ch. 4.

33. See Bastide, *Le Candomblé De Bahia (Rite Nagô)*, 109ff.; 282, etc.

but radical extensions of the worldview and rituals of ATR.[34] However, their increasing popularity and the confusion among Christians over their status argue for more attention to the social expectations that are redefining religion in West Africa. They argue for the urgent need of healthy assimilation of West African ATR concerns into Christianity. AICs' leading role in this project—expanding and redefining God's Holy Spirit—should be recognized. Charismatic movements and new African Pentecostals (grudgingly) learned from them. What insight does their procedure in assimilating the multiplicity of spirits in the West African cosmos into Christianity, bring to Trinitarian theology?

ONE HOLY SPIRIT AND MULTIPLE DEITIES— THE MELODY OF PNEUMATOLOGY

The *Celestials'* theology of *One Holy Spirit instead of the multiplicity of divine beings* is shared by most AICs explicitly or implicitly. The Holy Spirit, in the overall structure of AICs and those communities not controlled by the doctrinal precision of the mainline churches, as well as the popular religion of the Catholic and Protestant Charismatic movements, is ever present but difficult to grasp. The presence of the Spirit is better experienced rather than described. All gifts, inspirations, visions or auditions, dreams and other charisms are attributed to the Holy Spirit. The Holy Spirit is the sum total of the charisms, just as the Christ is the sum total of all the virtues (Origen). The Holy Spirit participates in the denominations of Christ, and through the Holy Spirit the saints participate in God and in Christ.

At the risk of repetition, I think one needs to expand Origen to fill out the identity of the Holy Spirit that emerges in West African Christianity. This may create problems for neo-Pentecostalism; but I think it is theologically justifiable. It is consonant with the creativity pre-exilic and exilic prophets displayed in forging the image of one and only Yahweh and also the creativity of the Fathers in describing the Triune God and the rituals surrounding every aspect of the Christian life. AICs boldly provide us with the material to forge the image of the Holy Spirit who is the point of entry into Trinitarian life. I stay with examples drawn from AICs in Benin Republic and Nigeria.

---

34. See Kalu, "Estranged Bedfellows?" 131, 133. See also Hurbon, *Dieu Dans Le Vaudou Haïtien.*

James Fernandez in his study of the *Celestial Church of Christ* correctly noted that their approach to ATR is synthetic rather than syncretistic. Instead of the syncretistic theology of the *Candomblé* mentioned above, the *Celestials* subject ATR spirits to "higher order integration in a Generalized Holy Spirit." The characteristics of the West African deities are subsumed under the one Holy Spirit. *Sango* and *Ogun* (deities of thunder, iron mongering or war), *Agwu, Ifa-Orunmila,* and *Sakpata* or *Soponna* (deities of divination and healing of smallpox and other diseases), etc., are no longer named and worshiped. Their powers are not recognised in their individuality. *Celestials* and other AICs no longer acknowledge spiritual inspiration, possession or seizure as originating from the West African deities that are diabolised. Rather "the diversity of animistic spirits receive, taxonomically, a higher order integration in a Generalized Holy Spirit . . . a unity out of multiplicity which is intellectually attractive." Nevertheless, this poses the problem of the spirits manifesting at times their parallel (even though subordinate) influence and creates "spiritual schizophrenia in the religion—a shifting back and forth of focus and a recurrent uncertainty as to the true subordinance of what may be parallel powers still potent in their spheres of influence."[35] The popularity of Archangel Michael—leader in the war against Satan— in all the denominational Churches and AICs in Benin Republic and other West African countries could represent the transformation of war deities into warrior angels. Archbishop Sarpong agrees with this solution: "In place of the gods and the divinities, we might also substitute the Saints and the Angels in globo, specifically or individually, by mentioning names as we do in libation."[36] The Jewish-Christian Holy Spirit receives qualitative development through the Christianization of West Africa. This emergent pneumatology satisfies AICs' Spirit-focus through assimilation of characteristics of deities into the Holy Spirit. It is implicitly if not explicitly endorsed by Charismatic movements, and also by the healing liturgies of Charismatic Catholic priests.

"Spiritual schizophrenia" of another type exists and is hard to resolve. Experts elected by deities (called *dibia* or *nganga* or *babalawo)* want to *remain Christian while rendering services to the wider community.* Some converted to Christianity and continued their practice; while others, like Madugwu Ufondu, received their call as Christians. Should

---

35. Fernandez, "Cultural Status of a West African Cult Group," 249.

36. Sarpong, "Libation and Inculturation in Africa," 334–35.

Christian clients continue to receive ministrations from these elect of deities and still remain Christian? Pastoral practice presents a picture that opens a window for resolving the theological logjam. In times of need Christians do not ask the theoretical question about the identity of the health-generating *spirit*—they address themselves to healers who operate in the name of *agwu, vodhun* or *orisa* as well as those who act in the name of the Holy Spirit of Christ. Frans Wijsen reports that in Sukumaland, East Africa, Christians have no scruples about going to the diviner-healer (*wanganga wa kinyeji*) and frequenting the catholic priest. "Priests and healers do not exclude each other, they are not competitors but partners."[37] This reflects African flexible attitude to God and deities—"when something stands, something else stands beside it" for the integral good of the community. Eric de Rosny, initiated as *ngambi* (seer), supports this procedure. He discerns the cause of illnesses and sends patients either to the *nganga* or to the orthodox medical practitioner and psychiatrist or to the priest/pastor depending on the dominant worldview of the patient. His concern is with effectiveness rather than with developing a pneumatology. While Central and East Africa locate the potency of *nganga* in ancestral power, West Africa locates it in deities. This raises the issue not just of traditional medicine and cult of ancestors but also of the worship of deities that take possession of the elect who minister as diviner-healers in the community.

AICs successfully integrate the ministry of diviner-healers into the structures of the church. The strong positioning of the *nganga, dibia,* or *babalawo* in ATR who, because of their therapeutic function, provide attractive answers in the age of confusion (the collapse of African socio-politico-economic structures) is replicated in AICs. Indeed some *dibia, nganga,* or *babalawo* may have simply relocated into the new patterns of African Christianity. AICs reinterpret the ministry of diviner-healers—named visionaries and prophets—as falling under the operations of the One Holy Spirit that indwells "the open space in the mind" and bestows gifts and charisms. This successfully transforms the powers attributed to *Sakpata, Ifa-Orunmila* or *Agwu* into dimensions of the Holy Spirit. Wisdom, discernment, and especially vision, audition, prophecy and healing that were dependent on the powerful deities now depend on the one and only Holy Spirit. Those Christian diviner-healers whose ministry involves divination, herbal medicine and healing and

37. Wijsen, *There Is Only One God*, 201.

who received their call from deities like *Agwu*, must reinterpret these deities as subordinated to or rather subsumed under God's Holy Spirit. The diviner-doctors want to remain Christian; therefore the qualities of their tutelary deities are assimilated into the Holy Spirit, and the deities are denied the perks of independent existence: gifts and sacrifices. To retain the flexibility characteristic of West Africa and the "pagan-ness" of Catholicism (Gesché) as opposed to the purity of evangelical-ism, the deities are reduced either to dimensions of God's Holy Spirit that heals, or to God's angels of health under God's Holy Spirit. This is a theologically satisfactory and Catholic way of integrating the ministry of diviner-doctors into the church. Therefore the gifted Christian members of mainline missionary churches, Catholic and Protestant, who render services that manifest the "fruits of the spirit," fruits that are "soteriologi-cally effective," who relate their history of divination-healing as originat-ing from tutelary deities of health, join the pioneer theological effort of forging a new flexible language and epithets for the Holy Spirit of God.

The West African tolerance and flexibility with regard to am-bivalent deities that contrasts sharply with the exclusivist stance of Christianity (moderate in Catholicism and extreme in evangelicalism) that may exacerbate "spiritual schizophrenia" could find containment. "Spiritual schizophrenia" as pathology is neither good for the individual nor for the community. The solution of One Holy Spirit recognized in multiple gifts or charisms, a melody or harmony of epithets, for the good of the community and humanity, is the contribution West African insight makes to the pneumatology of the Great Christian tradition. Process thought could help explain the ambivalent dimensions of *vod-hun* still encountered in aspects of "possession" by God's Holy Spirit as energies of the divine in the process of development. God on the level of existence contains no ambiguity or evil, while in actuality the change-ability and fickleness that accompany our daily existence are acceptable as dimensions of evolving divine energy or spirit. Christians, while set-ting boundaries with the ATR cult, assimilate into God's Holy Spirit the fundamental life-generating insight of the ATR vision of deities that may still require refinement in the process of ongoing conversion of the ancestral world of dynamic therapeutic spirits into the domain of the Holy Spirit. The ministry of oversight, guided by flexibility, establishes structures for the discernment of spirits to clarify Christian boundaries. *Celestials* are aware of the need for oversight. They leave this to pastors who never experience trance (similar to the shrine priests of *vodhun*) while visionaries and prophets experience frequent trances (similar to devotees or initiates of *vodhun* cult) but do not exercise the ministry of oversight.

The need for discernment of spirits should not be interpreted negatively. It should not prevent the mainline Churches from boldly affirming every good work, especially of divination or healing, as coming from the Holy Spirit. For "[to] each is given the manifestation of the Spirit for the common good"! (1 Cor 12:7) The positive discernment or acknowledgment of God's Holy Spirit at work in the community arises from the optimistic assurance that "*it is that very Spirit bearing witness with our spirit* that we are children of God" (Rom 8:16). The special favors granted through gifted Christians come from God through Christ in the Holy Spirit. Structural integration into the church by way of ordination or appointment to healing ministries and services, the sphere of operation of the Holy Spirit, reduces the chances of "spiritual schizophrenia". In this way the perspective of a Generalized Holy Spirit who bestows all gifts of healing and divining becomes a creative pneumatological contribution from West African Christianity to the great Christian tradition. This procedure is consonant with the OT creative integration of Canaanite religion into mono-Yahwism and the assimilation of epithets of powerful female deities into the concept of Wisdom. It is also consonant with the radical Christian redefinition of the relational God received through Judaism as Trinitarian and the creativity of Origen who defined the Holy Spirit as the sum total of charisms. The leading contribution of AICs in this creative pneumatology should be recognized. While the legitimacy of ATR spirits that produce fruits that are soteriologically effective is not denied, the Christian community affirms the Holy Spirit as the source of all gifts and charisms for the common good.

In the next chapter I focus on the impact of the Holy Spirit that descends on and empowers gifted people with charisms to promote the overall good of individual Christians and the Christian community to ensure their comprehensive security in a world made dangerous by evil spirits and mystically empowered evil people.

7

God's Power Manifest in the Holy Spirit for Human Wholeness

The identity of God's Holy Spirit is filled out or expanded through the interaction of Christians in West Africa with their context. What one expects of deities, that embody specific characteristics for the fulfillment of the individual's and community's destiny, is creatively transferred to God's Holy Spirit, for human wholeness. The discernment or divination of the origin of fortune and misfortune, the realization of the destined course in life in the form of progress in one's enterprise, protection from the fear of evil spirits or evil forces and evil people, and especially protection from witchcraft and sorcery, are under (the cool protecting wing of) God's Holy Spirit. In a world dominated by ambivalent deities, ancestral spirits, and forces that have not been grounded, in a world where powerful experts could misuse their healing power to kill and evil people practice witchcraft, an assurance of the powerful shade of the Holy Spirit (cf. Psalm 91) is a major priority of Christian practice. AICs, charismatic movements, neo-Pentecostals, claim protection under the expansive wing of the Holy Spirit. The ministry of prophets and visionaries prove this. Their charisms are for the common good. How does this ministry work out on the ground? What insight does one gain into the economy of the Triune God from the practice?

In this chapter, I begin by highlighting the preoccupation of a typical AIC—the *Celestial Churches of Christ* in Benin Republic—with the ministry of visionaries or prophets that reveal their confidence in God's protection. The *Epiclesis* or Consecratory Prayer pronounced over those being ordained *Visionaries* calls for the descent of God's Holy Spirit. Underlying the prayer is fear of evil spirits and evil people that God's Spirit engages in combat through his ministers. Life is a spiritual combat

(Origen). It becomes necessary to address, name and identify the evil, in order to expel it. Evil in its most frightening dimension is witchcraft that mystically inhabits the witch (in "the open space in the mind") who mystically destroys or "eats" the victim. The gifted and ordained prophets-visionaries, inhabited by the special power of the Holy Spirit, lead the community's spiritual combat. Finally, I describe the spirituality or mysticism of descent that is enjoyed by the elect, possessed by God's Holy Spirit—mysticism with a social agenda.

THE MAKING OF THE CHRISTIAN PROPHET, HEALER AND VISIONARY—PUBLIC OR OVERT EMPOWERMENT BY GOD'S SPIRIT FOR THE "COMMON GOOD"

The prayer for the descent of God (the Holy Spirit) during the ordination liturgy of visionaries in the *Celestial Church of Christ* is a captivating rhetorical merging of the Bible idioms and the universe familiar to West African peoples. *Celestials* name their visionaries *woli* (Yoruba for seer, visionary and prophet). Their call by the Holy Spirit must be revealed through visions, auditions or dreams. The text of the consecratory epiclesis (invocation of God in the ordination liturgy) pronounced over the ordinands lying prostrate on the floor opens as follows:

> God, save us for we are your children. Save us from evil spirits. Save us from evil people. And help us to worship you, as we should unto our death . . . You that spoil the works of Satan, come and show your laborers (those who through suitable intercessions contribute to the extension of the kingdom of God) the plan to be followed. Come and stay with your laborers. Your servants (the visionaries) are prostrate on the floor in your name. Descend and enter into them . . .[1]

The emphasis in this opening paragraph is that the community, a gathering of God's children, reposes total confidence in God to cage Satan. "For you did not receive a spirit of slavery to fall back into fear, but you have received a spirit of adoption. When we cry, 'Abba! Father!' it is that very Spirit bearing witness with our spirit that we are children of God" (Rom 8:15–16). Fear among God's children is caused by evil spirits and evil people; evil that thrives in poisoned relationships (see below). God's power, manifest through God's Holy Spirit, is demonstrated in the labor-

---

1. Surgy, *L'église Du Christianisme Céleste*, 205.

ers who in their ministry contribute to the "extension of the kingdom of God." The phrase "descend and enter into them" is typical of *vodhun* rhetoric. God-Spirit or God's Spirit or the Holy Spirit descends into the elect.

As "Spirit Churches" as well as "Bible Churches," AICs, rooted in their context, legitimately claim continuity with the apostolic church on whom the Holy Spirit "descended" on Pentecost (Acts 2) and with the Spirit-community of Corinth (1 Cor 11–12). This convergence of Bible and context is clear in the *epiclesis*. However, neat Trinitarian distinctions are not made. The preoccupation is with the power of God and the process of coming into contact with this power through God's "descent." The fluid, free-flowing and flexible language of the *epiclesis* is a feature of AICs' understanding of God-Christ-Spirit, with the focus on Spirit dominating. Olayiwola has drawn attention to this characteristic language of AICs that attributes power as coming from the Holy Spirit, while not mentioning explicitly the name of Jesus Christ. This is comparable to the language and theology of the Black Church of the USA that is focused on Jesus. In prayer there is no neat differentiation between the persons of the Trinity—Jesus, God or the Holy Spirit. "All of these proper names for God were used interchangeably in prayer language." But the concentration or focus is on Jesus—Jesus "was all one needs"![2]

What is clear from the opening paragraph of the *Celestials'* epiclesis is that to overcome evil and Satan structurally, God's Holy Spirit who enters into the ordinands bestows the power of seeing; this echoes more or less the impact of *vodhun* on possessed diviners. Next, the tempo increases; the ordination prayer displays increased confidence in the gift-giving God and the pride of place vision occupies, and the importance and urgency of this particular ministry in God's Church:

> Vision is the most important thing in your Church. Vision is the basis of her glory. Put it into your Church [Response of the assembly—*Nishé* or *atché*—"so be it"!].
>
> You spoke and said that vision gives weight to your Church. You said that a Church that has no vision is lost. This is why we put into your hands your laborers who provide accurate predictions.[3]

2. Grant, *White Women's Christ and Black Women's Jesus*, 212, 229 n. 53; Olayiwola, "Aladura Christianity in Dialogue with African Traditional Religion," 354.

3. Surgy, *L'église Du Christianisme Céleste*, 205.

The strategic position of dreams, visions or auditions in the *Celestial Church* and other AICs is remarkable. These mystical experiences played decisive roles in the call and definition of the mission of prophetic figures like Josiah Oluwalowo Oshitelu, founder of the *Church of God (Aladura)* in Nigeria, and Samuel Oschoffa, founder of the *Celestial Church of Christ* in Benin Republic. For example, the overpowering vision/audition of Samuel Oschoffa on September 29, 1947 was decisive for his vocation. The similarities with the experience of Moses at Horeb are striking. Oschoffa heard a voice saying:

> Samuel, Samuel, Samuel the Blessed has confided a mission in you on the part of Jesus Christ—because many Christians die without having seen the presence of Christ, because illness drives them towards fetish and diabolic things—and they are thus marked for death and hell. I give you the power to make miracles of healing through the power of the Holy Spirit.[4]

The value *Celestials* attach to dreams or visions is shown in the care to record and document. They are revelations from the Holy Spirit. They have weight comparable to the Bible that is a repository of "all previous visions of the Holy Spirit."[5]

In defense of their practice, AICs highlight the importance of dream-vision in the Bible to reveal God's will: God prepared Peter through dream-vision for the encounter with Cornelius (Acts 10); Jacob's dream-ladder linking earth and heaven is fondly recalled as God's medium of imparting blessings on Jacob and his descendants (Gen 28:12–22).[6] ATR world vision (functioning as pre-text) and Biblical idioms constitute the fertile background for reinterpreting mystical manifestations connected with those ministries that AICs need to make sense of their world. Victor Turner suggests, from East African evidence, a dual function of the ATR diviner-healer, *nganga*—that is useful in analyzing the AIC mystics-prophets. These are the functions of divination and revelation—on the one hand, the explanation of the way life is, and on the other hand, the revelation of the way life might be. The *nganga* (at conversion) could easily transform into prophets of AICs because they

---

4. Fernandez, "Cultural Status of a West African Cult Group," 245.

5. Ibid., 250.

6. Bishop R. Mirinda of the *Zion Apostolic Church* in Zimbabwe discusses many themes dear to AICs, including the importance of dreams, Mirinda, "Good News in Zion," 237–39.

reveal the way life might be.[7] In contradistinction from the mainline churches, where the prophetic function is limited to the proclamation of the Word, AICs' prophets, enabled by vision, freely enter into the problems of individuals to divine, predict, warn, and provide healing services. Moved by the *sound* or rhythm of the *drum,* the descending Spirit impels them to minister. That is why the "galaxy of prophets and founders" (Kä Mana[8]) of AICs embodies features associated with leading Hebrew prophets like Elijah and Elisha. It is not surprising that as the ordination prayer of the *Celestials'* visionaries reaches a crescendo, God is requested to transfer into the ordinands the prophetic spirit and power of known OT prophets.

> This is why we put into your hands your laborers who provide accurate predictions. Come and watch over them. Put Ezekiel into them [*Nishé* or *atché*]! Put Jeremiah into them [*Nishé* or *atché*]! Put Isaiah into them [*Nishé* or *atché*]! Put Amos into them [*Nishé* or *atché*]! Put Obadiah into them [*Nishé* or *atché*]! God of glory [Assembly response—*wiwe*—"holy one"], come down and penetrate/remain [in them?] for our sake in our Church.[9]

The close link between vision, prophecy and healing in the ordination rite presents AICs' visionaries and prophets not only as functioning in continuity with the *dibia, nganga, or babalawo;* they function also in continuity with OT prophets and even in imitation of the Crucified-Risen Jesus Christ, the Healer. The intertestamental literature of Judaism captures the cosmological assumptions prevalent in the time of Jesus relevant to healing. The Targum of Numbers 6:24 expands the priestly blessing of Aaron to include protecting people from the demons that terrorize during the night, midday, morning and evening, and from "evil spirits." The perception of the messiah, "son of David" and even "son of Solomon," is connected with healing. David through playing the harp healed Saul, and Solomon's great wisdom is linked to discovering medicinal herbs with healing powers. When the blind beggar, Bartimaeus, called out to the passing Jesus, "Son of David, have mercy on me," the

---

7. Wijsen, *There Is Only One God,* 217, citing Turner, *Revelation and Divination in Ndembu Ritual,* 15–33.

8. Mana, *La Nouvelle Évangélisation En Afrique,* 122ff.

9. Surgy, *L'église Du Christianisme Céleste,* 205–6. The last sentence of the prayer is not clear, "Dieu de gloire (w), descends et entre pour nous dans notre église." The sense of "entre" is not clear.

critical request he made of the "son of David" was, "My teacher, let me see again" (Mark 10:47, 51).[10]

The above helps one to appreciate the importance of AICs' healing ministry in the troubled context of West Africa; it is comparable to the practice of prophetic-healing ministry during the fertile period of Judaism before and in the time of Jesus. I agree with John Mbiti that the mainline churches must courageously face the pastoral urgency of creating a ministry of "Christian medicine men and diviners." Medical practitioners are doing a praiseworthy job, but this all important ministry cannot be left in their hands alone.[11] A brand new "ministry of healing" is not to be confused with the appointment of exorcists whose traditional role is nevertheless a support for the ministry; the idea of "Christian diviner-doctors" is not farfetched. The mainline churches learn from the experience of the AICs' prophets-visionaries and healers that embed their new structures in the Bible and the African context.

The *Celestials* and other AICs are aware that the Bible condemns divination (Deut 18:10–14). But they insist that as "seers" they are in the line and tradition of prophets who consulted God in favor of the people as they struggle against evil forces. They cite 1 Cor 14:1: "Pursue love and strive for the spiritual gifts, and especially that you may prophesy." This text is for them a clear demonstration that prophecy is the highest of the gifts of the Spirit. They claim that they are witnesses to the fulfillment of the prophecy of Joel (Joel 2:28–29). However, they are careful to distance themselves from and to denounce charlatans, at the service of Mammon, who, seeing the good deeds done by *Celestials,* also claim to be visionaries.[12]

There is no doubt that the area of vision-dream-prophecy is slippery and open to abuse. *Celestials* are aware of the fact that it calls for community discernment—a discernment controlled by the *social agenda* that is the essential requirement for the bestowal of gifts of the Spirit. In addition, the focus of this ministry captures the overriding *social agenda* of AICs' existence: "Vision is the most important thing in your Church. Vision is the basis of her glory." The *woli* (seer) enables healing and ex-

10. See Déaut and Robert, *Targum Du Pentateuque*—vol. III—Nombres; see also Tassin, "Jésus, Exorciste Et Guérisseur."

11. Cited by Berends, "African Traditional Healing Practices and the Christian Community," 285.

12. Surgy, *L'église Du Christianisme Céleste,* 206–7.

orcism: "*Spiritual healing,* in most of the AICs, is in a literal sense, the principal focus of our worship and liturgical practices, being the main cause of our impressive growth."[13] In countries like Benin Republic and Nigeria, the prophet-seer (*woli*) of the AICs and the devotee of *vodhun* or *orisa* (especially *Sakpata* or *Soponna*—deity of health) interpret their role in society in a similar way. Through initiation or ordination they are "born" into "a new life": "the life of initiation and the penetration of the world of spirits."[14] The penetration of the world of spirits is crucial for the services they render to the community. Life is a spiritual combat; to identify and name the evil in order to expel or overcome it increases the profile of visionaries and prophets.

AICs find justification for their beliefs and practices in the Pauline recommendation: "Pursue love and strive for the spiritual gifts, and especially that you may prophesy" (1 Cor 14:1). How do people in this region name or identify the evil that is confronted in daily life viewed as a spiritual combat?

LIFE AS SPIRITUAL COMBAT—NAMING THE DEVIL TO MYSTICALLY EXPEL OR OVERCOME IT

The concerns expressed in the ordination of visionaries in the *Celestial Church of Christ* sharply evoke a West African universe that is peopled by good and bad spirits, by good and bad people. In a period of generalized distress, an "age of confusion"—marked by political upheavals, wars, massive economic downturn and endemic corruption, breakdown in social relationships and especially breakdown in family life—pessimism and disillusionment prevail. The phrase "age of confusion" is used by Peel to describe mid-nineteenth century destabilized Yoruba land characterized by "the breakdown of public order and social trust," of "communities racked by internal conflict or destroyed altogether, of families broken up," of "radical changes in personal circumstances, of the norms of social life challenged or overthrown," of intimate friends accusing one another of poisoning. Claffey used the same expression to describe nineteenth century Dahomey and the contemporary distressed Benin Republic. Dodds' description of the upheavals that characterized the sunset of the Roman Empire that signaled the phenomenal conver-

---

13. Pobee and Ositelu II, *African Initiatives in Christianity*, 71.

14. Tidani, "Rituels," 305.

sion to Christianity as "the age of anxiety" says the same thing.[15] The West African deity accused of provoking the confusion is *Eshu* (also called *Legba*), named the Devil by Christians.

The "age of confusion" or "age of anxiety" has dominated the West African region from the 1970s; it reached its peak in the mid-1980s. For example in Nigeria, the Nigeria-Biafra war (1967–1970) was followed by endless military interventions and misgovernment. From the mid-1980s, the introduction of unsuccessful and anti-people economic reforms—Structural Adjustment Programs—caused incredible social distress and insecurity in all segments of the Nigerian society. In a society structured by a worldview that is dominantly non-secular, religious answers to social problems are popular. While the mainline churches and AICs struggle to cope with the crisis using familiar templates, the 1980s saw the rise of the new African Pentecostalism that operated with a radical dualistic perception of the universe divided between God-Christ-Spirit and Satan. The reinterpreted world is the theatre of spiritual combat—the struggle against evil, especially the evil of witchcraft and occultic powers. Pentecostal pastors, recruited from among young university graduates, learn from (and radically adapt to the Nigerian world) the sophisticated pattern of American televangelists.

In the West African region, and indeed throughout sub-Saharan Africa, the experience of evil people and spirits is real. Mystical possession by evil spirits and mystical cannibalism is accepted. The door is wide open for fear and superstition. The fear of evil and occultic powers is popularized and perhaps further engineered by home video films produced mainly in Nigeria and Ghana.[16] The "powerful" men and women gifted with the art of penetration into the world of spirits—be they neo-Pentecostal pastors, Charismatic Catholic priest-healers, AICs' visionaries-prophets, or *nganga, bokọnọ, babalawo,* and *dibia* that some pastors (especially neo-Pentecostals) classify among the agents of the Devil—assume a larger than life profile.

Mediators, therapists or experts, have always been crucial to life and religious practice in the region of West Africa (see chapter 3 above). In an age of anxiety their services to the community in general and to individuals in particular to enable them understand, predict, control and

---

15. See Peel, *Religious Encounter and the Making of the Yoruba,* 48–53; Claffey, "Looking for a Breakthrough"; Dodds, *Pagan and Christian in an Age of Anxiety.*

16. See Ukah, "Advertising God"; and also Ojo, *End-Time Army.*

reinvent the world, are highly appreciated. Neo-Pentecostal-inspired home video films evoke the shadow side of ATR; they focus on occultic practices (widely connected with secret societies) that enable people to acquire wealth, power, and upward social mobility. The video-films also focus on issues such as distress in family and social life, on barrenness and marital infidelity, all connected with witchcraft and sorcery. Video-films are popularly viewed in homes or in video-viewing centers found in university campuses, etc. They make abstract doctrines concrete; and the moral or ethical positions of "born again" Pentecostalism are carefully transmitted. Through the booming film industry (1,000 films are estimated to be produced annually in Nigeria since 1997) filmmakers (secular and Pentecostal) smile to their banks! For a good number of the viewers the truth-value of what is screened is beyond doubt. Video-films go beyond entertainment and become "a source of truth and value." A young viewer confided: "they enlighten me to know when what I cannot see begins to hit me from behind."[17]

My approach to naming the reality of *evil* in order to capture the dynamics of the spiritual combat is first to describe this "ontological evil" (Hebga), i.e., the evil of witchcraft that mystically inhabits the individual either from birth or through initiation. I draw from a sample myth-narrative of the Beti of Cameroon. Next, I address the process of mystical possession of the elect by God's Holy Spirit, the enabler of the combat against evil—this highlights the peculiar but controversial "mysticism of descent" as an African, or precisely West African, contribution to the experience of the Holy Spirit (or the experience of the Triune God in the Holy Spirit). It is interesting that the language of possession is used to describe the process of contamination with evil and of the experience of the life-generating indwelling of God's Holy Spirit to combat evil. Meyer rightly observed, from the missionary impact on the Ewe (Togo and Ghana), that by expanding the semantic range of a secular term *gbɔgbɔ* and giving it "a suprasensory sense" the foundation was laid on the level of language "for a theory of spirit possession" by God's Holy Spirit, by West African spirits and by evil spirits. Consequently, in the spiritual combat (Origen), "possession" is the language to express empowerment by conflicting entities opposed one to another "on a single, spiritual battlefield."[18]

17. Ukah, "Advertising God," 225.
18. Meyer, *Translating the Devil*, 146.

Describing the Evil of Witchcraft and the Occult

The phenomenon of witchcraft and the proliferation of witchcraft accusations cut across Africa. Confessional statements and anti-sorcery campaigns multiply. Every one of the Christian Churches has a charismatic wing that ensures healing-exorcism, or more accurately "deliverance ministry," as more people, young and old, including mere children, make confessions or are prodded by prophets and their assistants to do so. As unusual as it sounds, children are targeted in places like Democratic Republic of the Congo (DRC). Videotapes of confessional statements are routinely sent by pastors of Pentecostal churches from Brussels to Kinshasa to help in the resolution of witchcraft palaver![19] A Congolese Catholic priest involved in deliverance ministry recounted how a self-confessed witch—a ten year old boy—announced to him after a healing mass in DRC (c. 2001), "Father, today you have effectively destroyed my airport"! Child-witches claim to take off or are accused of taking off (in form of cockroaches) from their airport anywhere (Belgium or Congo) to attack victims located anywhere! Parents routinely accuse their children of witchcraft and exile them from the home onto the streets, or even throw them into the river Congo. The *International Herald Tribune* of April 22, 2004, carried a report by Somini Sengupta of a tearful seven-year-old Alfie, who had been thrown into the river Congo by her father, but was rescued by a gang of street children: "My father took me to the river," "He said I was a witch."[20] Mary Douglas' longitudinal study of the Lele of DRC in the mid-1980s shows that, compared to forty years earlier, witchcraft accusations have dramatically increased with the unusual development of including the traditional victims—women and children—as perpetrators.[21] All over Africa, family members (extended family), business and political associates accuse or are accused of witchcraft, poisoning and sorcery. Are neo-Pentecostals therefore right in their campaign to get church members and clients "untied" from the extended family structure, "the enemy within," to be limited to one's

19. See Boeck, "Le 'Deuxième Monde' Et Les 'Enfants-Sorciers' En République Démocratique Du Congo," 32–57.

20. Sengupta, "River is Witnessing the Rebirth of Congo."

21. Douglas, "Problem of Evil among the Lele." See her other studies of the question, Douglas, *Risk and Blame*, 88–91.

nuclear family, in order to enjoy the "prosperity" won by Christ?[22] Is witchcraft, the new language of the "age of confusion"?

Witchcraft was always part of the African experience of the world; but when the traditional system was operative, like among the Lele of DRC, false accusations were sanctioned. Palaver ethics (Bujo) dominated. Families or clans stood behind their own kin, and this reduced the number and frequency of accusations. Douglas is probably right that a highly developed judicial system and improved laws and requirements of evidence could reduce the phenomenon of irresponsible accusations as it did in Western Europe.[23] Such laws, as in Cameroon and Cote d'Ivoire, accept the reality of witchcraft and therefore the moral responsibility for witchcraft. But the situation today is that no one or very few people are ready to come forward to defend the accused. In the absence of an effective judicial system, deliverance ministry takes over, and in many instances free reign is given to jungle justice.

There is no doubt that this evil is fundamentally connected with social, economic, political and religious problems that need to be courageously addressed. For example, the novelty and frightening reality of the power of the youth at war, some of them mere children, is closely connected with the "age of confusion" that peaked in the mid-1980s. This helps one to appreciate the expansion of the territory of evil. The former victims of witchcraft, women and children, changed roles in places like the DRC, Angola, Mozambique, Liberia, Sierra Leone, and Côte d'Ivoire. The war gave new power to women, in the vanguard of commerce and trafficking between Kinshasa and Luanda (Angola); it also revealed the new power of children. The situation of absolute poverty that came with the war led to the break-up of families and values. Women and children therefore entered the table of perceived threats expressed in the language of witchcraft. They are part of the aggregate existential situation that calls "the tradition into question," they become blamable for illnesses, natural disasters, economic downturn, death, etc.[24] They are accused of, and sometimes confess to, deploying phantasmic power to eat their victims or diminish their life, property or potency.

22. See Claffey, *Christian Churches in Dahomey-Benin*, 238–48.

23. Douglas, *Risk and Blame: Essays in Cultural Theory*, 93; and Douglas, "Problem of Evil among the Lele," 22, 31–33.

24. See the reflection of Bujo on sorcery within the wider dimension of "the limits of African tradition" in his Bujo, *Foundations of an African Ethic*, 134ff.

Social disorganization and stress make it easier to withdraw from the real but intolerable world of corruption, ethnic conflict and crushing global economic transformations. There is no viable State to provide a functioning legal system to deal with the accusations in order to protect the weak. One inhabits or finds it convenient to retreat or escape into the world of the night, the phantasmagoric second and third worlds of witchcraft, into the battle of the night that disorganizes family and clan solidarity, a battle that dominates the social imaginary.[25] Apart from this popular view of witchcraft as a *function* of resolving social problems of inheritance, problems of political and generational succession in matri-lineal societies, or explaining the "age of confusion," what is this evil in its origin? Is it "objectified evil" that exists deep within each person as Hebga argued?

The structuralist approach underlines the pervasive dimension of witchcraft and sorcery. Interpretation of myth-narratives suggests that one could become a witch through *ritual inversion of the birth process.* In other words instead of "normal" birth from womb through the va-gina, the evil enters through the vagina for the "abnormal" birth in the womb. It is structural evil. Popular perception of witchcraft in parts of central Africa—Cameroon and Gabon—and parts of West Africa con-firm this. The myth of the origin of *Evu (Witchcraft)* among the Beti of Cameroon describes *Evu* as "an invisible, voracious, carnivorous, and powerful spirit" that hates "daylight." It was introduced into the village by *woman*, the wife of *Okombodo* (God—ancestral hunter) who then "lived with humans." *Evu* entered the village through a free choice or decision of *woman* brought about by curiosity or jealousy. The mode of transport by which *evu* entered the human society is shocking. *Evu* (resembling an ugly shapeless toad) refused the suggestion to be put into the hamper of the woman, or to hang onto her arm, or to be carried on her back. Rather *evu* proposed its own means of transport, telling the unsuspecting woman to spread out her legs (as in labour). Through the vagina *evu* entered her stomach for the unnatural inverted birth that is radically different from the wish of God the creator (*Nzambi*). This is at the same time perversion and transgression. The narrative concludes:

---

25. See the study of Boeck, "Le 'Deuxième Monde' Et Les 'Enfants-Sorciers' En République Démocratique Du Congo."

"*Evu* multiplied and transmitted itself to the descendants of the woman, soon each person has his own."[26]

What the narrative of the origin of *evu* (also called *hu*) appears to assert is not only the fact of the existence of witches, but also of the phenomenon (some say the ontological reality) that each person has the witchcraft virus in him/her. In other words, the power of the occult, sorcery and witchcraft is virtually embedded in all humans; it needs only to be activated. *Hu* is the "principle of evil," Hebga asserts. He draws attention to *soul-shadow* that empowers one for self-deployment beyond the body, in describing the components of the human person (see chapter 6 above). This enables one to act beyond the normal spatial constriction of the body. It is however a capacity or virtuality, activated when ordered by the person. Hebga, thereby, accepts the presupposition that the power of *evu* is in each person.[27] André Mary's study of *Bwiti* anthropology (a syncretistic cult in Gabon that merges Mitsogho myth-ritual, Fang ancestral cult and Christian practice) classifies humans in relationship to *evu*: the *nnem* have a strong, uncontrollable and evil *evu*; the *ngolongolo* are masters of the art of dual personality enabling them to overcome the *beyem* (witches); and finally the naïve *miêmiê* either have no *evu* or have very weak ones. It is interesting that the prophet that combats evil forces is not the naïve person, but one that is holy and also wise as a serpent, even sly like the *beyem mam* who knows all things, able to master the two faces of reality that the possession of *evu* guarantees.[28] The *beyem mam* is the counterpart of the diviner-doctor, *dibia*, *nganga*, *babalawo*, or *bokǫnǫ*, whose personality is ambivalent. Mary Douglas is of the view that both the diviner-doctor and witch draw from the same resources; the sorcerer is "a spoiled priest": "As power is one, and knowledge is one, the sorcerer taps into the same channels as the priest and diviner . . . The more he is trained in religious techniques for more ensuring fertility, curing sickness, and sterility, the more he has at his fingertips the techniques for striking with barrenness and killing. The difference

---

26. Drawn from Mary, "Le Schème De La Naissance À L'envers," 254–55, citing Guillemin, "Les superstitions encore en usage en pays Yaoundé," 22–37; and Guimera, *Ni dos, ni ventre. Religion, magie et sorcellerie evuzok*, 41–42.

27. Hebga, *La Rationalité D'un Discours Africain Sur Les Phénomènes Paranormaux*, 115. See a detailed description of activated potency of this element in the witch in Hebga, *Sorcellerie Et Prière De Délivrance*; Hebga, *Sorcellerie, Chimère Dangereuse?*

28. Mary, *Le Défi Du Syncrétisme*, 65–66.

is entirely moral."[29] Hebga's view that everyone has the witchcraft virus therefore appears defensible. Bujo supports Hebga's position but from a wider perception of evil,

> It is also important to note that every individual has the potential to become a sorcerer: the power of evil slumbers within him and can awaken at any moment. This power is the chief enemy of life and finds expression in envy, jealousy, hatred, wrath, desire, or pleasure in evil, etc. One who does not exercise self-control, but allows these dispositions to grow unchecked, becomes a sorcerer.[30]

Bujo talks about "self-control," the AICs add intensive "prayer" to good moral life as a safeguard against evil. The "open space in the mind," a magnetic field or the spirit-dimension of the person, is never left empty. Prayer ensures the indwelling of God's Spirit, while the absence of prayer is an invitation to evil spirits to take up residence.

The Beti myth-narrative is however specific and focused on *woman* as mediating the entrance of *Evu* into human society; the evil spread to all her children. Mary Douglas gives an alternative narrative from the DRC (the Lele) that appears to take the woman totally off the table of blame. It is God's doing! "It was God who made sorcery. He gave it to a Lele chief (the chiefs are all sorcerers to this day); the chief revealed the secret to his friend, and so knowledge of sorcery spread."[31] This is a legitimate functionalist narrative that suspects the powers of male political leaders and uncles who exercise power and authority in a matrilineal society. But the connection of the Beti narrative with *woman* is not fortuitous. It highlights the ambivalence that characterizes West African, and perhaps African, perception of commerce with spirits and deities. The symbolism of woman, of the vagina/vulva and the womb, the strategic position of women and female deities in the critical areas and periods of human life, lead one to believe that the narrative goes beyond gender. It introduces the riddle of the human journey from dreaming innocence to the real imperfect world, by an obscure or shady passage (choice— through an orifice) that is foundational to being human. The passage or choice brings to awareness the difference between good and evil. Female elements capture the symbolism of this passage. The meaning of life as a

29. Douglas, "Problem of Evil among the Lele," 29.
30. Bujo, *Foundations of an African Ethic*, 128.
31. Douglas, "Problem of Evil among the Lele," 29.

spiritual combat that one goes through to achieve one's destined course in life, involves decision (combat) either to attract God's Holy Spirit into the "open space in the mind" or to invite habitation by the spirit of evil. The female orifice symbolizes the struggle in this passage—the combat between good and evil, between life and death with life predestined to win because backed by spiritual allies. Life is predestined to overcome shapeless toads (witchcraft) blocking the orifice (vagina) through which one effects passage into life. Sabine Jell-Bahlsen in her study of female deities among the Igbo underlines how crucial "Female elements, like water spirits, have a very special place in Igbo cosmology, with regard to the circular flow of time, reincarnation, challenge, and innovation. . . . The water goddess embodies female control over the crossroads between the ordinary and the extraordinary, between spirits and humans, between life and death." Therefore one can legitimately interpret *Woman* in the Beti narrative as the innovative, inventive mother-ancestress at the crossroads that opens human eyes to right and wrong. Despite the threat of patriarchy, men and women cooperate to reinvent the world. Jell-Bahlsen argues,

> The female side of the universe is not only complementary to the male but also pivotal to man, for his procreation, reincarnation, and continued existence within the circular flow of time. This is expressed in ritual and in the water goddess's power to challenge man's destiny. By balancing patrilineal kinship structures, women's ritual leadership reiterates the concept of complementarity between static and dynamic elements, conservative and creative forces, continuity and change, ancestors and water spirits, men and women.[32]

The carving or opening up of *woman*, by giving her vagina, a strategic symbol of birth-death, invention and reinvention, is captured in the syncretistic ritual of *Bwiti*. Initiation is imaged as regression or inverted birth through the vagina into the womb—the initiate assumes the form of the shapeless fetus, at the same time weak but dangerous. The orifice (vagina) that mediates this passage is crucial. *Bwiti* liturgy opens with a song emerging from the chamber of the women ministers (*yombo*): "God has slit open the woman, he has opened her; O God my

32. Jell-Bahlsen, "Lake Goddess, Uhammiri/Ogbuide," 48. See also the highly suggestive and interesting study of Nnobi, another Igbo village-group, by Amadiume, *Male Daughters, Female Husbands*.

sex (vagina) pains; the sacrifice made her woman, before then she did not know that she was woman."[33] This strategic and originary orifice, the door to life and death, ensures the passage into the womb—a regressive or inverted birth through initiation into the ideal shapeless fetus that in liminality represents strength in utter weakness. To describe *evu*, the "principle of evil," as taking a similar initiatory channel sharpens the complexity, ambivalence and ambiguity of language and behavior in the African world even with regard to the aporia of evil. It also heightens the ethical, aesthetical, and religious sensibility required to contain evil that is intimately connected with relationship. In relationship there is always the need for the second point of view, "something stands and another stands beside it." The prophet-visionary is empowered by God's Holy Spirit not only to have knowledge of curative plants but also the wisdom of serpents and simplicity of doves, to be holy and still have the ability to master the two faces of reality.

The Power of Evil Possession—The Witch in Action

Though the narratives about the origin of witchcraft may vary, African traditions are unanimous in the struggle against this "objectified evil." They deploy an array of therapeutic tools to counteract it. Before moving on to discuss the ministry of "deliverance," I draw attention to the psychology of the one who has the witchcraft virus. The resilient notion of person outlined by Hebga rationally comes to terms with the non-visible activity of those whom Africans call witches. For example, the language of cannibalism is connected with the non-visible aspect of the person. The cannibalism is mystical; an action performed from a distance. This is characteristic of the *soul-shadow* that overcomes the limits imposed by space and time. But for one 'to eat' another means that *evu* or *hu* (quality of perversion) is directly criminal. In other words, keeping to Hebga's language, the "breath" (equivalent to *psyche* and *pneuma* in Greek, *anima* and *spiritus* in Latin), i.e., the person that has *evu* or *hu*, proceeds 'to eat' another through the *soul-shadow* by deploying energy on the victim (energy from one field deployed against energy in another field).[34] The traditional expert, *dibia/nganga/babalawo/bokọnọ*, operates within this world to fight the evil.

33. Mary, "Le Schème De La Naissance À L'envers," 242.

34. Hebga, *La Rationalité D'un Discours Africain Sur Les Phénomènes Paranormaux*, 314–22.

One can bring the discussion on the psychology of the "witch" closer to the familiar language of West Africa, expanded through Christian missionary impact: the ability to deploy negative energy against another presupposes that one's "open space in the mind," the spiritual quality of one who has breath (*gbɔgbɔ* of the Ewe), has given residence to or is "possessed" by a spirit of evil that empowers one to attack others. This is the world presumed by AICs' prophets-visionaries (*woli*) and Catholic priest-healers who are involved in anti-witchcraft campaigns and deliverance ministry. Neo-Pentecostalism recognizes but radically excoriates this world as the field of the agency of Satan; it deploys spiritual energy (exorcism) to battle this world and to deliver its members and clients from Satan. This description of the psychology of the witch that I find satisfactory combines Hebga's explanation and the radical modification of West African cosmological ideas of groups like the Ewe, under the impact of missionary Christianity. But what then happens to the person attacked?

According to Asante (Ghanaian) notion of "breath," each human is endowed with a spiritual (pre-existent) principle, "breath" or *sunsum* (the individualizing principle equivalent to the Greek *nous*). "Breath" can be trained to be "heavy" to resist malevolent witches. When *sunsum* is not trained through discipline, it is "light" and liable to attacks. The person is attacked precisely because *sunsum* has not been trained to be "heavy" through self-discipline and especially through fidelity to one's destined course in life, enabling one to be under the shadow of God's providence. For AICs and the Pentecostals close to the African universe, one is attacked because one left the self without the protecting shield of God's embedding Holy Spirit acquired through ceaseless prayer. "Prayer" ensures that the *self* attracts the Holy Spirit to reside in the "open space in the mind." The attack is therefore a tragedy in which the victim is implicated; the victim is partly to blame.

Blaming the victim has been part of the interpretive, diagnostic and healing tools used by experts. Deliverance centers of AICs, neo-Pentecostals, Catholic Charismatic movements, insist that the most effective way to eliminate witchcraft is through the admission of the evil in oneself and renouncing it! For does each person not have the virus? The late Albert Atcho, prophet and pastor of the Harrist church at Bregbo (Cote d'Ivoire, derived from the movement of William Wade Harris), had a highly organized system of deliverance through confessions. The strategy is to hurl back the accusation of witchcraft onto the accuser. Only a witch can complain of witchcraft attack! This produces what Andras Zempléni qualified as "freedom" from a "persecution" complex obtained only through imprisonment in "diabolical responsibility."[35] For example, out of 3,618 recorded confessions from the Harrist Church studied by sociologist Colette Piault and colleagues, three categories of sin of sick persons and sick villages emerge, in the following order: (a) being a "devil" or "container of the devil" (*en diable*) or "having a devil"; (b) being involved in immoral sexual acts; and (c) cult of fetishes.[36] Only through confession, ritual purification, and abundant use of water from Bregbo would a person or a community be purified of the evil of witchcraft. The healing addresses both the community and the individual. Hurling the blame back on the victim does not exonerate the witch nor does it reduce accusations. Victims and experts claim the attacks have palpable effects.

The effect of the mystical attack of witchcraft is diagnosed as disequilibrium. The organs do not disappear, rather they are more or less disorganized. The Yaka (DRC) describe the victim as follows: he or she experiences "a state of lightness, aimlessness, disorientation, excessive heat, and effusion." These sensory experiences are symptomatic of the inversion of "body order." The process could degenerate and end up in what is called death.[37] The inversion of body order explains the language of cannibalistic feasts and also phantasmagoric copulation! One may be alive but already eaten. Witches could invade the sanctuary of marriage to engage in sexual intercourse with a woman or a man and thereby destabilize a person or a relationship for a whole lifetime.[38]

The above diagnostics follow Hebga's anthropological, psychological and metaphysical framework. This framework, dependent on a flexible and relational notion of person, where ambivalence is the norm, helps one to make sense of the discourse on morally imputable actions that nevertheless fall within the domain of the paranormal. Cote d'Ivoire and Cameroon include witchcraft on the table of their criminal code. How possible is this? Is it possible that the witchcraft virus, *evu* or *hu*,

35. Zempléni, "De La Persécution À La Culpabilité," 216.

36. Piault, *Prophétisme Et Thérapeutique*.

37. Devisch, *Weaving the Threads of Life*, 271. See also Hebga, *La Rationalité D'un Discours Africain Sur Les Phénomènes Paranormaux*, 321–22.

38. Devisch, *Weaving the Threads of Life*, 91, 99.

can take possession of a person (witch) and lead him/her to cause such devastating havoc: sterility and barrenness, mystic enslavement or magical conversion of the "victim's" energies to increase the wealth of the "criminal" (ogwu ego—popular in Nigeria and popularized by home-video films)? Is it possible that through witchcraft and sorcery one can seize the vital parts of another (genitals) to increase one's wealth? By extension, is it possible that those who actually commit murder and remove the vital parts of their victims, or who desecrate burial grounds for the same purpose, in order to fabricate *medicine* to increase wealth and power really do so? Home-video films, dominated by the ethics of "born again" Christian of neo-Pentecostalist strain, popularize and engineer this interpretation.[39]

The study of deities and the role of the elect and devotees of deities crucial in the West African world (chapter 3) underline the power, attraction and proliferation of possession. One could be possessed by spirits that need to be named and grounded, or by familiar deities. Possession linked with the capacity for good or for ill is taken for granted in the West African region. Therefore, though one cannot accept the narratives of the origin of witchcraft as proven scientifically (myths do not require proofs, rather they structure our understanding of life and inspire our behavior), one is not mistaken to note with Buakassa: behind any kind of magical thinking and practice "there always lies something *not put into words*."[40] The 'unfathomable' that is part and parcel of life and death imposes modesty in our approach to this aporia that generates so much ritual and ethical energy in the community.

Despite the excesses of witchcraft accusations, there is a positive intentionality that must be noted. According to Bujo,

> The fundamental intention of sorcery is to draw attention to evil, which can totally destroy human relationships, and hence the entire community; this positive intention should be interpreted anew in a Christian ethic, so that exaggerated beliefs in sorcery can be corrected by its understanding of evil.[41]

The community's rejection of evil as destructive of human relationships, as radically disruptive of the structures of the very definition of being

39. See Ukah, "Advertising God."

40. See Bujo, *Foundations of an African Ethic*, 134 referring to Buakasa, *L'impensé Du Discours. "Kindoki" Et "Nkisi" En Pays Kongo Du Zaïre*, 283ff.

41. Bujo, *Foundations of an African Ethic*, 140.

human, underlies anti-witchcraft campaigns. The mystical deployment of energy to block relationality is a structural evil that must be resisted at all costs. The ideal human bodily order that exudes gentleness and kindness, well-spoken-ness, peace or "coolness" is proposed in ritual and ethical practice. These are fundamental for the realization of communal and individual destiny. While the distortion of "body order" manifest in lightness, aimlessness, "disorientation, excessive heat, and effusion" experienced by the victim of witchcraft, is ritually and ethically rejected. African (particularly Southern African) wisdom tradition sum up the ideal in ritual and ethical practice as *ubuntu:* being generous, hospitable, friendly, caring and compassionate. "My humanity is caught up, is inextricably bound up, in yours." We belong in a bundle of life. "A person is a person through other persons." "I am human because I belong. I participate, I share."[42]

How does God's Holy Spirit enable or possess prophets-visionaries, charismatic priest-healers, Pentecostals who have received the "baptism in the Holy Spirit" or the Church as a whole to propose and practice the human ideal and neutralize the negative occultic powers for the common good? How does the prophet experience the empowerment to lead the spiritual combat? What insight does the prophet's mystical possession give us into the Christian experience of the Triune God through the Holy Spirit?

MYSTICAL POSSESSION BY GOD'S HOLY SPIRIT, ENABLER OF THE COMBAT AGAINST EVIL

The major point to note in the discussion so far is the recognition of the reality of occultic powers that threaten life because they threaten relationship and the destiny of the individual and community. Life is a spiritual combat. The understanding of the demography of evil varies. The radical dualistic focus of neo-Pentecostalism that I disagree with defines the territory of evil (Satan) in its widest terms; it covers any world that does not come under their fundamentalistic interpretation of the Bible. This includes visions of the universe of the AICs' and Roman Catholics ("the great Babylon"[43]) that recognize good and bad spirits and ancestral spirits. Neo-Pentecostalism regards all these spirits

---

42. Tutu, *No Future without Forgiveness*, 32.
43. See Ojo, *End-Time Army*, 80.

as under the agency of Satan. The reality of occultic forces and the reality of human weakness led the *Celestial Church of Christ* in Benin Republic to establish "holy ground" within their Church compound or "parish enclosure." The enclosure, under the protective wing of the Holy Spirit, is a secure buffer zone; the diverse services conducted within the secure enclosure are totally sealed from the effects of evil spirits. Within the enclosure are designated centers—"prayer ground" and, especially, "place of security." The image is not dissimilar to the sacredness associated with *vodhun* shrines under the security of a particular *vodhun*. Most *Aladura Churches* in Nigeria possess a secluded place called "mercy ground" for the protection of the distressed; these places are totally secured from the hostile attack of witches and evil spirits. Catholic priest-healers regard their centers of prayer as "holy ground." Catholic Parishes have not only adoration chapels (where the Blessed Sacrament is exposed) but also "Gethsemane" and "Golgotha," where one could find wells from which to draw "holy water." Claffey finds it particularly interesting that architectural designs of some Catholic parishes in Benin Republic (e.g., St. Michel, Cotonou) copy the pattern of the *Celestial Churches* (e.g., Akpakpa Center, Cotonou). The idea behind such structural designs is the assurance of the presence of God's Holy Spirit that gives protection to the sick and distressed, to pregnant women and people having difficulty living within their families. Prophets-visionaries of AICs, charismatic priest-healers, and gifted people within the charismatic movements counsel or give directed retreats or prayer sessions to people who spend days in seclusion and prayer within the enclosure. The *Church of the Lord (Aladura*—Nigeria) pays special attention to the spiritual and material care of pregnant women. During the final 3 months of pregnancy the expectant mother may go to reside in the faith-home where she will engage in more frequent spiritual exercises, learn more about child-care from experienced women who are in charge of this particular ministry: "The time of delivery is felt to be a crisis when a woman is especially susceptible to the attacks of witchcraft and enemies, but prayer and faith, assisted sometimes by a dream or vision, set her free from the resultant inhibitions and tensions, so that labour is facilitated."[44] In this way, Christianity, like ATR, is becoming a therapeutic religion. This is the

---

44. Turner, *African Independent Church*, vol. II: The Life and Faith of the Church of the Lord (Aladura), 152–53. See also Surgy, *L'église Du Christianisme Céleste*, 101f., 106, 262ff. Claffey, *Christian Churches in Dahomey-Benin*, Appendix 10A and 10B.

context within which one should understand the "descent" of the Holy Spirit on the elect to enable them render services to the community—the elect have a true mystical experience but it is an experience with a radical social agenda.

The Descent of the Holy Spirit—Ritual Drama

The ordination liturgy of visionaries in the *Celestial Church of Christ* invokes God: "Come and stay with your laborers. Your servants (the visionaries) are prostrate on the floor in your name. Descend and enter into them. . . ." The ministry of visionaries involves frequent experiences of the "descent" of the Holy Spirit registered through trance. The experience of trance generated by being possessed by God's Spirit involves the disquieting temporary loss of memory—a major point of criticism of AICs by the Catholic Church. But as will be discussed below, the ATR background that constitutes the pre-text for the experience of visionaries sees no problem in the temporary loss of memory. The assembly that is integral to the mystical experience has clear memory of what happened and is focused on the therapeutic reasons for the possession of the initiates or the elect by the spirits. AICs, one has to insist, are "Spirit-Churches." The presence of God's Spirit throbs within the Church; and then the Spirit's goodwill to heal becomes manifest through the "possession" of visionaries. The assembly's groaning "with eager longing" (cf. Rom 8:19, 22) for the indwelling Holy Spirit is captured in seductive prayers for the Spirit to descend like the following hymn:

> Heavenly Dove come down,
> Come down, come down
> I open my heart to you
> Holy Spirit, come down.[45]

"I open of my heart to you" is facilitated not only by the attraction which "the open space in the mind" has for God's Spirit but also by the assurance of God's protecting power in the community through the gift of ordained ministry of visionaries-prophets. The ordination prayer of the *Celestials* is insistent: "You spoke and said that vision gives weight to your Church. You said that a Church that has no vision is lost. This is why we put into your hands your laborers who provide accurate predic-

---

45. Olayiwola, "Interaction of African Independent Churches with Traditional Religions in Nigeria," 368.

tions. . . . Put Ezekiel into them. . . ." The Holy Spirit is *enticed* by *sound* and rhythm to descend and possess or indwell the "open space in the mind" of the chosen one. A leader of the *Church of the Lord, Aladura*, underlined sound as a key attraction for the descending Holy Spirit:

> Why do you need to sing, dance, clap and engage in all sorts of lively entertainments before the Holy Spirit could descend? Because sweet songs, drums, and the like are relished goods of the Holy Spirit. The Spirit would therefore descend on hearing them.[46]

AICs recapture the dimension of *sound* in the African world that attracts the descending *orisa* or *vodhun* to take possession, enter or "mount" the head of the devotee. This is transferred to the descending Holy Spirit. The descent of the Holy Spirit is preceded by the correct dispositions that make the Spirit "laugh." Access to God, in this mystic experience of descent, is a rhythmic or throbbing experience that is full of play (making humans and God's Spirit laugh). I borrow the language of play or "laughter" from the Rwandan ATR as observed by Alex Arnoux in the early twentieth century. The ritual texts of initiation into *Lyangombe* and other cults recorded by Arnoux contain prayers of thanksgiving and request in favor of a petitioner such as: "Be favorable towards him, deliver him from all evils; laugh and laugh loudly [boisterously]."[47] The sound of the drum, in West African ATR, radically adapted by the AICs, links deities, initiates and the whole assembly into healthy merriment. Through diligent training the initiated woman or man internalizes the rhythm of the talking drum, leaves herself open to be entered or "mounted" by the spirit, and thereby to double as the spirit. Whether the initiate is male or female she becomes *vodhunsi* or *iyawo*—"wife" of the possessing *orisa* or *vodhun*. In the liturgy of AICs and Charismatic movements the dispositions that attract God's Spirit are prayer, songs and sustained percussion with the talking drum. With these on the ground, trance, ecstasy and glossolalia testify to the presence of or possession by God's Holy Spirit. Paul told the Ephesians to

---

46. Turner, *African Independent Church*, 127.

47. See Arnoux, "Le Culte De La Société Secrète Des Imandwawa Au Ruanda" (1912); and Arnoux, "Le Culte De La Société Secrète Des Imandwawa Au Ruanda," (1913). The texts concern a confirmation ceremony that few fulfill scores of years after initiation as devotees of Lyangombe—Arnoux, "Le Culte De La Société Secrète Des Imandwawa Au Ruanda," 7 (1912) 841.

be "filled with the Spirit, as you sing psalms and hymns and spiritual songs among yourselves, singing and making melody to the Lord in your hearts" (Eph 5:19). Christianity in West Africa welcomes *sound* as melody mediating or attracting the Holy Spirit. *Sound externalizes* the internal life (orthopraxis) of a church that God's Spirit enables to be vibrant with one heart and one soul.

Philosophers from the West African region have tried to construct a theory of knowledge of and access to the universe through the symbol of Sound or Drum. K. C. Anyanwu (Nigeria) proposes that *sound* mediates the "participant-performer" dynamics of knowing. Since knowledge is never experienced in total detachment, the ambivalence or conflict in the experience of the self and the other becomes reconciled through *sound. Sound* is Life-force; humans are life-ing (as opposed to Be-ing) who through music and dance access "the universe of Sound," which is ultimate reality.[48] Niangoran-bouah (Côte d'Ivoire) focuses on the *Drum* as the overriding symbol of access to life and to the sacred in Africa. Drum-texts that accompany the initiation of boys and girls, coronation of kings, funerals, New Year and New Yam festivals, and so on, display the "Bible" or the "Quran" of ATR.[49]

> Bible, Quran, and Drum have the same vocation; these are fundamental sacred 'books' venerated by their respective peoples ... The discourse of the drum, unchangeable and conventional, is not a discourse of an isolated man, but a real ideology of several thousand years which the memory of a whole people preserves with piety from generation to generation.[50]

Sound as life-force materialized in the *drum* is ungraspable, like the *spirit* that is *life* (*ruah* or *pneuma*). This ungraspable *Sound* (Spirit) has ultimately its origin in God—God's Spirit that is drawn or attracted by the *sound-symbol* or *drum* to descend and inhabit the throbbing personality of the assembly and to manifest its healing power through the ministry of the elect. The divine source of this experience in West Africa

---

48. See Anyanwu, "Response to A. G. A. Bello's Methodological Preliminaries," 67. Anyanwu's principal argument is in Anyanwu, "Sound as Ultimate Reality and Meaning."

49. See Niangoran-bouah, "La Drummologie Et La Vision Négro-Africaine Du Sacré." An English version of this article is available Niangoran-bouah, "Talking Drum."

50. Niangoran-bouah, "Talking Drum," 92.

is illustrated in the Abron (Ghanaian) drum-text that chants the origin of the drum in words that evoke Proverbs 8:22–31:

> While organising the world,
> God-the-Creator
> Has suffered to create.
> What did He create?
> He has created the Word
> And the Word-carrier,
> Has created the drum and
> The drummer. . . .
> Divine Drum,
> Wherever you be
> In nature,
> We call upon you, come!
> Divine drum,
> We shall wake you up
> And make you heard" (*Abron drum text*)
>
> "I am coming from my dream
> And find myself
> In the hands
> Of the drummer." (*Abron drum*)[51]

In traditional Igbo culture this "language of the drum," especially the *ikolo,* is understood "by the neighbouring villages": "Its sound invigorates and stirs up the people to mad action irrespective of consequences, especially when the beater causes it to vibrate the gallant names of persons, age grades, villagers and the town at large." As the drums call these names they stir also to violence and war and not only to merriment. In olden times, at a village-group such as Umuchu in Anambra State of Nigeria, "human skulls" hung as trophies of war around the *ikolo* that is "carved out of a strong heavy log of wood and measured eighteen and half feet long [c. 5.6m], five and half feet high [c. 1.6m], and carved-in about two and half feet [76cm] deep."[52]

The radical adaptation of *sound* in AICs and Charismatic movements and in general liturgical inculturation in the Catholic Church still retains the *Drum* as a potent symbol attracting the assembly and God's Spirit into deep encounter. This plays a strategic role in the descent of the

---

51. Ibid., 86.

52. Nnolim, *History of Umuchu, 32*; also Achebe, *Arrow of God*, 79–80.

Holy Spirit on prophets and visionaries, or rather in the ecstatic experience of these ministers. This should not sound strange or heterodox. The Hebrew tradition is replete with the evidence of *sound* of the harp or lyre as relished goods of God's Spirit. Prophets routinely played these instruments to pass into trance or "prophetic frenzy" (cf. 1 Sam 10:5–6). David's extraordinary skill "in playing the lyre" (cf. 1 Sam 16:16–23) and its therapeutic results converted him into a healer in later Judaic tradition. Even a prophet of the standing of Elisha who inherited "a double share" of Elijah's spirit needed the mediation of *sound* to be possessed by the Spirit of Yahweh. In the process of giving accurate predictions of a military campaign to the kings of Judah and Israel who went to consult him, music was required to dispose both the prophet and the Spirit. "But get me a musician." "And then, while the musician was playing, the power of the LORD came on him. And he said, 'Thus says the LORD . . .'" (2 Kgs 2:14–16). Christians in West Africa are in very good company when they insist on music and songs as means to clear the ground for the descent of the Holy Spirit.

Mysticism with Social Agenda

The focus on mysticism with a social agenda runs through AICs and the Charismatic movements in the mainline churches. In other words, the descent of the Holy Spirit is for the common good—principally for the therapeutic good of members of the community. There is a radical continuity between what happens among the AICs and in the ATR worship. The Holy Spirit descending on the chosen 'mediums' or prophets follows the traditional pattern of "mounting the head" of the *vodhun-si* (wife of the spirit; or wife of the *orisa*—*iyawo-orisa*). However, the intentionality of the mystic experience is not to escape (flee) from the world (like the familiar Western Christian image of the mystic) but to participate in the divine nature, represent the deity, and transmit saving messages to the laity.[53]

The clear divergence of West African mystical experience, as mediated through ATR memory, from the Jewish-Christian heritage is manifest in AICs despite their strong appeal to Scripture as warrant for the experience of the Holy Spirit. This fundamental ancestral spirituality, that is pre-text for the popular appeal to the Spirit among AICs,

---

53. See Parrinder, "Le Mysticisme Des Médiums En Afrique Occidentale," 137.

Charismatics and neo-Pentecostals (though neo-Pentecostals would be horrified at such a suggestion), illuminates pneumatology. Among the AICs the descent of the Spirit (trance) is always accompanied by utterances (the language of angels—according to the *Celestial Church of Christ*) for the benefit of those present. This expands tradition; and is carefully recorded.[54]

The experience of possession, manifest in trance or ecstasy, a key block in ATR ritual practice, enjoys profound dignity and influence and is assimilated into Christian practice. Issiaka Lalèyê and Kabasele-Lumbala argue that possession is the peak experience towards which African ritual practices tend. It is a realization of human closeness to God through divinization. ATR mysticism of "descent" demarcates itself from the Jewish-Christian "ascent" of the soul to God—e.g., Origen's *ascensiones in corde*. It also differs from the Hindu "descent" of the self into the One (atman becoming Brahman). It rather prefers "prayer" for the descent of the deity into the beloved. Possession is therefore cherished by the African religious imagination. Kabasele and Lalèyê would agree with Zahan that the "beatific vision" projected in African spirituality is "this worldly." In Zahan's view, the distance or "withdrawal" of God in ATR intensifies the human need for God, intensifies the human aspiration (groaning "with eager longing," cf. Rom 8:19, 22) "to become God." However, this does not imply abandoning the "human condition" so as to "rise to the sky in order to peacefully bask in the beatific vision." "Rather, he [the African] obliges God to come to earth, to renew his closeness to man, to descend to him in order to divinize him."[55] Zahan may be adapting the Greek *homoiôsis* to the African context. I already noted above that there is a fundamental homology between Origen's *human pneuma* and the West African *ori, okra, chi, aklama, se,* the *personal spirit*. Both provide enabling anthropological grounding for the magnetic pull of God's Holy Spirit. In the mystical experience, both traditions represent the mystic in intimate rapture. While Origen's *ascensiones in*

---

54. See the interesting pictorial documentary along with commentary on the religious traditions of Benin Republic in Christoph and Oberländer, *Vaudou—Les Forces Secrètes De L'afrique*, esp. 83–95; see also Surgy, *L'église Du Christianisme Céleste*, 205ff. and the whole of chapter 8.

55. Zahan, *Religion, Spirituality, and Thought of Traditional Africa*, 16–17. For the views of Lalèyê and Kabasele see Laléyé, "L'accès À Dieu Dans Les Religions Négro-Africaines Traditionnelles"; and also Laléyé, "De La Quête Spirituelle De L'afrique Contemporaine," 54–68. Kabasele Lumbala, *Alliances Avec Le Christ En Afrique*, 317–48.

corde displays the mystic pulled upward to pneumatic life, the ATR inspired model represents the Spirit descending into the mystic. While one
may call Origen's "ascent" a transcendent mysticism, one could call ATR
inspired Spirit's "descent" a kenotic mysticism. In the former the Spirit
captures the *nous* (the intellectual soul and hegemonic principle) to the
point that the *psyche* and *soma* become spiritualized or divinized. In the
latter the descending Spirit enters into or possesses the person, shares
human fragility, and transforms and gives new energy (spiritualization)
to the fragile human condition, healing and empowering the community. This mystical experience confirms the divine companionship,
the embedding and indwelling Providence very dear to West Africans
and Diaspora Africans. Equiano expresses this indwelling Providence
in terms of being "a *particular favorite of heaven.*" James Cone refers to
it as a fundamental dimension of the spirituality of the *Black Church:*
"God did not bring us this far to leave us." This spirituality or mysticism
embodies liberation, love and hope;[56] a kenotic mysticism, mediated by
God's Holy Spirit, in which the Triune God suffers with us and for us, to
heal and divinize us.

Ecstasy, trance or possession in AIC practice is always a mystical
experience with a social agenda. One may even suggest (in view of the
ATR matrix) that it is an experience under social pressure—the song and
prayer for the Spirit to come down make the suggestion credible. The
reason for the descent of the Spirit on "his laborers" is more often than
not the prediction of illnesses, healing, discovering of medicinal herbs,
and driving away evil people or spirits. This is a creative Christian appropriation of the dimensions of ATR mysticism. Western Christianity
regards all possession as diabolical and tries to distinguish possession
from the quiet and private feelings that accompany ecstatic experiences
of saints, which in most cases do not go beyond levitation or tears. This
Western experience with its focus on the individual is legitimate, but
must not be allowed to override the imaginative creativity of the African
mystical experience.

Africa provides a legitimate and interesting viewpoint on mystical
experience that should stand alongside genuine mysticism in world religions, because of the intensity and extensity of the experience in West

---

56. See Equiano, *Interesting Narrative of the Life of Olaudah Equiano*, 33; also Cone,
Martin & Malcom & America, chapter 5.

Africa and in the diaspora.[57] The strategic position of the social agenda of this mystical experience, despite the disquieting loss of memory, imposes a this-worldly stamp on mysticism. Mysticism and integral human liberation are bedfellows. Roger Bastide, initiate and expert in Candomble, cast suspicion on Western Christian mystical experience because of the facility with which it can slip into the selfish and egotistical that John of the Cross also denounced. Bastide points out two qualities that differentiate Western Christian and African experience. First, in ATR, the focus is on spirits or deities that enter or "mount the head of the chosen"; the Christian, on the other hand, focuses on the Absolute or transcendent one. In the African mystical experience the Transcendent One God, the "Supreme Being"—*Chukwu, Onyame, Amma, Mawu,* or *Olodumare*—never "mounts" or enters anybody; only God's emissaries mount and give messages for the good of the community. Second, the social agenda of all possession or manifestation of the spirit through the medium makes the sociological the overriding concern. On the other hand, Christian mysticism possesses no clear social agenda and leaves itself open to pathology. No doubt Christian mysticism, a true experience of the sacred, is orientated to "saving the world," saving souls or saving the dead. But these do not equate clearly with (or give priority to) the sociological. In African mysticism the sociological dominates a genuine spiritual experience.[58] This has been creatively assimilated into West African Christianity.

This social dimension of the mystical experience frees African mysticism from the danger to pathology that threatens mystical experiences. Pathological disorder accompanies the initial impact of deities that have to be grounded, molded in clay, installed in a shrine, worshipped and have devotees who, after initiation are periodically possessed during ritual. As the deity builds the community, the community and devotees build the image of the deity. Possession outside the normal ritual drama, after one has gone through initiation, not predicated in the sound and rhythm of the drum, is symptomatic of infidelity of the initiate. Ecstasy and trance therefore do not arise from the effect of psychological disorder; they are rather understood as mystical experiences that are expected and that could arise from social pressure.

57. See Olupona and Rey, Òrìsà Devotion as World Religion.

58. Bastide and Parrinder expressed their views in discussion following the paper of Parrinder, "Le Mysticisme Des Médiums En Afrique Occidentale," esp. 138–42.

The impact of the social does not minimize the individuality of the mystical experience. Trance is the privileged occasion for the communion of the initiated with the possessing spirit; and this forms the most important dimension of the initiates' religious life.[59] The trance or possession is particularly important for the analysis of the state of the individual who loses memory during the momentary period of the experience. First, "breath," or the person's non-visible dimension (*shadow-soul*), has been providentially enabled to receive the kind of indwelling called possession, ecstasy or trance. In AICs, spiritual exercises ("prayer") ensure that the *self* (e.g., of the *woli* or prophet/seer of the *Celestial Church Christ*) is opened up so that the Holy Spirit takes residence in the "open space in the mind." Mystical experience enables a deep spiritual life while fulfilling a sociological function.

The Holy Spirit, following the descending order of Trinitarian economy, descends to dwell in the elect or the laborers for the function assigned to them by God (the extension of the Kingdom of God). The difference between Origen's picture of the mystical experience and the West African Christian mysticism is that in Origen the "Holy Spirit" through the human *pneuma* draws the saint upwards (ascent) to holiness, while in West Africa the descending Holy Spirit takes possession of the elect. The Holy Spirit "fills the earth" (descending and remaining) to empower the community through the elect to resolve problems of this world. Or, in the *Celestials'* evangelistic terms, the Holy Spirit descends on the laborers who "through suitable intercessions contribute to the extension of the kingdom of God."

Instead of being relegated to a purely private experience, African religious mystical experience notoriously dominates the public arena; and, predictably, comes into conflict with mainline Christian spirituality. The Catholic Church in particular suspects the trance whether in the charismatic movements or in the AICs. First, they are overtly public and boisterous (as prayer, chants, and percussion from the drum and other musical instruments speak to attract the Holy Spirit). Furthermore, the Catholic Church objects to the depersonalizing aspect of possession. The elect of the Spirit experiences loss of memory concerning what happened during trance or possession. This renders possession less controllable.[60] But, as noted above, the loss of memory poses no problem in the

59. Ibid., 137.

60. See Eric de Rosny's interesting comments on this: Rosny, *L'afrique Des Guérisons*,

world-vision of ATR, because the assembly that fully participates in the mystical experience has clear memory of what happened and is focused on the therapeutic reasons for the possession of the initiates or the elect by the Holy Spirit. This irreplaceable community (social group) lays the foundation, draws up the parameters and even determines the nature of spiritual experience in its totality.[61] AICs, Pentecostals, and Charismatics hold on to trance or possession that includes loss of memory. They claim that these are totally consonant with the biblical faith and are indispensable for the extension of the Kingdom of God. In addition, they claim that a clear boundary is set between the charlatan and the beloved of the Spirit, based on the social agenda of the manifestation of the Spirit—for or against the common good.

There is no doubt that a ministry of discernment of spirits is necessary in any Christian community that welcomes this particular dimension of African and biblical religion. AICs, the Charismatic movements, and Pentecostals are guided by the unimpeachable logic: the intention of God for religions, including the Christian religion, is the healing service for humans. This is realized in mysticism that is the peak of religious experience, the peak of communing with the Triune God in the Holy Spirit.

INCULTURATION IN HARMONY
WITH THE CATHOLIC TRADITION

The previous chapters tried to clarify the AICs' pneumatological procedure, dependent on the ATR worldview, but at the same time capable of being aligned with the Trinitarian imagination of the great Christian tradition. This pneumatological procedure, shared in varying degrees by Charismatic movements and Pentecostals, should be more widely discussed and critiqued so that their insight into Spirit-directed Church Order could be integrated into the mainline Church Order. The prophetic theological option of converting Semitic deities into allies or foes of Yahweh and the assumption of epithets of deities into the personality of Yahweh has been creatively replicated in AICs. While mainline churches (Evangelicals more than Catholics) and neo-Pentecostalism

---

129–32, and especially chapter 7 with title, "Renouveau charismatique et transe en Afrique."

61. Laléyé, "De La Quête Spirituelle De L'afrique Contemporaine," esp. 62–63.

favor a dualistic approach, AICs adopt a flexible relational approach. This appears to me to be closer to the Catholic character of the Church.

The labor of developing an acceptable pneumatology in the West African region is helped along with the sophisticated but lucid analysis of Origen on God-Word-Spirit, spirit-soul-body, and especially on the oneness and multiplicity of the Son and the Holy Spirit. Only the Father is absolutely One (*ho theos*—"the" God—the origin of origins), while the other persons of the Trinity are multiple in their denominations. But God's absolute oneness rather than turning God inwards turns God naturally outwards: God suffers! Moltmann and others talk about the "Suffering God." Origen, immersed in Greek culture, gave priority to the Christian Scriptures, and, in opposition to Greek philosophical mono-theism, made extraordinary non-Greek statements about God's human-ity. In his *Commentary on Matthew* 22:1–14 (the royal wedding feast), he declared: "Just as God, who governs human beings is called a man in the parable, perhaps he does indeed become one in some way."[62]

AICs like other Christians do not question the Incarnation of the Son of God—a revelation that is unique to Christianity and "completely incomprehensible" to the "traditional Kikuyu" or African.[63] In West Africa, God alone can be called God (*Chukwu, Olodumare, Onyame, Mawu, Amma,* etc) in the *exercise of supreme power*. Other deities or spirits derive existence from God (even though there are areas where they exercise autonomous, plenipotentiary, though not supreme, power.) The West African context encourages developments in pneumatology. God's healing and consoling power or presence is displayed as Spirit, assimilated and radically transformed in Christianity as the Holy Spirit. Just as the power of the plenipotentiary deities, focused on given areas of healing services within the community, does not threaten the One God, the Holy Spirit revealed as the Spirit of God encompassing all these areas of healing services, does not threaten the One God. Rather the Holy Spirit owes existence to God through the Son, the Crucified-Risen One. The multiple deities, in their variety of operations in favor of the community, are transformed into the operations and denominations of the Holy Spirit of God. They are aspects of the Holy Spirit or charisms through which the Holy Spirit is operative within the Christian com-

---

62. Figura, "Suffering of God in Patristic Theology," considers this statement "as-tonishing," 378.

63. See Kibicho, "Interaction of the Traditional Kikuyu Concept of God," 226.

munity. This transformation is not only possible but is already on the ground, despite the schizophrenia that accompanies practice.

I do not share the dualistic pessimism of the new African Pentecostalism; it introduces a radical reorganization of African cosmology and demonizes all spirits in the ancestral religious universe. For these Christians, there is a sharp divide between covenanting with Christ (that radically excludes ancestral world of spirits) and covenanting with the African ancestral world of spirits (or stewing in "paganism").[64] This radical discontinuity between the Gospel and the religions, the stock-in-trade of radical evangelicalism, has never been the Catholic viewpoint. I opt for the hermeneutical principle of always looking at everything twice and reject the practical dualism propagated by missionary Christianity and exaggerated in Pentecostalism. Evangelization is always confronted with "the unknown God" (cf. Acts 17:22–31). It has never been the Catholic practice to insulate the message narrowly within the terms set by and comprehensible to the world of the messenger. Going elsewhere, engaging in intercultural dialogue, and being involved in the difficult task of the discernment of spirits contain risks. Ultimately the risky venture presents "the unknown God" and perhaps proposes the therapeutic God we want to know.

It will be a tragedy to dismiss the wealth of God's gift to West Africa—the religion that is accessible through the multiplicity of operations of God's Spirit in the various deities that populate the region. I agree with Adolphe Gesché that the genius of Catholicism, as displayed in the history of Christian thought, is ensuring the preservation of the "pagan heritage." In the West, the "pagan heritage" ("the pagan-ness" of ancestral tradition) "remained the Christian heritage so as not to be lost to humanity." The option to preserve this treasure ensured that the Christian religion escaped a death-dealing self-insulation, "a solitary identity robbed of the presence of a regenerating otherness, of a challenging vis-à-vis."[65] Similarly, one of the pillars of the "pagan heritage" of West Africa that should not be lost to humanity is the flexible, relational and dynamic perception of hierarchy in divinity. This has been carried by AICs into the reception of God-Christ-Spirit. The overriding focus is God-Spirit for human wholeness. Christians have access to God's many blessings through the Spirit's gifts or charisms for the common good.

---

64. See Kalu, "Estranged Bedfellows?" esp. 137–38.

65. Gesché, "Le Christianisme Comme Athéisme Suspensif," 206–7.

The Spirit is the entry point to the Triune God. Catholic and Protestant Charismatic movements agree! The adoption of such pneumatological procedure in mainline churches facilitates the inclusion of the ministry of diviner-healers within the structures of the church.

The above exploration retains and radically transforms the picture and mediatory pattern of the universe of West Africa. It evokes other viewpoints, especially those of Origen, in searching the Scriptures, to propose alternative ways of perceiving the divine in being and operation. It emphasizes that God is the mystery that is approached only by way of multiplicity. In the West African perception of dynamic hierarchy and flexibility in divinity, the multiplicity of spirits and the distance of God are valid ways of stressing transcendence, communion and mystery. Basically, in West Africa, as elsewhere in the world, God remains unknowable. However, for the West African heritage to remain the "Christian heritage so as not to be lost to humanity," it is radically being assimilated into Christianity. In the *spirit-oriented* West African Christianity, the God revealed in Jesus Christ, assimilates the providential qualities of God in West Africa, transcendent and yet mystically close to the community and to each individual human, generating human wholeness in the Holy Spirit.

Conclusion

Re-appropriating the God of Wholeness in the Spirit

Contribution to World Theology

WHEN FRANCISCAN MISSIOLOGIST AND theologian, Walbert Bühl-mann, announced the *Coming of the Third Church* (1976), few anticipated the theological implications. It was precisely at that point in time that the Ecumenical Association of Third World Theologians (EATWOT 1976, Dar-es-Salaam) drew a line of demarcation between their theological methodology and the dominant Western method in theology. They opted for a radical epistemological break that makes theology a reflection on praxis. The epistemological break has taken diverse trajectories.

The argument of this book is that the life of West African Christians on the ground, i.e., their practice and perception of God's redemptive action in Jesus Christ, translates into an approach to God as author of wholeness in the Spirit of the Crucified-Risen Jesus Christ. It is an experience of the *same* Triune God of the great tradition; an experience that is certainly Christian but very much dependent on the West African constituency—a constituency that lays high premium on *spirit*. Has this any impact on world theology or world Christianity? Is it of interest only to missiometrics? [Missiometrics 2008 and 2009[1] show that Africa has more Christians than Asia; Africa's total population is barely 25 percent of Asia]. What would Western Christian theology, that provided the re-

---

1. See *International Bulletin of Missionary Research* 32 (2008) and 33 (2009).

source for the evangelization of West Africa, learn from this orientation? How would Western theology challenge this approach to God?

In my conclusion I do not intend to take up methodological issues discussed in my opening chapter. I conclude by making three points related to how theologians from other regions of the world could benefit from the main body of this book: (1) the importance of constituency in every theology; (2) the need to put the Holy Spirit on the driving seat of any theology that critically analyses the impact of God on the life of Christians redeemed by the death-resurrection of Jesus Christ; and flowing from the inspiring God's Spirit, (3) the reshaping or remapping of the human, and the entire world, thanks to the embedding of the Holy Spirit that enables divine human encounter: an encounter mediated or experienced as God's outpouring of God's self, a kenosis that first generates the story of God's self as God for us, and then displays the God that heals and renews us, the God that builds us as community and enables generosity in us for the transformation of life in the world.

CONSTITUENCY AS INSPIRATIONAL AND LIMITING TO THE THEOLOGICAL TASK

Western theology is profoundly marked by modernity, by the Western enlightenment logic. Theologians from the region, whether liberal or evangelical, devote enormous energy to elaborate philosophical reasoning in order to accept or modify it, or in order to declare reason inadequate as starting point for the discussion of God's revelation that creates/recreates human life lived in the faith. The question Rahner addressed at the beginning of his *Foundations of Christian Faith* could apply to peoples anywhere in the world, but certainly arises from the Western life-experience and horizon of understanding: "What is a Christian, and why can one live this Christian existence today with intellectual honesty"?[2] French theologian, Joseph Moingt, argues that one cannot discuss redemption in Jesus Christ, that one cannot discuss the Trinity in the West without facing up to the enlightenment challenge: Faith as an intellectual act requires that my belief accords with my reason and not simply with the reason of "others"; without this, faith would not be "an integrally human act." Familiarity with philosophical reasoning is therefore the prerequisite or basis to display the reasonableness of faith

---

2. Rahner, *Foundations of Christian Faith*, 2.

that accords with one's reason. It enables one to discuss with those who do not share our beliefs but communicate with the language of reason alone. In this perspective Moingt disagrees with the evangelicalism of Eberhard Jüngel. Jüngel's consuming passion to make faith in the Crucified-Risen God the starting point of the definition of the human in the world led him to reject the priority of philosophical reasoning in Christian theology. For Moingt such arrogant faith that, in the name of revelation, determines or regiments thought and denies philosophical reason competence to name God fails to display the reasonableness of the faith to the believer.[3] I think the above samples illustrate how Western theologians relate to their constituency.

Three young African theologians, Bede Ukwuije, Augustin Ramazani Bishwende, and Benoît Awazi Mbambi Kungua, recently published their dissertations that focused on the Triune God revealed in the Crucified-Risen Jesus. All three show familiarity with Western philosophical reasoning. Nevertheless, they are all profoundly concerned with the inculturation of Trinitarian life in the African context. By extension they would see Western theology as embodying a particular viewpoint in world theology. In their view Trinitarian life that is a life of creative self-emptying and communion, revealed on the Cross of Jesus Christ, stands either as entry point for discussing theology or as focal point for the radical holistic transformation of African life and world.[4] My interest in these three new generation African theologians (who defended their dissertations in French and Belgian universities) arises from their patient exploration of the African and Western thought, the critical analysis of both, their firm conviction that theology in Africa must distance itself from self-defensive (negative) apologetics, and that the object of theology should either be the starting point or the focal point of theological discourse.[5]

Going through the works of the new generation African theologians convinced me of the value of my book as an important contribu-

3. Moingt, *Dieu Qui Vient À L'homme*, 39; 58–59.

4. Ukwuije, *Trinité Et Inculturation*. Ramazani Bishwende, *Pour Une Ecclésiologie Trinitaire Dans La Postmodernité Et La Mondialisation*, vol. 1: De R. Bellarmin à Y. Congar. Ramazani Bishwende, *Pour Une Ecclésiologie Trinitaire Dans La Postmodernité Et La Mondialisation*, vol. 2: De la Déconstruction à la Réception de Vatican II. Kungua, *Le Dieu Crucifié En Afrique*.

5. See my review of their works in Uzukwu, "Trinity in Contemporary African Theology."

tion to a new approach to the task of theology from the perspective of West Africa. The "second point of view" is particularly vital in theology. The consummate passion of my constituency, made up of practicing and reflecting Christians, does not take off from or anchor on rationally justifying to "my reason" why I should believe with intellectual honesty. This is important and valuable; and is not ignored by African theology that considers the Western enlightenment logic one of its conversational partners. However, my West African constituency is primarily preoccupied with the Holy Spirit of God, revealed in the Crucified-Risen Jesus Christ, as enabler of intensive communion; the Spirit that completely takes over the life of the Christian for holistic growth and healing of the community and individual. The Holy Spirit naturally, for my constituency, becomes the entry point to explore the Triune God. To ensure that the context and background of the West African Christian is clearly accessible to my readers, I made a detailed analysis of the pattern of communication with the divine; and I showed how this communication with the divine is fundamentally spirit-directed, spirit-focused and spirit-embedded. This is why my analysis and narrative culminated in spirituality: the inhabitation of the Holy Spirit of God in the "open-space in the mind" of the Christian faithful ensures life in the Triune God and transformation of the community and the individual.

Has my interest in my constituency perhaps made me take my eye off the object of theology? I do not think so; unless one imagines that the discourse on West African approach to the divine that is spirit-embedding is a distraction. Nor do I think that philosophical theology, an orientation that characterizes Western theological thinking, has no place in the theology of God. But I do think that any theology that takes its eye off the directing and abiding Holy Spirit is endangering its definition as Christian theology: the reflection on the faith-encounter of the community with the revealing God of the Crucified and Risen Jesus. The Holy Spirit is the enabler of Christian communities—creating the possibility for Christians to immediately relate to the power of the Crucified and Risen Jesus, appropriate the self-emptying of the Triune God that engenders generosity within the Christian community and the world, and embrace the mission to live this relationship that translates into the transformation of the world. This informs my next point, for it is necessary for me to clarify my agreement and disagreement with some of my younger colleagues; and by extension to stress what world theology should learn from my book.

POSITIONING THE HOLY SPIRIT ON THE DRIVING SEAT OF THEOLOGY

In my reflection on the theological orientation of my younger colleagues, I summed up what emerges from their critical evaluation of both African and Western systems of theological thinking as a preoccupation with "repositioning God on the driving seat of theology." The tenor of my book is not very different from the intentionality of their project. However, my evaluation of what is on the ground, from the West African Christian perspective, is that the Holy Spirit should be on the driving seat of theology. I do not derive this principle only from Origen's position that the Holy Spirit is closest to humans in the Trinitarian order of relationship. Rather I am confirmed in this by the overwhelming spirit-directed approach to the divine in West African traditional religion that in my view is the horizon of appropriating the Christ event; this strongly influences Christian life in the West African region. Some of my younger colleagues will quarrel with me over this position. And Western theology, especially of evangelical leaning, will distance itself from what I am saying.

The three African theologians that I mentioned above approve of or at least draw from the theological assumptions of Reformed theologian Karl Barth. (Here I summarize what I detailed in my review of the three theologians.) Against Schleiermacher and the protagonists of liberal theology, Barth insisted that theology must be concerned with its object, "the Word of God" addressed to humans: God alone tells humans who God is (not philosophy, not sociology; and by extension not ATR). Jürgen Moltmann and Eberhard Jüngel regard the historical incarnational act of God on the Cross of Jesus as the pivot of God's self-disclosure (and not simply the incarnation of the Logos that is the focus of Rahner's Trinitarian meditation). The Crucified God is for us the beginning of beginnings; God tells us who God is for us in the historical identification of God with Jesus on the Cross, and in the historical identification of God eternally with suffering humans. This application by Moltmann of Karl Rahner's maxim, "the immanent Trinity is the economic Trinity and vice versa," to the revelation of the immanent and economic Trinity on the Cross, forms the foundational molding block of the Trinitarian theology of my three colleagues. It points to the ecumenical focus of theology in Africa and of world theology. The consequences of this Trinitarian theology for the creation or recreation of humans and the shaping/reshaping of the Church are clear: ecclesial-human renewal and transformation depend on appropriating the revelation of God who died on the Cross. The emergent community called Church, the product of the Trinity, gathered in its Eucharistic celebration, replicates in the world, in order to transform the world, the self-emptying and communion of the Trinitarian God. Trinitarian communion impacting Church and world sets aside the excessive centralization and monarchical autocracy that characterized the a-Trinitarian socio-political ideology of Christendom dominant from Constantine to Vatican II. Indeed Congar refers to this ideology as embedded in political and social monotheism, based on Greek cultural assumptions, introduced into Christian theology.[6]

The above Trinitarian statement embraced by my colleagues is not contradicted by the positions I developed in this book. However, there are stress areas, not just matters of detail, in which we disagree. The major point is evaluating the relationship between the crucial and central revelation of the Triune God on the Cross of Jesus Christ, the revelation of God's self-identification with humans that Moltmann argues to exist eternally in God, and the story of God, narrated and lived in West African religions, that impacts on Christian life and reflection in the continent. The West African position is captured by Mbiti in a statement that is quoted more than once in this book: "Western missionaries did not introduce God to Africa—rather, it was God who brought them to Africa, as carriers of news about Jesus Christ." In my review of the works of my younger colleagues, I pointed out that Bede Ukwuije challenges Mbiti's theological assumption more clearly than the two other colleagues. This is a revisiting of the lingering debate over the viability and correct way of naming God in African theology.

Ukwuije's central argument is that pioneer theologians like John Mbiti, and their followers, have not carefully weighed the imperatives of the dogmatic responsibility of all theology: the death of Jesus the Son of God as the Death of God on the Cross. Discourse on continuity between ATR and Christianity, on the identification of God or the divine expe-

---

6. See Congar, "Le Monthéisme Politique Et Le Dieu Trinité." Among the three young theologians, Ramazani makes the best argument for a world transforming Trinitarian ecclesiology.

rienced in ATR and the God of Jesus Christ, is, to say the least, taking the eye off the novel image of God who died on the Cross. Even if one abandons the language of continuity, as Benezet Bujo did, in order to affirm the shattering of ancestral religious experience in the revelation of the Triune God in the Crucified and Risen Christ, any insinuation that the God of ATR constitutes a substratum for the novel experience of God on the Cross, as contained in Bujo's theology, remains a betrayal of the dogmatic responsibility of theology. Ukwuije's embrace of evangelicalism led him to reject Bujo's reasoning that the God of ATR could be promoted to such a privileged position of a prerequisite, a pre-comprehension to demonstrate the novelty of the Christian Trinity.[7] Such *vestigia trinitatis* is nothing more and nothing less than self-defensive or negative apologetics; it is not Christian theology; it gives priority to ATR, to African systems of thought, to the African approach to the divine, rather than to the Word of God. Kungua and Ramazani, especially Kungua, will not go as far as Ukwuije. Kungua follows the path traced by pioneer African theologians in affirming identity between the God of our ancestors and the God of Jesus Christ; but he carefully (like Bujo and Bimwenyi) outlines the radical nature of the Cross that displays the Crucified God. He will therefore agree with Ukwuije that Christian theology in Africa must not be the prolongation of ATR. But Ukwuije, in his dialogue with, or rather critical "reception" of, pioneer African theologians, demonstrates the radical distancing that characterizes new generation African theologians.

The argument of my book is different from the evangelical thesis and from the position of Ukwuije: there is continuity, though radical break, between the God-Spirit experienced in ATR and the revelation of God-Spirit in Jesus Christ. Trusting the creative power of the Holy Spirit, whose thousand names West African Christians proclaim in the denominations or qualities (*epinoiai*—cf. Origen) derived from the multiplicity of deities-spirits, Christians live wholesome life in a world that has changed and is changing thanks to their new Spirit-directed faith. For Christians, the deities that represent in the West African universe God-Spirit's benevolent shadow or presence are totally denied airtime. They are not accorded independent existence; rather they transform into qualities of the ever present and embedding Holy Spirit. African Christianity (represented by AICs) cautiously but serenely declared in

---

7. Ukwuije, *Trinité Et Inculturation*, 173.

their 1996 manifesto: "*The renewal of the Holy Spirit* is continuous with and greater than the spirits around us." Indeed the Holy Spirit makes it possible for Christians to have the new experience of the Crucified-Risen God in Jesus Christ.

I have no illusions that pitfalls and stumbling blocks litter the pathway of this theological elaboration. Would it not be better to adopt the principle of radical dethronement or displacement of the Baals once and for all like Elijah or like the nineteenth century German Pietist mission to the Ewe of Togo and Ghana (with regard to the deities, *trowo)?* Kungua is inclined to the latter viewpoint; he even goes on to support Elijah's war as revealing God at war with the Baals. I critiqued the Elijah project, showing how the novel revelation of God as "sound of sheer silence" is a sharp rebuke of Elijah's violent projection of Yahweh: Religion that is for the service of the human, which humanizes and divinizes, is life-giving, life-affirming and not life-denying. That is why, in my view, Elijah's mystical experience illustrates how little we know God and how mysticism shatters cultural boundaries bringing peoples, cultures and religions together. This not only mediates the revelation of the God beyond God—i.e., beyond all our habitual patterns of naming God; this also blazes the trail for healthy interreligious relations and dialogue! The emerging face of God, the unknown God, the God we want to know or rather who wants to be known, is displayed in *discrete withdrawal, distance, and transcendence or silence.* I make bold to not only study the story of God in the Old Testament, the gradual purification of the faith of key Old Testament prophets, especially those within the Elijah circle and the Deuteronomistic historians, but I also point out that ultimately Israelite faith in the One and Only Yahweh, as displayed by Second Isaiah, is by way of witness. Only a life of humble witness demonstrates the credibility of the faith in God's self-giving, God's covenant relationship with Israel, and ultimately the self-manifestation of God powerfully weak on the Cross of Jesus Christ.

There was patient pedagogy in this *story of God in Israel* that peaked during the exile. This patient pedagogy involved the transformation of the multiplicity of deities into angels (messengers), opponents, or qualities (denominations). Instead of radical displacement characteristic of evangelicalism, learning from the Hebrew tradition, one should patiently be attentive to the process of divine pedagogy narrated in West African ATR. The dominance of relationality, the overflow of epithets such as "grandeur, mercy, patience, goodness, tenderness and sweet-ness," addressed to *Mawu-Lisa* (God—*Chukwu, Olodumare, Amma, Onyame*), in cosmic non-threatening relationship with deities that oper-ate with liberty and responsibility for the good of humans in the areas of their competence, demonstrate God powerfully weak. This moves the exercise of God's "supreme power" to a new key: God is not rendered "less" but "more" in the relational hierarchy! From this perspective, preoccupation with exclusive supremacy, as opposed to the flexible, re-lational and dynamic hierarchy in divinity, is a sign of weakness. It is a mark of competition or the struggle for airtime that characterizes the fight among devotees to make their "god" (*orisa* or *vodun*) important. Such struggle is totally nonexistent between God, the origin of origins, and the deities (God's children). The relational and inclusive exercise of supreme power that fosters human flourishing is suggestive of a unique West African contribution to the meaning of religion: Religion intends the realization of human destined course in life, to promote peace and exclude conflict. West African religious experience promotes harmony and not violence.

It is the argument of my book that West African Christians ap-proach the novelty of Jesus Christ from this experience of relationality. Furthermore, the divine personalized spirit-companionship that domi-nates West African myths is not lost in or expunged from the experience of the novelty of Jesus Christ. Rather it transforms into the embedding of the Holy Spirit of God in each Christian: "it is that very Spirit bear-ing witness with our spirit that we are children of God" (Rom 8:16)! This is the Spirit that overshadowed the incarnation and the Cross; the Spirit that is Gift of the Risen Christ; the Spirit that is the enabler of the Christian community to be aware of and to live divine generosity that is radically displayed on the Cross. From this perspective, Christian life and Christian theology takes off from the action of the Holy Spirit of God. I do not have the intention of calling the West African experience *vestigium trinitatis*. But even if I do so, there is really nothing wrong with that. I present it as part of the genius of Catholicism: the commitment to preserve the "pagan heritage," "the pagan-ness" of every ancestral tradi-tion, no longer as just ancestral, but as Christian; the ancestral heritage remains "the Christian heritage so as not to be lost to humanity."[8]

---

8. See Gesché, "Le Christianisme Comme Athéisme Suspensif," 206–7.

ATTENTIVENESS TO THE RESHAPING OR REMAPPING
OF THE HUMAN THROUGH ENCOUNTER
WITH THE TRIUNE GOD

Ultimately the intentionality of religion, the experience of God's self-disclosure in Jesus Christ who died on the Cross, the operation of God-Spirit in human and Christian life, is the integral liberation of humans. This is the principle focus and concern of religion in West Africa. It is the concern of both evangelical and catholic theology.

One may wonder why my younger colleagues are all interested in foremost evangelical theologians; especially Karl Barth, Jürgen Moltmann, and Eberhard Jüngel. One thing is clear from their works, and from the use of African and Western resources: contact with the person of the Crucified God mediates or generates holistic liberation (Kungua); it leads to authentic inculturation (Ukwuije) and radical "contexturation" (Ramazani). Ramazani's critical evaluation of ecclesiology from Vatican I to Vatican II came to the conclusion that to effect radical transformation of social structures in this era of globalization one needs to radically change the structures of the church to enable the church change society. This change is what Ramazani calls "contexturation": the Church that emerges from the Trinity, that lives Trinitarian self-emptying and communion, actualized in the Eucharist, transforms its structures to become more resilient to change the globalised world. Though Vatican II enabled cultural transformation in the church it totally ignored transformation of structures. Only a new reception of Vatican II, open to structural transformation, carries the hope of moving Church and world forward.[9]

Kungua is particularly interesting for the project I pursued in my book. He not only elaborated Moltmann's *Crucified God*, in view of holistic liberation, but insisted on giving airtime to the voices of the poor through the dangerous narrative and memory of the powerless of our world as outlined in the political theology of Johannes Baptist Metz. Though I disagree with his projection of Elijah's war as Yahweh's war in the mystical experience of the prophet at Horeb, I agree with him that the pattern of revelation, "audition" as opposed to "vision," is divine confirmation of the revelatory viability of mysticism. On the ground

---

9. *Pour Une Ecclésiologie Trinitaire Dans La Postmodernité Et La Mondialisation,* vol. 1, 93–95.

African Christianity that is Spirit-driven flourishes within mystical experience. In the descending Holy Spirit, and filled with the Spirit's gifts or charisms, mystics practice healing and exorcism that display the liberating, healing or therapeutic hand of God.

In the final analysis the pre-eminence of the Holy Spirit is not only informed by the desire to transform "the spirits around us." The intentionality of the spirit-focused, spirit-directing and spirit-embedding Christian life is holistic liberation: the Spirit bestows gifts, material and spiritual, and frees individuals and the community from satanic or spiritual powers. AICs in their manifesto captured this: "Our dependence on the Holy Spirit for protection from evil forces has liberated us to share with others our freedom from fear, a very enticing proposition in the African context, as well as in the rest of the world."[10]

This sums up the purpose of my research. This explains why I believe that the Holy Spirit is at the driving seat of theology. I think world Christianity, African and Western theology, driven by the Holy Spirit of Truth, under the shadow and presence of the Crucified-Risen God, will learn-live communion-relationship more intensely renewed by the vigor of God who is powerfully weak in Jesus Christ.

---

10. The manifesto is recorded in Pobee and Ositelu II, *African Initiatives in Christianity*, 71. Anderson develops AICs' theology in Anderson, *African Reformation*.

Glossary

Adama: a clan linked with the Nri village group of the Igbo of Nigeria.

Adja-Fon or **Fon**: ethnic nationality found principally in Benin Republic, West Africa.

Adro: "guardian spirit," Lugbara of Uganda.

Afa: *divination*, esoteric lore among the Igbo, Nigeria.

Agbara: deity of coercion, generic term for unnamed and undomesticated spirit-force, Igbo of Nigeria.

Agwu: deity of divination, knowledge and health, Igbo of Nigeria.

Akan: ethnic nationality found in West Africa especially in Kumasi (Ghana) and also in Cote d'Ivoire, same as Asante.

Aklama: *(or kla) personal spirit given by God to each person at creation among* Ewe of Ghana and Togo

Ala: Earth deity, the most powerful spirit in Igbo religion.

Ama: *herbs,*among Ewe of Togo & Ghana.

Amadioha: Thunder deity, Igbo of Nigeria.

Amma: God, Dogon of Mali.

Anagono Bile: primordial ancestors of the Dogon myth of origin created in 4 pairs.

Anyanwu: Sun deity, Igbo of Nigeria.

Asante: ethnic nationality found in West Africa especially in Kumasi (Ghana) and also in Cote d'Ivoire, same as Akan.

Asantehene: the Asante king, Ghana.

Babalawo: expert in all medicine and healing in the Yoruba religious world.

Bambara: ethnic nationality found in Mali, West Africa.

Beyem: witches, in Bwiti cult of Gabon.

beyem mam: the counterpart of the diviner-doctor in Bwiti cult of Gabon.

Bokǫnǫ: expert in all medicine and healing in the Adja-Fon religious world.

Bome: ancestral location or bosom of pre-existence of the Ewe of Togo and Ghana, West Africa.

Bwiti: syncretistic cult and ritual of the Fang in Gabon.

Candomblé: worship of African religion in communities of Brazil.

Chi: in Igbo religion (Nigeria), dominant personal spirit given by God to each person at creation; also used to denote Chukwu (God).

Chineke: Chi the creator, God, Igbo of Nigeria.

Cuku or **Chukwu**: God in Igbo religion.

Dahomey: ancient West African kingdom, flourished during the period of slavery, whose center is in the present West African country of Benin Republic, but extended beyond Benin.

Dibia: expert in all medicine and healing in the Igbo religious world.

Dogon: ethnic nationality found in Mali, West Africa.

Ebora: spirits subordinates of the *orisa, in Yoruba religious world.*

Egbesu: deity of war, Ijaw ethnic group, Nigeria.

Ekwensu: deity of war, associated with violence, Igbo of Nigeria.

Elêgbara or **Lêgba:** same deity or spirit as Eshu.

Eshu: very popular deity or spirit in Yoruba religious world also called Elêgbara or Lêgba among the Fon and diaspora Africans in Brazil, Cuba and Haiti.

Evu: Witchcraft virus in everyone among the Beti of Cameroon.

Ewe: ethnic nationality found principally in Togo and Ghana, West Africa.

Ezenri and **Ezeadama:** king of Nri & king of Adama—Nri village-group, sometimes linked with Adama clans, possesses the better known myth of origin of some segment of Igbo ethnic nationality.

Fonio: grain, found in the original egg at creation, Dogon of Mali.

Ganda: dominant ethnic nationality of Uganda (East Africa).

Gbo: medicine, charms, magic in the Ewe religious world.

gbogbo: breath, a secular term transformed by missionaries to signify spirit among Ewe of Togo and Ghana.

Hevioso, Thunder deity, Fon of Benin & Togo.

Hu: another name for *Evu, witchcraft* virus among the Beti of Cameroon.

Ibiniukpabe: oracle, deity of the Arochukwu village group, Igbo of Nigeria.

Idemili: Pillar of Water, daughter of *Chukwu* and *Ala,* divinity of peace, Igbo of Nigeria.

Ifa: divination, esoteric lore among the Yoruba, Nigeria.

Igbo: ethnic nationality found in Nigeria, West Africa.

Igwe: Sky deity, Igbo of Nigeria.

Jelgobe: an ethnic group within the wider Fulani nationality in Mali and Burkina Faso; Fulani are also spread through Nigeria and Cameroon.

Ka: Egyptian, one's double.

Kola nut: fruit from the kola tree found all over West Africa, but used in ritual among the Igbo.

Luvo: shadow, Ewe of Togo and Ghana; modified by missionaries to mean soul.

luvoagbetɔ: soul as shadow of life, Ewe of Togo & Ghana.

luvokutɔ: soul as shadow of death, Ewe of Togo & Ghana.

Mgbologwu: *herbs among* Igbo of Nigeria.

Miêmiê: naive person, does not have or has low level witchcraft virus, in Bwiti cult of Gabon.

Nana: Ancestor, Akan of Ghana.

Ndi-ichie: *Ancestors,* i.e., Elders also *Nna-a-ha* i.e. the Fathers: Igbo of Nigeria.

Ngambi: seer, religious world of Cameroon.

Nganga: expert in all medicine and healing in the Bantu religious world.

Ngolongolo: masters of the art of dual personality, in Bwiti cult of Gabon.

Njoku-ji: Yam deity overseeing agriculture, Igbo of Nigeria.

Nnem: one who has a strong, uncontrollable and evil *evu, or witchcraft virus in Bwiti cultu.*

Nommo Anagono: primordial deities of the Dogon of Mali created by God in 4 pairs (Nommo=deity).

Nri: a village group among the igbo of Nigeria.

Ñutila: body, Ewe of Togo & Ghana.

Nyamedua: God's tree, Akan of Ghana.

Nzambi: God the creator among Bantu speaking peoples of Africa.

Oba: the Yoruba king, Nigeria.

Odomankoma: creator God, Akan of Ghana.

Oduduwa: mythical hero, founder of kingship and of Ile-Ife, Yoruba of Nigeria.

Ogun: deity of iron and war, Yoruba of Nigeria.

Ogwu: medicine, charms, magic in the Igbo religious world.

Ogwugwu: deity in Igbo religion of Nigeria, West Africa.

Okra: (or kra) personal spirit given by God to each person at creation among Asante of Ghana.

Olodumare: God, Yoruba of Nigeria; also *Olorun.*

Olorun: God, Yoruba of Nigeria; also *Olodumare.*

Olugbala: savior in Yoruba religious culture of Nigeria, West Africa.

Onile: Earth mother, Yoruba of Nigeria.

Onyame: God, Akan of Ghana *also Nyame or Onyankopon.*

Onyankopon: God, Akan of Ghana; also *Onyame.*

Òògun: medicine, charms, magic in the Yoruba religious world.

Ori: head, human or spiritual, Yoruba of Nigeria.

Orisa: spirit or deity worshipped among Yoruba of Nigeria (also written, orisha).

Orunmila or *Ifa:* deity of divination, wisdom and health, Yoruba, Nigeria.

Sakpata or *Soponna*: deities of divination and healing of smallpox and other diseases, vodhun religion, Benin Republic and Togo.

Santeria: Saints, Worship of African religion in Cuba.

Se: *personal spirit given by God to each person at creation among* Adja-Fon of Benin Republic.

Segbo: the Great *Se;* another name for Mawu, God, among the Fon of Benin Republic & Togo.

Shango: deity of thunder, Yoruba of Nigeria.

Suman: medicine, charms, magic in the Akan religious world.

Tali: "personality," Lugbara of Uganda.

trowǫ: deities among the Ewe of Togo and Ghana.

Udo: deity in Igbo religion of Nigeria, West Africa.

Vodhun: Spirit, deity—in the practice of religion in Togo, Benin, Ghana & Haiti (also written as vodun; and misrepresented as voodoo)

Woli: seer, visionary and prophet, Yoruba religious universe.

Wuro: hut—of which woman has total proprietorship, Jelgobe symbol of culture.

Yoruba: ethnic nationality found in Nigeria and also in Benin republic of West Africa.

Bibliography

Achebe, Chinua. *Anthills of the Savannah*. London: Heinemann, 1987.

———. *Arrow of God*. New York: J. Day, 1967.

———. *Home and Exile*. New York: Anchor, 2000.

———. *Hopes and Impediments: Selected Essays, 1965–1987*. London: Heinemann Educational, 1988.

———. *Morning yet on Creation Day: Essays, Studies in African Literature*. London: Heinemann Educational, 1975.

Adamo, David Tuesday. *Reading and Interpreting the Bible in African Indigenous Churches*. Eugene, OR: Wipf & Stock, 2001.

Adoukonou, B. *Jalons Pour Une Théologie Africaine: Essai D'une Herméneutique Chrétienne Du Vodun Dahoméen*. 2 vols. *Le Sycomore. Série "Horizon" 4*. Paris & Namur: Lethielleux ; Culture et Vérité, 1980.

Afigbo, A. E. "The Dialogue of Civilizations: Aspects of Igbo Wisdom Knowledge." *Bulletin of Ecumenical Theology* 13 (2001) 3–17.

Afigbo, A. E., and Toyin Falola. *Igbo History and Society: The Essays of Adiele Afigbo*. Trenton, NJ: Africa World, 2005.

Agbasiere, Joseph-Thérèse. *Women in Igbo Life and Thought*. Edited with a Foreword by Shirely Ardner. New York: Routledge, 2000.

Agossou, Mèdéwalé-Jacob. *Christianisme Africain: Une Fraternité Au-Delà De L'ethnie*. Paris: Karthala, 1987.

Aguwa, Jude C. U. *The Agwu Deity in Igbo Religion: A Study of the Patron Spirit of Divination and Medicine in an African Society*. Igbo Life and Culture Series. Enugu: Fourth Dimension, 2002.

Albertz, Rainer, and Bob Becking, editors. *Yahwism after the Exile: Perspectives on Israelite Religion in the Persian Era (Papers Read at the First Meeting of the European Association for Biblical Studies, Utrecht, 6-9 August 2000). Vol. 5, Studies in Theology and Religion (Star)*. Assen, The Netherlands: Royal Van Gorcum, 2003.

Ali, Tariq. *The Clash of Fundamentalism: Crusades, Jihads, and Modernity*. New York: Verso, 2002.

Allen, Judith van. "'Aba Riots' or Igbo 'Women's War'? Ideology, Stratification and the Invisibility of Women." In *Women in Africa: Studies in Social and Economic Change*, edited by Nancy J. Hafkin and Edna G. Bay, 59–85. Stanford: Stanford University Press, 1976.

Amadi, Elechi. *Ethics in Nigerian Culture*. Ibadan, Nigeria: Heinemann Educational Books, 1982.

Amadiume, Ifi. "Igbo and African Religious Perspectives on Religious Conscience and the Global Economy." In *Subverting Greed: Religious Perspectives on the Global*

Economy, edited by Paul F. Knitter and Chandra Muzaffar, 15–37. Maryknoll, NY: Orbis, 2002.

———. *Male Daughters, Female Husbands: Gender and Sex in an African Society*. New Jersey: Zed, 1987.

———. *Re-Inventing Africa: Matriarchy, Religion and Culture*. New York: Zed, 1997.

Amaladoss, Michael. *Making Harmony: Living in a Pluralist World*. Delhi: IDCR/ISPCK, 2003.

Anderson, Allan. *African Reformation: African Initiated Christianity in the 20th Century*. Asmara, Eritrea: Africa World, 2001.

Anderson, Gary A. "Introduction to Israelite Religion." In *The New Interpreter's Bible* (Electronic Edition), vol. 1. Nashville: Abingdon, 1995–2002.

Anderson, Victor. *Creative Exchange: A Constructive Theology of African American Religious Experience*. Minneapolis: Fortress, 2008.

Anyanwu, K. C. "The Meaning of Ultimate Reality in Igbo Cultural Experience." *Ultimate Reality and Meaning* 7.2 (1984) 84–101.

———. "A Response to A. G. A. Bello's Methodological Preliminaries." *Ultimate Reality and Meaning* 14 (1991) 61–69.

———. "Sound as Ultimate Reality and Meaning: The Mode of Knowing Reality in African Thought." *Ultimate Reality and Meaning* 10 (1987) 29–38.

Arinze, Francis. *Sacrifice in Ibo Religion*. Ibadan, Nigeria: Ibadan University Press, 1970.

Arnoux, Alex. "Le Culte De La Société Secrète Des Imandwawa Au Ruanda." *Anthropos* 7 (1912) 273–95; 529–58; 840–74.

———. "Le Culte De La Société Secrète Des Imandwawa Au Ruanda." *Anthropos* 8 (1913) 110–34; 754–74.

Babalola, S. A. *The Content and Form of Yoruba Ijala*. Oxford: Clarendon, 1966.

Babut, Etienne. *Le Dieu Puissamment Faible De La Bible, Coll. Lire La Bible 118*. Paris: Cerf, 1999.

Baëta, C. C., editor. *Christianity in Tropical Africa: Studies Presented and Discussed at the Seventh International African Seminar at the University of Ghana, April 1965*. London: Oxford University Press, 1968.

Balthasar, Hans Urs von, editor. *Origen: Spirit and Fire: A Thematic Anthology of His Writings*. Edinburgh: T. & T. Clark, 1984.

Bamikunle, Aderemi. "Priest-Heroes in the Nigerian Novel: A Comparative Study of Achebe's Arrow of God and Ibrahim Tahir's the Last Imam." In *Reconstructing the Canon: Festschrift in Honour of Professor Charles E. Nnolim*, edited by Austine Amanze Akpuda, 325–41. Owerri, Nigeria: Skillmark Media, 2001.

Barber, Karin. "How Man Makes God in West Africa: Yoruba Attitudes Towards the Òrìsà." In *Perspectives on Africa: A Reader in Culture, History, and Representation*, edited by Roy Richard and Christopher B. Steiner Grinker, 392–411. Oxford: Blackwell, 1997.

Basden, George T. *Among the Ibos of Southern Nigeria*. 1966 ed. London: Frank Cass, 1921.

———. *Niger Ibos*. 1966 ed. London: Frank Cass, 1938.

Bassler, Jouette M. "God in the NT." In *The Anchor Bible Dictionary* (Electronic Edition), edited by David Noel Freedman. New York: Doubleday, 1997, 1992.

Bastide, Roger. *Le Candomblé De Bahia (Rite Nagô)*. Paris-La Haye: Mouton, 2000.

Bediako, Kwame. *Christianity in Africa: The Renewal of a Non-Western Religion*. New York: University of Edinburgh Press, 1995.

————. "How Is Jesus Christ Lord?: Aspects of an Evangelical Christian Apologetics in the Context of African Religious Pluralism." *Exchange* 25 (1996) 27–42.

————. *Theology and Identity: The Impact of Culture Upon Christian Thought in the Second Century and in Modern Africa.* Costa Mesa, CA: Regnum, 1992.

Berends, Willem. "African Traditional Healing Practices and the Christian Community." *Missiology (An International Review)* 21.3 (1993) 275–88.

Bimwenyi-Kweshi, O. "Religions Africaines, Un 'Lieu' De La Theologie Chrétienne Africaine." In *Religions Africaines Et Christianisme: Colloque International De Kinshasa, 9–14 Jan. 1978.* Kinshasa: Faculte De Theologie Catholique Vol. 2, 1979.

Bimwenyi-Kweshi, O. *Discours Théologique Négro-Africain : Problème Des Fondements.* Paris: Présence africaine, 1981.

Boeck, Filip de. "Le 'Deuxième Monde' Et Les 'Enfants-Sorciers' En République Démocratique Du Congo." *Politique Africaine* 80 (2000) 32–57.

Bosch, David. *Transforming Mission: Paradigm Shifts in Theology of Mission.* Maryknoll, NY: Orbis, 1991.

Brueggemann, Walter. "The Book of Exodus." In *The New Interpreter's Bible* (Electronic Edition), vol. 1. Nashville: Abingdon.

Buakasa, T. K. M. *L'impensé Du Discours. "Kindoki" Et "Nkisi" En Pays Kongo Du Zaïre.* 2nd ed. Kinshasa: Facultés Catholiques de Kinshasa, 1980.

Bühlmann, Walbert. *The Coming of the Third Church : An Analysis of the Present and Future of the Church.* Maryknoll, NY: Orbis, 1977.

Bujo, Bénézet. *Foundations of an African Ethic: Beyond the Universal Claims of Western Morality.* Translated by Brian McNeil. New York: Crossroad, 2001.

Bujo, Bénézet, and Juvénal Ilunga Muya, editors. *Théologie Africaine Au Xxie Siècle: Quelques Figures.* Vol. 1. Fribourg, Switzerland: Éditions Universitaires Fribourg Suisse, 2002.

Burrell, David B. *Friendship and Ways to the Truth.* Notre Dame, IN: University of Notre Dame Press, 2000.

Carrière, Jean-Marie. "De l'un à l'autre testament : le travail de l'unicité." In *Le Fils Unique Et Ses Frères: Unicité Du Christ Et Pluralisme Religieux,* edited by Michel Fédou, 49–73. Paris: Éditions faculté jésuites, 2002.

Chinweizu. "Gender and Monotheism: The Assault by Monotheism on African Gender Diarchy." Lagos, 1993.

Christoph, Henning, and Hans Oberländer. *Vaudou: Les Forces Secrètes De L'afrique.* Köln, Paris: Taschen, 1996.

Claffey, Patrick. *Christian Churches in Dahomey-Benin: A Study of Their Socio-Political Role.* Edited by Paul Gifford. Vol. 31, *Studies of Religion in Africa—Supplements to the Journal of Religion in Africa.* Boston: Brill, 2007.

————. "Looking for a Breakthrough: The Role of Christian Churches in the Socio-Political Development of Danxomè—Benin." PhD diss., University of London, 2004.

Clifford, R. J. *Fair Spoken and Persuading. An Interpretation of Second Isaiah.* New York: Paulist, 1984.

————. "The Hebrew Scriptures and the Theology of Creation." *Theological Studies* 46 (1985) 507–23.

Cone, James H. *Martin & Malcom & America. A Dream or a Nightmare.* London: Fount, 1991.

Congar, Yves. "Le Monthéisme Politique Et Le Dieu Trinité." *Nouvelle Revue Théologique* 103 (1981) 3–17.

Crenshaw, James L. "The Book of Sirach." In *The New Interpreter's Bible* (Electronic Edition), vol. 5. Nashville: Abingdon, 1995–2002.

Cross, F. M. *Canaanite Myth and Hebrew Epic.* Cambridge: Harvard University Press, 1973.

Crouzel, Henri. *Origène.* Paris, Namur: Lethielleux, Culture et Vérité, 1985.

Daigne, P. *Pouvoir Politique Traditionnel En Afrique Occidentale.* Paris: Présence Africaine, 1967.

Danet, Henriette, and Éloi Messi Metogo. "L'afrique Francophone." In *Le Devenir De La Théologie Catholique Depuis Vatican Ii—1965-1999,* edited by Joseph Doré, 201–24. Paris: Beauchesne, 2000.

Day, John. *Yahweh and the Gods and Goddesses of Canaan, Journal for the Study of the Old Testament—Supplement Series 265.* Sheffield, UK: Sheffield Academic Press, 2000.

Déaut, Roger Le, and Jacques Robert. *Targum Du Pentateuque: Traduction Des Deux Recensions Palestiniennes Complètes Avec Introduction, Parallèles, Notes Et Index.* Vol. III - Nombres, *Sources Chrétiennes.* Paris: Cerf, 1979.

Dedji, Valentin. *Reconstruction and Renewal in African Christian Theology.* Nairobi: Acton, 2003.

Des Pêtres Noirs S'interrogent. Paris: Cerf, 1956.

Devisch, René. *Weaving the Threads of Life: The Khita Gyn-Eco-Logical Healing Cult among the Yaka.* Chicago: University of Chicago Press, 1993.

Dickson, Kwesi A., and Paul Ellingworth, editors. *Biblical Revelation and African Beliefs.* London: Lutterworth, 1969.

Diop, Cheikh Anta. *Civilization or Barbarism: An Authentic Anthropology.* Translated by Yaa-Lengi Meema Ngemi. Brooklyn: Hill, 1991.

————. *The Cultural Unity of Black Africa: The Domains of Patriarchy and Matriarchy in Classical Antiquity, Karnak History.* African Studies. London: Karnak House, 1989.

————. *Precolonial Black Africa: A Comparative Study of the Political and Social Systems of Europe and Black Africa, from Antiquity to the Formation of Modern States.* Westport, CT: Hill, 1987.

Dodds, E. R. *Pagan and Christian in an Age of Anxiety.* Cambridge: Cambridge University Press, 1965.

Douglas, Mary. "The Problem of Evil among the Lele: Sorcery, Witch-Hunt, and Christian Teaching in Africa." *African Christian Studies* 4.3 (1988) 21–38.

————. *Risk and Blame. Essays in Cultural Theory.* New York: Routledge, 1992.

Dupuis, Jacques. "L'esprit De L'homme": *Étude Sur L'anthropologie Religieuse D'origène, Museum Lessianum. Section Théologique* 62. Paris: Desclée de Brouwer, 1967.

Eboussi Boulaga, F. *Christianity without Fetishes: An African Critique and Recapture of Christianity.* Maryknoll: Orbis, 1984.

————. *La Crise Du Muntu: Authenticité Africaine Et Philosophie: Essai.* Paris: Présence africaine, 1977.

Echeruo, M. J. C. *A Matter of Identity, 1979 Ahiajoku Lecture.* Owerri, Nigeria: Ministry of Information, Culture, Youth, and Sports, 1979.

Echeruo, Michael J. C. "Religion, Imperialism, and the Question of World Order." Paper presented at the Religion in a World of Change: African Ancestral Religion, Islam and Christianity—International Symposium, Owerri, 8th–12th October 2002.

Edwards, Paul, and Rosalind Shaw. "The Invisible *Chi* in Equiano's *Interesting Narrative*." *Journal of Religion in Africa* 19.2 (1989) 146–56.

Eggen, Wiel. "Mawu Does Not Kill: On Ewe Kinship-Focused Religion." *Exchange* 31.4 (2000) 343–61.

———. "Parenté Du Dieu Qui Ne Tue Pas." In *Anthropologie Et Missiologie—Xixe-Xx Siècle: Entre Connivence Et Rivalité*, edited by Olivier Servais and Gérard Van't Spijker, 119–35. Paris: Karthala, 2004.

Ejizu, Christopher I. "Down but Not Out: Contemporary Forms of Igbo Indigenous Religion." Paper presented at the Religion in a World of Change: African Ancestral Religion, Islam and Christianity—International Symposium, Owerri, 8th–12th October 2002.

Ela, Jean Marc. *African Cry*. Maryknoll, NY: Orbis, 1986.

———. *Repenser La Théologie Africaine: Le Dieu Qui Libère*. Paris: Karthala, 2003.

Eliade, Mircea. *Fragments D'un Journal*. Paris: Gallimard, 1973.

———. *Patterns in Comparative Religion*. London: Sheed & Ward, 1979.

Equiano, Olaudah. *The Interesting Narrative of the Life of Olaudah Equiano—Written by Himself*. Edited with an Introduction by Robert J. Allison. Boston: St. Martin's, 1995.

Ezekwugo, Christopher U. M. *Chi, the True God in Igbo Religion*. Kerela, India: Alwaye, 1987.

Fabella, Virginia, and Sergio Torres, editors. *Irruption of the Third World: Challenge to Theology. Papers from the Fifth International Conference of the Ecumenical Association of Third World Theologians, August 17-29, 1981, New Delhi, India*. Maryknoll: Orbis, 1983.

Fashole-Luke, Edward, editor. *Christianity in Independent Africa*. Indianapolis: Indiana University Press, 1978.

Fédou, Michel, ed. *Le Fils Unique Et Ses Frères: Unicité Du Christ Et Pluralisme Religieux*. Paris: Éditions faculté jésuites, 2002.

Fernandez, James W. "The Cultural Status of a West African Cult Group on the Creation of Culture." In *African Religious Groups and Beliefs: Papers in Honour of William R. Bascom*, edited by Simon Ottenberg, 242–60. Meerut, India: Archana, 1982.

Figura, Michael. "The Suffering of God in Patristic Theology." *Communio* 30 (2003) 366–85.

Fisher, Robert B. *West African Religious Traditions: Focus on the Akan of Ghana*. Maryknoll: Orbis, 1998.

Fortes, M., and E. E. Evans-Pritchard. *African Political Systems*. Oxford: University Press, 1961.

Freedman, D. N., and M. P. O'Connor. "Yahweh." In *Theological Dictionary of the Old Testament*, edited by G. J. Botterweck and Helmer Ringgren, 500–21. Grand Rapids: Eerdmans, 1986.

Gesché, Adolphe. "Le Christianisme Comme Athéisme Suspensif: Réflexions Sur Le 'Etsi Deus Non Daretur.'" *Revue Théologique de Louvain* 33 (2002) 187–210.

———. "Le Christianisme Comme Monothéisme Relatif: Nouvelles Réflexions Sur Le 'Etsi Deus Non Daretur.'" *Revue Théologique de Louvain* 33 (2002) 473–96.

Gibellini, Rosino, editor. *Panorama De La Théologie Au Xxe Siècle, Théologies*. Paris; Montréal: Cerf ; Médiaspaul, 1994.

———, editor. *Percosi Di Teologia Africana*. Brescia: Queriniana, 1994.

———, editor. *Paths of African Theology*. Maryknoll: Orbis, 1994.

Gikandi, Simon. *Reading Chinua Achebe: Language & Ideology in Fiction, Studies in African Literature Series*. Oxford; Portsmouth, NH, 1991.

Glasswell, Mark E., and Edward Fashole-Luke, editors. *New Testament Christianity for Africa and the World*. London: SPCK, 1974.

Gnuse, Robert Karl. *No Other Gods: Emergent Monotheism in Israel, Journal for the Study of the Old Testament—Supplement Series* 241. Sheffield, UK: Sheffield Academic Press, 1997.

Gottwald, N. K. *The Tribes of Yahweh. A Sociology of the Religion of Liberated Israel 1250–1050 B.C.E.* Maryknoll: Orbis, 1979.

Grant, Jacquelyn. *White Women's Christ and Black Women's Jesus: Feminist Christology and Womanist Response*. Atlanta: Scholars, 1989.

Grinker, Roy Richard, and Christopher B. Steiner, editors. *Perspectives on Africa: A Reader in Culture, History, and Representation*. Oxford: Blackwell, 1997.

Guillemin, R. P. "Les superstitions encore en usage en pays Yaoundé." *Le Cameroun catholique (Yaoundé)* (VII/3: 1943) 22–37

Guimera, L. Mallart. *Ni dos, ni ventre. Religion, magie et sorcellerie evuzok*. Paris: Societé d' Ethnographie, Société africaine 5, 1981

Guisimana, Bartholomé. "L'homme Selon La Philosophie Pende." *Cahiers des Religions Africaines* 2.3 (1968).

Hammond, Dorothy, and Alta Jablow. *The Africa That Never Was; Four Centuries of British Writing About Africa*. New York: Twayne, 1970.

Hearne, Brian, and Nsolo Mijere, editors. *Celebration*. Vol. 2, *Spearhead* 42. Eldoret, Kenya: Gaba, 1976.

Hebga, Meinrad P. "Christianisme Et Négritude." In *Des Prêtres Noirs S'interrogent*, edited by Présence Africaine. Paris: Cerf, 1956.

———. *La Rationalité D'un Discours Africain Sur Les Phénomènes Paranormaux*. Paris: l'Harmattan, 1998.

———. *Sorcellerie Et Prière De Délivrance: Réflexion Sur Une Expérience*. Paris; Abidjan: Présence africaine; Édition Inades, 1982.

———. *Sorcellerie, Chimère Dangereuse—?* Abidjan, Côte d'Ivoire: Éditions Inades, 1979.

Hegel, G. W. F. *Lectures on the Philosophy of World History: Introduction*. Translated by H. B. Nisbet. 1975 ed. New York: Cambridge University Press, 1830.

Held, David, Anthony McGrew, David Goldblatt, and Jonathan Perraton, editors. *Global Transformations: Politics, Economy, and Culture*. Stanford: Stanford University Press, 1999.

Hillaire, Jacques. "Quand L'homme Africain Parle De Dieu." *La Maison Dieu* 116 (1973) 130–40.

Horton, Robin. "African Conversion." *Africa* 41.2 (1971) 85–108.

———. "African Traditional Thought and Western Science—Part 1. From Tradition to Science." *Africa* 37 (1967) 50–71.

———. "African Traditional Thought and Western Science—Part 2. The 'Closed' and 'Open' Predicaments." *Africa* 37 (1967) 153–87.

———. "Judaeo-Christian Spectacles: Boon or Bane to the Study of African Religions." *Cahiers d'Etudes Africaines* 96.27 (1984) 391–436.

———. "Ritual Man in Africa." *Africa* 34 (1964) 85–103.

Hountondji, Paulin "Reason and Tradition." In *Philosophy and Cultures*, edited by O. Oruka, 136–37. Nairobi: Bookwise, 1983.

Hurbon, Laënnec. *Dieu Dans Le Vaudou Haïtien, [Bibliothèque Scientifique].* Paris: Payot, 1972.

Idowu, Bolaji. *African Traditional Religion: A Definition.* London: SCM, 1973.

———. *Olódùmarè: God in Yoruba Beliefs.* London: Longmans, 1962.

Isichei, E. *Igbo Worlds. An Anthology of Oral Histories and Historical Descriptions.* Philadelphia: Institute for the Study of Human Issues, 1978.

Jell-Bahlsen, Sabine. "The Lake Goddess, Uhammiri/Ogbuide: The Female Side of the Universe in Igbo Cosmology." In *African Spirituality: Forms, Meanings, and Expressions, World Spirituality ; V. 3,* edited by Jacob Obafemi Kehinde Olupona, 38–53. New York: Crossroad, 2000.

Jenkins, Philip. *The Next Christendom: The Coming of Global Christianity.* New York: Oxford University Press, 2002.

Kabasele Lumbala, François. *Alliances Avec Le Christ En Afrique : Inculturation Des Rites Religieux Au Zaïre.* Athènes: Editions historiques S.D. Basilopoulos, 1987.

Kagamé, Alexis. *La Philosophie Bantu Comparée.* Paris: Présence Africaine, 1976.

———. *La Philosophie Bantu Rwandaise De L'etre.* 2nd ed. New York: Johnson, 1966.

———. "La Place De Dieu Et De L'homme Dans La Religion Des Bantu." *Cahiers des Religions Africaines* 2 (1968) 213–22.

Kalu, Ogbu U. "Estranged Bedfellows? The Demonisation of the Aladura in African Pentecostal Rhetoric." *Missionalia* 28.2 & 3 (2000) 121–42.

Kane, Hamidou. *Ambiguous Adventure.* London: Heinemann, 1972.

Kaplan, Robert D. *The Coming Anarchy–Shattering the Dreams of the Post Cold War.* New York: Vintage, 2001.

Keel, Othmar, and Christoph Uehlinger. *Gods, Goddesses, and Images of God in Ancient Israel.* Translated by Thomas H. Trapp. Edinburgh: T. & T. Clark, 1998.

Kenzo, Mabiala Justin-Robert. "Thinking Otherwise About Africa: Postcolonialism, Postmodernism, and the Future of African Theology." *Exchange* 31.4 (2002) 323–41.

Kibicho, Samuel J. "The Interaction of the Traditional Kikuyu Concept of God with the Biblical Concept." *Cahiers des Religions Africaines* 2 (1968) 223–37.

Köstenberger, Andreas J. *The Missions of Jesus and the Disciples According to the Fourth Gospel.* Grand Rapids: Eerdmans, 1998.

Koyama, Kosuke. *No Handle on the Cross: An Asian Meditation on the Crucified Mind.* London: SCM, 1976.

Kungua, Benoît Awazi Mbambi. *Le Dieu Crucifié En Afrique: Esquisse D'une Christologie Négro-Africaine De La Libération Holistique.* Edited by François Manga-Akoa, Églises D'afrique. Paris: L'Harmattan, 2008.

La Notion De La Personne En Afrique Noire: Colloques Internationaux De Cnrs No. 544 Paris 11-17 Octobre 1971. Paris: CNRS, 1981.

Laléyé, Issiaka Prosper. "De La Quête Spirituelle De L'afrique Contemporaine. Repérage Des Fondements Pour Une Évaluation Critique." In *L'afrique Et Ses Formes De Vie Spirituelle: Colloque International Kinshasa 21-27/11/1983,* 54–68. Kinshasa: Faculté de Théologie Catholique, 1983.

———. "L'accès À Dieu Dans Les Religions Négro-Africaines Traditionnelles." *Mission de l'Église* 130—Supplément (2001) 49–55.

———. "Les Religion De L'afrique Noire." In *Le Fait Religieux,* edited by Jean Delumeau, 643–713. Paris: Fayard, 1993.

Lease, G. "Mithraism and Christianity: Borrowings and Transformations." In *Aufstieg Und Niedergang Der Römischen Welt*, edited by H. Temporini and W. Haase, 1306–31. Berlin: W. de Gruyter, 1980.

Lee, J. Y. *God Suffers for Us: A Systematic Inquiry into a Concept of Divine Passibility*. The Hague: Martinus Nijhoff, 1974.

Legrand, Lucien. *Unity and Plurality. Mission in the Bible*. Translated by Robert R. Barr. Maryknoll, NY: Orbis, 1990.

"Les Noms Théophores." *Afrique et Parole* 39–40 (1972).

"Les Noms Théophores Ii." *Afrique et Parole* 41–42 (1972) 69–118.

"Les Noms Théophores Iii." *Afrique et Parole* 43–44 (1973).

Lewis, Theodore J. "Mot (Deity)." In *The Anchor Bible Dictionary* (Electronic Edition), edited by David Noel Freedman. New York: Doubleday, 1997, 1992.

Lovell, Nadia. *Cord of Blood: Possession and the Making of Voodoo*. Sterling, Virginia: Pluto, 2002.

Luneau, René. *Laisse Aller Mon Peuple!: Églises Africaines Au-Delà Des Modèles?* Paris: Karthala, 1987.

———, editor. *Noms Théophores D'afrique, Série Ii, Mémoires Et Monographies*. Bandundu, Zaire: Ceeba, 1977.

Mana, Kä. *Christ D'afrique: Enjeux Éthiques De La Foi Africaine En Jésus-Christ*. Nairobi: CETA, 1994.

———. *Christians and Churches of Africa: Salvation in Christ and Building a New African Society*. Theology in Africa Series. Maryknoll, NY: Orbis, 2004.

———. *La Nouvelle Évangélisation En Afrique, Chrétiens En Liberté*. Yaoundé: Clé, 2000.

Manfredi, Victor. "Igbo Initiation: Phallus or Umbilicus"? *Cahiers D'Etudes Africaines* 145.37-1 (1997) 157–211.

Mary, André. *Le Défi Du Syncrétisme: Le Travail Symbolique De La Religion D'eboga (Gabon)*. Paris: Éditions de l'École des Hautes Études en Sciences sociales, 1999.

———. "Le Schème De La Naissance À L'envers: Scénario Initiatique Et Logique De L'inversion." *Cahiers d'Études africaines* 110.28-2 (1988) 233–63.

Mbiti, John S. *African Religions & Philosophy*. London: Heinemann, 1969.

———. *Bible and Theology in African Christianity*. Nairobi: Oxford University Press, 1986.

———. *Concepts of God in Africa*. London: SPCK, 1970.

———. "The Encounter of Christian Faith and African Religion." In *Third World Liberation Theologies: A Reader*, edited by Deane William Ferm, 199–204. Maryknoll, NY: Orbis, 1986.

———. *The Prayers of African Religion*. London: SPCK, 1975.

McKenzie, Peter. *Hail Orisha! A Phenomenology of a West African Religion in the Mid-Nineteenth Century*. New York: Brill, 1997.

Messi Metogo, Eloi. *Dieu Peut-Il Mourir En Afrique?: Essai Sur L'indifférence Religieuse Et L'incroyance En Afrique Noire, Chrétiens En Liberté. Questions Disputées*. Paris: Karthala, 1997.

Metuh, Emefie Ikenga. *African Religions in Western Conceptual Schemes : The Problem of Interpretation: Studies in Igbo Religion*. Ibadan & Jos, Nigeria: Pastoral Institute Bodija, 1985.

———. *Comparative Studies of African Traditional Religions*. Onitsha, Nigeria: IMICO, 1987.

———. *God and Man in African Religion: A Case Study of the Igbo of Nigeria.* 1999 ed. London: G. Chapman, 1981.

Meyer, Brigit. *Translating the Devil: Religion and Modernity among the Ewe in Ghana.* Edinburgh: Edinburgh University Press for the International African Institute, London, 1999.

Miller, Patrick D. "The Book of Jeremiah." In *The New Interpreter's Bible* (Electronic Edition) *Vol. 6.* Nashville: Abingdon, 1995–2002.

Mirinda, R. "The Good News in Zion." *Missionalia* 28.2 & 3 (2000) 233–41.

Moingt, Joseph. *Dieu Qui Vient À L'homme: Du Deuil Au Dévoilement De Dieu, Cogitatio Fidei 222.* Paris: Cerf, 2002.

Monastère bénédictin (Bouaké Ivory Coast). *Les Religions Africaines Traditionnelles.* Paris: Éditions du Seuil, 1965.

Mudimbe, V. Y. *The Invention of Africa: Gnosis, Philosophy, and the Order of Knowledge.* Bloomington and Indianapolis: Indiana University Press, 1988.

Mulago, Vincent. "L'union Vitale Bantu, Ou Le Principe De Cohésion De La Communauté Chez Les Bashi, Les Banyarwanda Et Les Barundi." *Annali Lateranensi* 20 (1956) 61–263.

———. *Un Visage Africain Du Christianisme. L'union Vitale Bantu Face À L'unité Vitale Ecclésiale.* Paris, 1965.

Mushete, Ngindu. *Les Thèmes Majeurs De La Théologie Africaine.* Paris: L'Harmattan, 1989.

Muzorewa, G. H. *The Origins and Development of African Theology.* New York: Orbis, 1985.

Mveng, Engelbert. "Impoverishment and Liberation: A Theological Approach for Africa and the Third World." In *Paths of African Theology*, edited by R. Gibellini, 155–65. New York: Orbis, 1994.

———. *L'afrique Dans L'eglise: Paroles D'un Croyant.* Paris: Editions L'Harmattan, 1986.

———. *L'art D'afrique Noire.* [Tours]: Mame, 1964.

———. *L'art D'afrique Noire. Liturgie Cosmique Et Langage Religieux.* Yaoundé: Clé, 1974.

Niane, D. T., editor. *General History of Africa. Vol. 4. Africa from the Twelfth to the Sixteenth Century.* New York: Routledge, 1984.

Niangoran-bouah, G. "La Drummologie Et La Vision Négro-Africaine Du Sacré." In *Médiations Africaines Du Sacré. Actes Du 3e Colloque International Du Cera, Kinshasa 16–22 Fév. 1986*, 281–95. Kinshasa: Faculté de Théologie Catholique de Kinshasa, 1987.

———. "The Talking Drum: A Traditional Instrument of Liturgy and of Mediation with the Sacred." In *African Traditional Religions in Contemporary Society*, edited by Jacob Obafemi Kehinde Olupona, 81–92. St. Paul, Minnesota: Paragon, 1991.

Nimisi, Mujynya. *L'homme Dans L'univers des Bantu.* Kinshasa: Presses Universitaires du Zaïre, 1972.

Nnolim, Charles. "Achebe's Tragic Heroes." In *"Wahlverwandtschaften": "Elective Affinities" Eine Gedenkschrift . Tributes and Essays on Germanic and African Studies in Memory of Edith Ihekweazu (1941–1991)*, edited by Willfred F. Feuser, Marion Pape, and Elias O. Dunu, 87–96. Norbert Aas: Boomerang, 1993.

———. *Approaches to the African Novel: Essays in Analysis.* 1999 ed. Owerri, Nigeria: Ihem Davis, 1992.

Nnolim, S. A. *The History of Umuchu. Second Revised and Enlarged Edition.* Edited by Charles E. Nnolim. Enugu, Nigeria: Ochumba, 1953.

Ntakarutimana, Emmanuel. *Vers Une Théologie Africaine: La Théologie Et Les Théologiens Au Congo : Projets Et Défis Dans La Période De L'après Indépendance (1960-1990).* Fribourg, Suisse: Éditions Universitaires de Fribourg, 2002.

Nwankwo, Lawrence Nchekwube. "From Power Christianity to Christianity That Empowers: Towards a Theology of Empowerment in the Nigerian Context." PhD, Katholieke Universiteit Leuven, 2004.

Nwodo, Christopher S. *Philosophical Perspective on Chinua Achebe.* Port Harcourt, Nigeria: University of Port Harcourt Press, 2004.

Nwoga, Donatus. *The Supreme God as Stranger in Igbo Religious Thought.* Ekwereazu, Nigeria: Hawks, 1984.

O'Day, Gail R. "The Gospel of John." In *The New Interpreter's Bible Vol 9* (Electronic Edition). Nashville: Abingdon Press, 1995–2002.

Oduyoye, Mercy Amba. *Daughters of Anowa. African Women and Patriarchy.* Maryknoll, NY: Orbis, 1995.

———. "Feminist Theology in an African Perspective." In *Paths of African Theology,* edited by Rosino Gibellini, 166–81. Maryknoll, NY: Orbis, 1994.

Oduyoye, Mercy Amba, and Musimbi R. A. Kanyoro, editors. *The Will to Arise. Women, Tradition, and the Church in Africa.* Maryknoll, NY: Orbis, 1992.

Ogot, B., editor. *General History of Africa.* Vol. 5. Africa from the Sixteenth to the Eighteenth Century. New York: Routledge, 1992.

Ojo, Matthews A. *The End-Time Army: Charismatic Movements in Modern Nigeria.* Trenton & Asmara: Africa World, 2006.

———. "Indigenous Gospel Music and Social Reconstruction in Modern Nigeria." *Missionalia* 26 (1998) 210–31.

Okonjo, Kamene. "The Dual-Sex Political System in Operation: Igbo Women and Community Politics in Midwestern Nigeria." In *Women in Africa: Studies in Social and Economic Change,* edited by Nancy J. Hafkin and Edna G. Bay, 45–58. Stanford: Stanford University Press, 1976.

Okpewho, Isidore. *African Oral Literature: Background, Character, and Continuity.* Indianapolis: Indiana University Press, 1992.

Okure, Teresa. *The Johannine Approach to Mission: A Contextual Study of John 4:1–42, Wissenschaftliche Untersuchungen Zum Neuen Testament. 2. Reihe; 31.* Tübingen: Mohr, 1988.

———. "Leadership in the New Testament." *Nigerian Journal of Theology* 1.5 (1990) 94–101.

Olayiwola, David O. "Aladura Christianity in Dialogue with African Traditional Religion (the Yoruba Example)." *Studia Missionalia* 43 (1994) 345–62.

———. "The Interaction of African Independent Churches with Traditional Religions in Nigeria." *Studia Missionalia* 42 (1993) 357–70.

Olupona, Jacob Obafemi Kehinde, and Terry Rey. *Òrìsà Devotion as World Religion: The Globalization of Yorùbá Religious Culture.* Madison: University of Wisconsin Press, 2008.

Onwuejeogwu, M. A. *An Igbo Civilization. Nri Kingdom and Hegemony.* London: Ethnographica and Ethiope, 1981.

Origen. "De Principiis." In *Ante-Nicene Fathers: Volume 4,* edited by Alexander Roberts and James Donaldson. Oak Harbor, WA: Logos Research Systems, 1997.

Origène. *Commentaire Sur Saint Jean: Tome1 (Livres I–V)*. Translated by Cécile Blanc. *Sources Chrétiennes* 120. Paris: Editions du Cerf, 1966.

———. *Homélies Sur Ezéchiel*. Translated by Saint Jerome (Latin Text) and Marcel Borret (French). *Sources Chrétiennes* 352. Paris: Editions du Cerf, 1989.

p'Bitek, Okot. *African Religions in Western Scholarship*. Kampala, 1971.

Parrat, John. *A Reader in African Theology*. London: SPCK, 1987.

Parrinder, Edward Geoffrey. "Le Mysticisme Des Médiums En Afrique Occidentale." In *Réincarnation Et Vie Mystique En Afrique Noire*, edited by Dominique Zahan and Roger Bastide, 130–42. Paris: Presses Universitaires de France, 1965.

———. *West African Religion, a Study of the Beliefs and Practices of Akan, Ewe, Yoruba, Ibo, and Kindred Peoples*. 2nd ed. London: Epworth, 1961.

Peek, Philip M., and Kwesi Yankah. *African Folklore: An Encyclopedia*. New York: Routledge, 2004.

Peel, J. D. Y. *Religious Encounter and the Making of the Yoruba*. Indianapolis: Indiana University Press, 2003.

Pernot, P., editor. *Tradition Et Modernisme En Afrique Noire: Rencontres Internationales De Bouaké*. Paris: Éditions du Seuil, 1965.

Piault, Colette, editor. *Prophétisme Et Thérapeutique: Albert Atcho Et La Communauté De Bregbo*. Paris: Hermann, 1975.

Pieris, Aloysius. *An Asian Liberation of Theology*. Edinburgh: T. & T. Clark, 1988.

Pobee, John S, and Gabriel Ositelu II. *African Initiatives in Christianity: The Growth, Gifts and Diversities of Indigenous African Churches—A Challenge to the Ecumenical Movement*. Geneva: WCC, 1998.

Prudence. *Psychomachie Contre Symmaque*. Vol. 3: Texte établi et traduit par M. Lavarenne. Paris: Les Belles Lettres, 1948.

Rahner, Karl. *Foundations of Christian Faith: An Introduction to the Idea of Christianity*. New York: Seabury, 1978.

Ramazani Bishwende, Augustin. *Pour Une Ecclésiologie Trinitaire Dans La Postmodernité Et La Mondialisation*. Vol. 2: De la Déconstruction à la Réception de Vatican II. Paris: L'Harmattan, 2008.

———. *Pour Une Ecclésiologie Trinitaire Dans La Postmodernité Et La Mondialisation*. Vol. 1: De R. Bellarmin à Y. Congar. Paris: L'Harmattan, 2008.

Ricoeur, Paul. *The Symbolism of Evil*. Boston: Beacon, 1967.

Riesman, Paul. *Freedom in Fulani Social Life* (Chicago: University of Chicago Press, 1977).

Roberts, Alexander and James Donaldson. *Ante-Nicene Fathers*. Volume 10, Book 2, 6. Oak Harbor, WA: Logos Research Systems, 1997.

Rose, Martin. "Names of God in the O T." In *The Anchor Bible Dictionary* (Electronic Edition), edited by David Noel Freedman. New York: Doubleday, 1997, 1992.

Rosny, Eric de. *L'afrique Des Guérisons*. Paris: Karthala, 1992.

———. "For a Mission of Vision: A Testimony." In *Africa: Towards Priorities of Mission—Acts of the Inter-Continental Congress of the Spiritan International School of Theology (Sist), Attakwu, Enugu, Nigeria, November 11–17 1996*, edited by P. Ikechukwu Odozor, Chinedu Amadi-Azuogu, and Elochukwu Uzukwu, 95–100. Enugu: SIST, 2000.

———. *Healers in the Night*. Translated by Robert R. Barr. New York: Orbis, 1985.

———. *Les Yeux De Ma Chèvre: Sur Les Pas Des Maîtres De La Nuit En Pays Douala*. Paris: Plon, 1981.

Ross, Kenneth R. "Grounding Theology in History: New Directions for Research." In *Jahrbuch Für Kontextuelle Theologien1999*, 121–36. Frankfurt: IKO—Verlag für Interkulturelle Kommunikation, 1999.

Ryan, Patrick J. "'Arise, O God!' the Problem of Gods in West Africa." *Journal of Religion in Africa* 11.3 (1980) 161–71.

Saggs, H. W. F. *The Encounter with the Divine in Mesopotamia and Israel, Jordan Lectures 1976*. London: Athlone, 1978.

Sanneh, Lamin O. *Encountering the West: Christianity and the Global Cultural Process: The African Dimension, World Christian Theology Series*. Maryknoll, NY: Orbis, 1993.

———. *Whose Religion Is Christianity? The Gospel Beyond the West*. Grand Rapids: Eerdmans, 2003.

Sarpong, Peter K. "The Individual, Community, Health and Medicine in African Traditional Religion: The Asante Model." *Pontificium Consilium Pro Dialogo Inter Religiones Bulletin* 28.3 (1993) 271–80.

———."Libation and Inculturation in Africa." *Studia Missionalia* 44 (1995) 305–35.

———. "Rôle Des Ancêtres Dans Une Religion Africaine: Le Modèle Ghanéen." *Mission de l'Église* 130.1 Supplément, janvier (2001) 8–15.

Scharbert, J. "Brk, Berakah." In *Theological Dictionary of the Old Testament*, edited by G. J. Botterwech and H. Ringgren, 279–80. Grand Rapids: Eerdmans, 1974–75.

Schmid, H. H. "Creation, Righteousness, and Salvation: 'Creation Theology' as the Broad Horizon of Biblical Theology." In *Creation in the Old Testament*, edited by B. W. Anderson, 104–17. Philadelphia: Fortress, 1984.

Semporé, Sidbe. "Barthélémy Adoukonou: Un Pionnier De L'inculturation En Afrique De L'ouest." In *Théologie Africaine Au Xxie Siècle: Quelques Figures*, edited by Bénézet Bujo and Juvénal Ilunga Muya, 142–56. Fribourg, Suisse: Éditions Universitaires Fribourg Suisse, 2002.

Senghor, L. S. "Problématique De Négritude." In *Colloque Sur La Négritude, Dakar 12–18-Avril 1971*. Paris: Présence Africaine, 1972.

Sengupta, Somini. "A River is Witnessing the Rebirth of Congo", http://iht.com/articles/516276.htm (Thursday, April 22, 2004).

Shorter, Aylward. *African Christian Theology*. London: Chapman, 1975.

Soyinka, Wole. *The Burden of Memory, the Muse of Forgiveness, W. E. B. Du Bois Institute*. New York: Oxford University Press, 1999.

———. "The Tolerant Gods." In *Òrìsà Devotion as World Religion: The Globalization of Yorùbá Religious Culture*, edited by Jacob Obafemi Kehinde Olupona and Terry Rey, 44. Madison: University of Wisconsin Press, 2008.

———. *Que Ce Passé Parle À Son Présent, Discours De Stockholm 1986*. Translated by Etienne Galle. Paris: Pierre Belfond, 1987.

Surgy, Albert de. *L'église Du Christianisme Céleste: Un Exemple D'église Prophétique Au Bénin*. Paris: Karthala, 2001.

Tassin, Claude. "Jésus, Exorciste Et Guérisseur." *Spiritus* 120 (1990) 285–303.

Tempels, Placide. *Bantu Philosophy*. Paris: Présence Africaine, 1969.

Thomas, Louis-Vincent, and René Luneau. *La Terre Africaine Et Ses Religions: Traditions Et Changements*. Paris: Larousse, 1974.

———. *Les Sages Dépossédés: Univers Magiques D'afrique Noire*. Paris: Éditions Robert Lafont, 1977.

Thomas, N. W. *Anthropological Report on the Ibo-Speaking Peoples of Nigeria.* Vol. 1. London: Harrison, 1913–14.

Tidani, A. Serpos. "Rituels." *Présence Africaine* 8–9, no. spécial - Le Monde Noir - dirigé par Théodore Monod (1950) 297–305.

Tshibangu, Tharcisse. *Théologie Comme Science Au Xxème Siècle.* Kinshasa, 1980.

———. *Théologie Positive Et Théologie Spéculative: Position Traditionnelle Et Nouvelle Problématique.* Paris: Léopoldville, 1965.

Tshibangu, Tharcisse, and Alfred Vanneste. "Débat Sur La Théologie Africaine." *Revue du Clergé Africain* 15.4 (1960) 333–52.

Turner, Harold W. *African Independent Church.* Vol. 2: The Life and Faith of the Church of the Lord (Aladura). Oxford: Clarendon, 1967.

Turner, Victor. *Revelation and Divination in Ndembu Ritual* (Ithaca-London: Cornell University Press, 1975)

Tutu, Desmond. *No Future without Forgiveness.* 1st ed. New York: Doubleday, 1999.

Uchem, Rose N. *Overcoming Women's Subordination: An Igbo African Perspective: Envisioning an Inclusive Theology with Reference to Women.* Parkland, Fl & Enugu: Dissertation.com USA & SNAAP Press, 2001.

Uchendu, V.C. *The Igbo of South-Eastern Nigeria.* New York: Rinehart & Winston, 1965.

Ukah, Asonzeh F.-K. "Advertising God: Nigerian Christian Video-Films and the Power of Consumer Culture." *Journal of Religion in Africa* 33.2 (2003) 203–31.

Ukpong, Justin. "Developments in Biblical Interpretation in Africa: Historical and Hermeneutical Directions." In *The Bible in Africa: Transactions and Trajectories and Trends,* edited by Gerald O. West and Musa W. Dube, 11–28. Boston: Brill Academic, 2001.

Ukwuije, Bede. *Trinité Et Inculturation.* Edited by Philippe Bordeyne and Henri-Jérome Gagey, *Théologie À L'université.* Paris: Desclée de Brouwer, 2008.

Ukwuije, Bede Uche. "L'humanité De Dieu : Pertinence De La Doctrine Trinitaire D'eberhard Jüngel Pour La Nomination De Dieu Dans Le Contexte De La Théologie Africaine De L'inculturation." Institut Catholique de Paris; Katholieke Universiteit Leuven, 2005.

Umeh, John Anenechukwu. *After God Is Dibia: Igbo Cosmology, Divination & Sacred Science in Nigeria.* Vol. 1. London: Karnak, 1997.

———. *After God Is Dibia: Igbo Cosmology, Healing, Divination & Sacred Science in Nigeria.* Vol. 2. London: Karnak, 1999.

Uzukwu, Elochukwu E. "Bible and Christian Worship in Africa: African Christianity and the Labour of Contextualization." *Chakana* 1.2 (2003) 7–32.

———. "Le Destin De La Personne Humaine Dans Une Religion Africaine: Les Igbo Du Nigeria." *Mission de l'Église* 130. Supplément—Les Religion des Ancêtres (1), (2001) 16–23.

———. "Food and Drink in Africa and the Christian Eucharist." *African Ecclesial Review* 22 (1980) 370–85, 98.

———. "Igbo World and Ultimate Reality and Meaning." *Ultimate Reality and Meaning* 5.3 (1982) 188–209.

———. "L'afrique Anglophone." In *Le Devenir De La Théologie Catholique Depuis Vatican Ii: 1965-1999,* edited by Joseph Doré, 225–55. Paris: Beauchesne, 2000.

———. *A Listening Church: Autonomy and Communion in African Churches.* Maryknoll, NY: Orbis, 1996.

————. "Trinity in Contemporary African Theology: Conversation with Augustine Ramazani, Bede Ukwuije, and Benoît Kungua." *Bulletin of Ecumenical Theology* 21 (2009) 23–40.

————. *Worship as Body Language: Introduction to Christian Worship: An African Orientation.* Collegeville, MN: Liturgical, 1997.

Uzukwu, Eugene E. "The Future of Foreign Missionary Congregations in Africa: A Nigerian Example." *African Ecclesial Review* 27.6 (1985) 331–44.

Walls, Andrew F. *The Missionary Movement in Christian History: Studies in the Transmission of Faith.* New York: Orbis, 1996.

Weinandy, Thomas G. *Does God Suffer?* Notre Dame, IN: Notre Dame University Press, 2000.

Westermann, C. *Genesis 1–11: A Commentary.* Translated by J. J. Sullivan. Minneapolis: Augsburg, 1984.

Wijsen, Frans Jozef Servaas. *There Is Only One God: A Socio-Scientific and Theological Study of Popular Religion and Evangelization in Sukumaland, Northwest Tanzania.* Nijmegen: Uitgeverij Kok-Kampen, 1993.

Zahan, Dominique. *The Religion, Spirituality, and Thought of Traditional Africa.* Translated by Kate Ezra Martin and Lawrence M. Martin. Chicago: University of Chicago Press, 1979.

Zempléni, Andras. "De La Persécution À La Culpabilité." In *Prophétisme Et Thérapeutique: Albert Atcho Et La Communauté De Bregbo,* edited by Colette Piault, 153–219. Paris: Hermann, 1975.

Zeusse, Evan M. "Perseverance and Transmutation in African Traditional Religions." In *African Traditional Religions in Contemporary Society,* edited by Jacob K. Olupona, 167–84. St. Paul, MN: Paragon, 1991.

Index